WHAT MEN DON'T TALK ABOUT

Maggie Hamilton is a writer, teacher and publisher, with a Masters in English Literature and expertise in self-development. She is a regular media commentator and a keen observer of social trends. Her books include *Coming Home: Rediscovering Our Sacred Selves*, *Magic of the Moment* and *Love Your Work, Reclaim Your Life*.

www.maggiehamilton.org

WHAT MEN DON'T TALK ABOUT

MAGGIE HAMILTON

VIKING
an imprint of
PENGUIN BOOKS

VIKING

Published by the Penguin Group
Penguin Group (Australia)
250 Camberwell Road, Camberwell, Victoria 3124, Australia
(a division of Pearson Australia Group Pty Ltd)
Penguin Group (USA) Inc.
375 Hudson Street, New York, New York 10014, USA
Penguin Group (Canada)
90 Eglinton Avenue East, Suite 700, Toronto ON M4P 2Y3, Canada
(a division of Pearson Penguin Canada Inc.)
Penguin Books Ltd
80 Strand, London WC2R 0RL, England
Penguin Ireland
25 St Stephen's Green, Dublin 2, Ireland
(a division of Penguin Books Ltd)
Penguin Books India Pvt Ltd
11 Community Centre, Panchsheel Park, New Delhi – 110 017, India
Penguin Group (NZ)
Cnr Airborne and Rosedale Roads, Albany, Auckland, New Zealand
(a division of Pearson New Zealand Ltd)
Penguin Books (South Africa) (Pty) Ltd
24 Sturdee Avenue, Rosebank, Johannesburg 2196, South Africa

Penguin Books Ltd, Registered Offices: 80 Strand, London WC2R 0RL, England

First published by Penguin Group (Australia), a division of Pearson Australia Group Pty Ltd, 2006

1 3 5 7 9 10 8 6 4 2

Cover design by Jo Hunt © Penguin Group (Australia)
Text design by Adam Laszczuk © Penguin Group (Australia)
Cover image by Steve Hunt, Pigs Might Fly
Typeset in 12.75/17 pt Perpetua by Post Pre-press Group, Brisbane, Queensland
Printed and bound in Australia by McPherson's Printing Group, Maryborough, Victoria

National Library of Australia
Cataloguing-in-Publication data:

Hamilton, Maggie, 1953– .
What men don't talk about.

Bibliography.
ISBN-13: 978 0 670 02879 5.
ISBN-10: 0 670 02879 7.

1. Men – Social conditions. 2. Masculinity. 3. Sex role. I. Title.

305.31

www.penguin.com.au

For Douglas and Derek,
and all the men
whose strength and decency help us thrive;
and for Matt and Stuart,
and all the beautiful boys who die too soon.

Contents

Acknowledgements

Nothing we achieve is simply through our own efforts. This has been a huge project that would not have been possible were it not for the wonderful support I have received from so many people. My heartfelt thanks to all the men who so willingly shared the intricacies of their lives – their triumphs and their defeats. And thanks to my dear friends, whose belief in this project has never wavered, and who have continued to encourage me from the moment I put pen to paper.

My thanks also to Bob Nelson, Bruce White, Bill O'Hehir, Marian Clarke, Carol George, Dr Sotirios Sarantakos, Marie M. Eadie, Professor Yeates Conwell, Julie Coates, Jan Backhouse, John Hanrahan, Lisa Hanrahan, Trena Clarke, Augustine J. Kposowa, Rev. Dave Smith, Steve Boston, Andrew King, Anne Willems, Ray Lenton, Murray Drummond, Susanne Gervay and Karen Reid, whose assistance with my research was invaluable. Thanks also to the staff at Balmain Library, who went out of their way to source books for me. Special thanks to Brad Mander and Dean Dyer, who took the time to read the manuscript and give me such valuable feedback.

Thanks to my dear friend and agent Selwa Anthony; to my wonderfully talented publisher Julie Gibbs; to my publicist Bridie Riordan and editor Claire de Medici, whose ongoing love and commitment mean so much. Thanks to the whole Penguin team – to Dan Ruffino, Sally Bateman, Nicola Young, Anne Rogan, Peg McColl and Frances Bruce for their excellent work.

My thanks to my father Douglas, the first man I loved, and to my husband Derek, whose unwavering belief in all I do never ceases to sustain me. My thanks to the Hopi people, where this book began; and to the Great Spirit, who inspires me to look more deeply at life, and see things not only as they are, but how they may yet be.

Introduction

Writing this book has been one of the most liberating, yet at times shocking projects I have undertaken. It was prompted by my growing unease at the many assumptions I had made about men. While I'd been happy to believe that men's lives were easier than those of women, that men were never vulnerable, when I took a closer look at men, I began to realise this wasn't the case. Up until this point I'd never *really* questioned why so many men and boys take their lives. Or why when relationships fell apart my focus was always on how my *girl*friend was coping. It was only when I took a step back that I realised that the many dilemmas men grappled with, the pain they felt, were largely invisible to me. This shook me.

I started to wonder what else I didn't know about men. As I began to examine the lives of men and listen to their stories, I realised that, like many women, I had very little understanding of them. And what I did know was mostly based on anecdote and stereotype, and my own experience of men. At a first glance, most of the men around me seemed to be coping and getting on with their lives, but once I scratched the surface, a very different picture emerged. I began to

see that, like women, most men have very real doubts and vulnerabilities. Like women, men long to be heard, to be held, to be loved,
to be accepted for who they are. They too struggle for acceptance
and meaning. And when given the chance they can reveal the depth
of their feeling, their courage, their humanity.

Time and again in my interviews with men, they were genuinely surprised that a woman was interested enough to listen to their
story, let alone write about it. Many men became extremely emotional during our time together. Some cried. For too many, this was
the first time anyone had asked them in depth about *their* lives and
their experience of the world. And as they recounted whole chapters of their lives, I found these men as open, vulnerable and frank
as any woman. Their candour and insight amazed me. As we talked I
discovered that they too had experienced many moments of doubt
and despair in life. They spoke of working hard at their relationships
with women, of doing their best to try to make the women they
loved happy, and of their bitter disappointment when their efforts
fell short of expectations.

As I contemplated everything these men shared with me, I began
to realise that in our desire to grasp the differences *between* the sexes,
we as a society have come to focus on what separates us, rather than
what joins us together. We have also fallen into the trap of competing for whose pain is the greatest, instead of seeking to alleviate pain
wherever we find it. I can see now that this lack of wider vision has
come at a great cost. I cannot help but wonder how many thousands
of boys in the past might have been spared sexual abuse had we not
held false notions about who was (and was not) vulnerable to such
things.

In my quest to understand how men experience life, in no way
do I wish to trivialise the many hurdles women have faced, and

continue to face. The women's movement remains essential, because it not only continues to liberate women, but also liberates how we as a society think and act. Its positive effects are ongoing and point us towards an even better future, as we utilise all we have learned for the good of everyone. I believe it is time now to take the many benefits women have gained, and enable men to enjoy more choice, more freedom than is possible within the current narrow definition of masculinity.

The way ahead also lies in realising that there are many more qualities that bind us, than separate us. We are first and foremost human beings, with all the potential and frailties that human life brings. This is not to suggest we ignore the nuances of gender. It is only by better understanding these differences that we are more able to comprehend them, learn from them and celebrate them.

From the earliest times we as a society have created stories to help make sense of those things we don't fully understand, including men. Most of us have devoured these stories without question, because this is one of the few means we had to try to explain what men were all about. But it's only as we dig deeper that we begin to see just how harmful and misleading many of these stories can be. In spite of the many necessary advances we have made, there have been casualties. We have come to view masculinity as something dark, dangerous and undesirable. While we must continue to strive to keep individuals and our communities safe, we need to be more imaginative about how we do this, so that there is room also to honour the many wonderful textures men bring to our lives.

I feel it is time for us to hold a more informed view of men's lives, for while it might be acceptable to make fun of men and to say we no longer need them, this isn't helpful. How quickly our focus changes when there is a major disaster — we're quite happy then for our fathers, sons and partners to risk life and limb to disperse hazardous chemicals, protect us from floods and fire, and shield us from the worst elements in our community. Women now also work in these roles, but still these tasks are largely carried out by men.

Although few men will admit it, many men's lives aren't particularly easy. Many don't enjoy the choices and success they had hoped for. But because others rely on them, somehow they summon what courage they can to get out of bed in the morning and do what they have to do. Few men rule the world. Most try simply to lead worthwhile lives, and deal with life's lacerations great and small.

There *are* dangerous and dysfunctional men in our communities, who do harm others and destroy lives. But there are many more good men, courageous men, decent men. The dozens upon dozens of men I spoke to impressed me with their depth of insight, their capacity for love, their desire to lead meaningful lives without the need for fame or glory. These men came from all walks of life: young and old, factory workers and professionals, men out of work and men with healthy incomes, single men and men in relationships, fathers and sons, and boys who were yet to make their own way in the world. Throughout the book you can read their thoughts for yourself, and discover more about who men are and what they long for.

Apart from my own extensive interviews with men, I immersed myself in the literature on men – in novels and works of nonfiction, in the way men are represented in popular culture. Wherever possible I sought to familiarise myself with the leading thinkers and practitioners in the topics covered, to give the book a wider perspective. Where local case studies and/or statistics were hard to access, I have used the most relevant overseas data. All the men I interviewed for the book, apart from experts, appear under pseudonyms to respect their privacy. The scope of the book did not allow sufficient space to examine the lives of homosexual men and boys, or those from indigenous or other cultural backgrounds. What this work has left me with, however, is an appreciation of how much more difficult the lives of these men and boys must be on occasion.

As I immersed myself in this material, the many differences and similarities between men and women began to emerge. Then, as I explored our differences, I started to better appreciate, understand and respect them, and to see the many qualities men have to offer.

I have written this book for men and women. I hope the men who read it will be heartened to discover they are not alone in the many issues they face. And I hope the women who read it will gain a far greater understanding not only of men, but of what it means to be a woman, because the more women comprehend the many subtle textures that make men who they are, the more they can in turn appreciate the gifts of their gender. Many of the issues covered in the book are shared by women and girls to a greater or lesser extent. I have refrained from this wider debate because there just wasn't the scope to do so, given the amount of material examined here.

One of the many bonuses of living in our society is the freedom and ability it offers to intelligently explore, understand and celebrate ourselves and others. Through this process we are then able to create something far more meaningful than is possible when we remain focused on our own individual needs and perspectives. This aim was uppermost when writing the book. I wanted to challenge our assumptions about men, and to stretch our imaginations, so we can better understand them and all they might bring to our lives. I hope I have succeeded.

What has been most rewarding about my time with the men who contributed to this book are the many ways I am now inspired to celebrate all that being a woman means, and to enjoy the company of men in ways I have never experienced before. My greatest hope is that the many insights contained in this book will touch all those who pick it up, and that they too will be inspired to learn from and celebrate each other more, as together we seek to create the kind of relationships and world we all long for.

What *is* it about men?

WHAT IS GOING ON WITH MEN RIGHT NOW?

What do men ache for, agonise over, aspire to? Why are men often silent in dark, dangerous or difficult situations? Why do so many men find it hard to express how much they care? Do they care? What do they look for in women? What do they want from committed relationships, from friendships? What motivates them? What do they worry about? How do they see their bodies, their world? Is it true that men's lives are much easier than women's lives – that they have 'got it made'? What do we *really* know about men when we take away the stereotypes, the anecdotes? Have we ever sat down with men and asked what is important to them? Do we care enough to discover what men long for, and what fills them with fear? Or are we happy to perpetuate the assumptions we have clung to for so long?

Every day we're bombarded with articles about men – men at home, men at work, men in bed – but still the confusion and frustration between the sexes remain. Can we simply put the differences between men and women down to the influence of Venus and Mars, or are there more profound dynamics at play? I now realise that if we want to get a grip on what men are about, we need to take time to listen to *their* stories — their collective story as well as their individual stories. Only then can we understand who they are, and who they most long to be.

A FRAGILE START

To understand men, we need to begin at the beginning — in the womb where, during the first few weeks of life, there are no visible differences between boys and girls. Then, around the seventh week, if the embryo is to be a boy testosterone kicks in, prompting the development of male genitals. Over the next few weeks and months, as these biological differences are fine-tuned, more male embryos will be spontaneously miscarried than female embryos. More male babies will be born dead. This mortality pattern will follow boys who survive through childhood into adulthood, for the rest of their lives.

Few of us realise how tenuous a start to life many boys have, because we tend to see them as strong. This belief affects how a boy is treated from birth. From here on in, a boy's parents will start to shape how he sees himself and the world. They will do this through the clothes and the toys and the decor they choose for him, in how they talk to and about this baby boy, and in the way they interact with him. Many of us assume baby girls are cute and vulnerable, while we see baby boys as naturally strong and well coordinated.[1] As a result, from birth baby boys often receive fewer cuddles, less attention, less interaction than baby girls. Parents who treat their baby boys like this do so not because they are unkind or thoughtless, but because they believe boys need less love and nurturing than girls.

'As a young boy there is a yearning for physical contact. You don't get embraced — not even by your parents.' *Tony, 26*

What perhaps most of us don't know is that generally more boys than girls die in their first twelve months of life. And even though frequently baby boys *seem* more robust, they are more likely than girls to suffer speech impediments and mental retardation, or to die from sudden infant death syndrome, injury or poisoning. A baby boy's testosterone can also place him at greater risk because it can depress his immune system, causing him to be more susceptible to leukemia, cancers of the lymphatic system, respiratory ailments, hepatitis and gastrointestinal illnesses.[2] Yet in spite of this, many parents continue to believe that infant boys are naturally stronger than infant girls.

> From birth baby boys often receive fewer cuddles, less attention, less interaction than baby girls.

WHEN PARENTS WITHDRAW

As a baby boy grows, he begins to absorb distinct messages about what it means to be male. His parents' facial expressions, for example, help teach him about rapport, tenderness and empathy. The quality of these and other exchanges he has with his parents will start to shape this baby boy's level of trust and feelings of security.[3] From around six months, this tiny boy will also begin to learn how to deal with his feelings of insecurity and, based on the emotional responses he receives from those around him, he will learn to adjust his behaviour accordingly.[4]

Babies soon learn to *respond* to these signals. According to noted American professor of psychiatry and human development Berry Brazelton, mothers are particularly important in these initial months, because a baby's emotions are directly related to the input he receives, relative to what he was hoping for. So, when an infant's needs are met, that infant is more able to handle stressful situations than infants who don't get this input.[5]

> Long before they go to school, parents start to withdraw
> from their little boys.

It is helpful for parents to know that by responding positively to the physical and emotional needs of their baby, they enable their baby to feel more secure. This is as true for baby boys as it is for baby girls, yet from birth we tend to give little girls far more positive input, perhaps because we assume they need more nurturing, more care. Little girls do need nurturing and care, but they have a head start because they also have a far greater ability than little boys to interact with those around them.

'Within hours of birth girls are more interested than boys in people's faces,' explains Professor Ross Parke, director of the Center for Family Studies, University of California. 'At only four months, baby girls can tell the difference between photographs of people they know, from those of strangers; boys can't.'[6] Baby boys aren't as aware of social nuances as baby girls, but this doesn't mean they *feel* less. Nor does it mean that tiny boys are strong enough to cope with things that baby girls are not. Like girls, boys need to be cuddled, loved, understood, appreciated, so they too can thrive.

> 'I still see the ways boys are brought up [as] cruel. I see it even with friends, who don't realise they are being cruel. Parents are less tolerant of weakness and vulnerability in boys. It really hits me.'
> Lawrence, 33

MAKING BOYS STRONG

Most parents do love their little boys. They do give them cuddles, and try to affirm what they do. But often these demonstrations of love are tempered by what parents *expect* of boys. Long before boys go to school, many parents start to withdraw from them, because they know how tough life can be for boys. They do this because they are worried that if they get too close to their son, he won't be able to stand up for himself. Many also fear that if they are tender with their son, he might grow up to be soft or gay.

My interviews with men showed me that boys are very aware of the emotional withdrawal of their parents when they are little, but because no-one explains why, they assume it's because of something they have done. While the ways parents withdraw from their sons may differ, the end result is the same: it is very painful and confusing for a boy. These boys soon get the very clear message that they are on their own in a whole range of areas, from dealing with scratches and scrapes, to facing unknown people and situations. Just seeing their boy being clingy can cause parents to worry. Out of a genuine concern for their son, parents start to gloss over his feelings. Even when boys try to tell their parents or other adults they are frightened, hurt or unsure, they are often told they are *not* scared, they are *not* uncomfortable, they are *not* out of their depth.

> 'There was a time when my father would carry me around on the top of his shoulders. It was great. Then there was the awkwardness, like he didn't want to touch me anymore.' *Tony, 26*

A number of men described to me their feelings of isolation from a very young age. Often it's not until we're aware of this dynamic that we can see how prevalent it is. When I was with a group of friends recently, one related how her son had started to cry when he went to kindergarten, saying he was frightened. She laughed, not unkindly, and said she'd told him he really wasn't scared at all. It's hard to imagine how any frightened little boy must feel when he is told he is not scared, when in fact he is terrified. The irony is that if a little girl says she's frightened, usually we don't hesitate to gather her up in our arms and reassure her.

'The one thought you have is you're the only one with the things you're worrying about. You think you're in a hole that you can't get out of. You're not able to talk to anyone. It can really get you down.'
Nathan, 19

There is nothing wrong with boys learning to be strong. The problem is that often we expect them to learn how to do this all by themselves. From early on, countless little boys experience this very real distancing from those they love. Small boys are sometimes hit or verbally abused if they cry. Most boys soon get the message and very quickly start to keep their pain and fear to themselves, because, like little girls, they want love and approval from those around them, and they will do whatever it takes to gain these.

If a little boy is repeatedly told to *deny* what he is feeling, he will soon learn to push his emotional needs aside. One of the most shocking themes to emerge from my interviews with boys and young men was the number of times they admitted to feeling completely on their own. Time and again they would mention something challenging that had happened to them, prefacing their experiences by saying there was nothing anyone else could do to help them. As they spoke it was clear that they saw much of their early life in terms of survival.

> *Even when boys try to tell their parents or other adults they are frightened, hurt or unsure, they are often told they are not scared, they are not uncomfortable, they are not out of their depth.*

BOYS ARE SENSITIVE TOO

Dealing with any emotions boys display is frequently harder for fathers than mothers, because fathers know intimately the many challenges their boys will face. Often they will come down hard on their sons when they are little to toughen them up, in the hope that they will then be able to deal with whatever is thrown at them. While most dads do this with the best of intentions, many have no idea the impact this has on their sons. This treatment is especially hard for boys who are not naturally aggressive, and for boys who have a strong need for protection and compassion from their parents.

Other fathers are very tough on their sons because they are driven by the need to compete — they end up competing with their young sons at every opportunity. Good competition is healthy for boys; it can be exhilarating for them to be stretched beyond what they thought they were capable of. But when fathers have to win all the games they play together, far from helping their boy progress by learning how to win and to lose, their son is left feeling demeaned and frustrated, because everything Dad does seems out of reach.

In his book *Raising Cane*, psychologist Dan Kindlon talks of boys as being 'exquisitely sensitive' to the way their father behaves.[7] Fathers aren't the only culprits. Often families, adult friends and teachers fail to show true regard for a boy's feelings. Because society *wants* to see boys as strong, that's how boys are being programmed. Academic Peter West agrees; he believes that softness in boys is being deliberately suppressed.[8] The tragedy is that when a boy's needs are neglected, it is harder for him to be interested in other people's feelings. And so begins what Dan Kindlon calls the 'emotional *mise-ducation*' of boys. When talking of this process at a Harvard forum, child and family psychologist Michael Thompson pointed out that while boys are born with the same emotional potential as girls, by kindergarten a girl is six times more likely than a boy to use the word 'love'. And by age 8 or 9 boys are already evaluating everything and everyone purely in terms of their strengths and weaknesses.[9]

> 'I didn't have a great upbringing. Mum and Dad had a few marital problems. I didn't feel a hundred per cent safe. I was always intimidated about expressing who I was. It was like I was expected to say nothing and stay out of the way. It was difficult. There was a real loneliness there.' *Robert, 30*

Most adults don't consciously set out to shut boys down. Yet from early on, this is what they end up doing, by failing to read their many cries as signs of distress. Frequently parents assume that because boys are far more action-oriented than girls, they are also naturally tough and endlessly resilient. There is something about the exuberance and sense of adventure that little boys possess that does often take your breath away. Society attempts to harness the huge energy boys have by encouraging risk-taking and independent play. There is nothing wrong with this approach, as long as it acknowledges that boys also have significant emotional lives.

As boys grow, they soon learn they are expected to *appear* capable at all costs. This message starts with small boys, and will be reinforced throughout their lives. The difficulty is that when boys are made to feel ashamed of their emotions, they become less able to express their needs with ease. And so begins their keen sense of isolation from those around them.

> 'There isn't much room to move as a boy. You can't ask anyone else for help, because it looks weak. It's like if you can't do it yourself, then you don't have the internal resources, so there's something wrong with you.' *Tony, 26*

EMOTIONS DON'T GO AWAY

Just because boys learn to suppress their emotions from an early age doesn't mean they stop *feeling* their emotions. Over time boys can become so good at disguising their feelings, even their parents and those close to them have no idea what is really going on with them. In a series of landmark experiments that began in the 1970s, Ross Buck, professor of communication sciences at the University of Colorado, tested mothers' ability to read the emotional response of their children while the children watched a series of slides. He then repeated this experiment with mothers and their boys aged 4 to 6 on the *20/20* television program. While the boys watched the slides they were hooked up to a polygraph so their physiological responses could be measured, and their mothers observed from another room. The mothers had to guess from their child's facial responses which slide they were viewing, and how they felt about that slide. While the boys had little *facial* reaction to these slides, the polygraph showed they clearly had an *emotional* response to what they had seen. Not surprisingly these mothers were unable to tell how the boys were feeling, because they were relying on how the boys *appeared*, to gauge their reactions.[10]

The ongoing suppression of a young boy's emotions leaves many boys with an intense sense of loneliness.

Like it or not, adults frequently have no idea what boys are feeling or the depth of emotion they are experiencing. The more we shut boys down, the more adept they become at masking their feelings. This shutting-down process doesn't serve the boys or their parents, because their parents then start to assume that because their boys *look* fine, they must *be* fine. And so the isolation boys feel intensifies.

'Our dog was run over. I didn't find out about this until I sat down at the dinner table. We'd had the dog a long time. I began to cry. My dad was an ex rugby player. He rammed his fist into the table and ordered me out of the room. It worked. For years I had an absolute intolerance of anyone who got emotional, and I would get very aggressive with them.' *Lawrence, 33*

With no training in emotional nuance or appropriate ways to express their emotions, boys have little choice other than to soldier on the best they can. Well aware of the need to appear strong and in charge at all times, they work actively to keep their feelings hidden. As professionals who work with boys know well, when their feelings do surface, they surface as anger, because this is the only emotion we have come to expect and accept from boys.

'It's a struggle as a young boy. A lot of young boys find it hard to control their anger. They are in a pretty powerless situation – it can be very frustrating. I just felt there was nothing much you could do about it.' *Jason, 22*

ON THEIR OWN

This ongoing suppression of a young boy's emotions leaves many boys with an intense feeling of loneliness. During my conversations with men I was surprised at how many could still recall the sense of isolation, even as grown men. When I asked Doug, 52, about his childhood, he admitted that his most significant memories as a little boy were of being lonely. Doug talked of his early years living with a working mother who was run off her feet, and a distant father who didn't engage in family life, as being plagued by a sense of 'insecurity' and 'embarrassment', and of the 'loneliness'. This left Doug with a 'dread of adulthood', and the impression that it was 'boring and uninspiring'.

> 'I even had a kid of ten in for a treatment the other week. It was his first visit. He looked pretty nervous, so I asked him if he was okay. Before he could say anything his mother piped up, telling him not to be such a girl. It was pretty terrible, but it happens to boys all the time.' *Mitchell, 26, complementary health practitioner*

When recalling his early years, Rowan, 41, described his boyhood as 'a struggle on every level', because no-one helped him work it out. Even though Ray, 50, came from a large family, his abiding memory was also of isolation. 'Never having my parents say "I love you,"' he explained. 'Never having my parents attend any school or sports event.' The irony is that when I met these men, they all talked initially as if they had trouble-free childhoods, until we got into the details. Often they went on to relate devastating situations they had experienced, as if these were perfectly normal, or as if this was all that boys could expect of life.

'I don't ever remember my parents ever having played with me.'
Ted, 65

'I recall being frightened much of my childhood.' *Kieran, 58*

As we have already noted, when boys become isolated it is hard for them to empathise with those around them, because they don't have much experience of empathy. This not only causes difficulties for the boys concerned, but for their families and friends. When boys fail to show empathy, they alienate those around them, and are then labelled uncaring. As family therapist Olga Silverstein points out, just as girls have been encouraged to be competent in many areas of life they were previously discouraged from, it is important we encourage boys to be caring.[11] To enable boys to be more thoughtful they need to *experience* more nurturing, and more one-on-one attention.

Most experts agree that when boys do experience good nurturing, they get a head start in life. This can be anything from parents and friends taking time to really listen to boys and encourage them to be more expressive, to enabling them to experience more physical warmth. Boys aren't naturally distant and uncaring, but over time this is what they can become. Too often boys are expected to be self-starters, without the right kind of direction and encouragement. When boys experience warmth and gentle encouragement, their experience of childhood is quite different.

Matthew, 27, feels that much of his success to date is due to his parents. 'They were always very loving and supportive, and I never felt any pressure to perform because of their expectations.' One of the things Matthew remembered most about his parents was the way they *actively* included him in family life and social situations. He has no doubt that this was a very important part of his personal development. 'Being encouraged by my parents to engage in conversation with their adult friends, so I could converse with anyone from a young age, made a big difference,' Matthew recalled.

> Boys need to be actively *included in family life.*

Lee also experienced a supportive childhood. 'I loved my dad. He knew everything – he would offer advice as to what he might do in my situation, then leave it with me.' Lee found his mother equally supportive during his formative years. He has no doubt that the encouragement of both parents – although they lived apart – enabled him to be a well-adjusted boy.

> 'Me and Dad would go away camping and fishing. If he was doing physical kind of work, we'd do it together. It was really good being with Dad.' *Jason, 22*

Part of the problem in raising boys is that parents often don't have the wider support networks of extended families and the community they enjoyed in previous generations, so all the parenting is down to them. Back-up from other family members can be a lifeline for a young boy. 'Giving the job of raising kids to one or two people is ludicrous, and it's not working well,' said Rowan, 41, when looking back on his own fractured childhood. 'It takes a whole group of loving, interested, dedicated people to raise a child.'

Learning to measure up

CHILD'S PLAY

As boys grow, they start to develop a more intimate sense of what being male means. They soon discover that the male world is dominated by competition, in which strength, self-reliance and invulnerability matter. And they quickly learn the importance of *appearing* stronger and more powerful than they feel. One of the most significant ways boys discover the world of men is through toys and games. Long before they reach school, many boys are introduced to violent toys, at a time when little girls are generally surrounded by dolls and soft toys.

Parents who buy boys these games often do so because their boys are drawn to them, and because they seem an ideal way to keep lively boys occupied. Too few parents give enough thought to what they are exposing their sons to. We only have to wander around a toy store to realise how violent toys for boys have become, as Professor Myriam Miedzian noted in *Boys Will Be Boys*: 'Today's toy manufacturers are not content to exploit traditional forms of violence in boy's toys – soldiers, military weapons, cowboys and Indian outfits. They have widened their horizons considerably. Toy manufacturers now often provide a violent storyline or characterisation that goes along with their toy.'[1]

From toys, boys progress to action-packed video games and movies. Here boys become immersed in a whole new level of violence. They watch the so-called heroes of these games solve their problems largely by obliterating their opponents. While these one-dimensional heroes may seem relatively harmless, they can have a huge impact on a young boy's psyche. Myriam Miedzian tells of the many men who went off to World War II and Vietnam with a clear determination to be just like the heroes John Wayne portrayed. What is concerning is that today's fictional action heroes – played by such iconic actors as Arnold Schwarzenegger and Jean-Claude Van Damme – are even more one-dimensional and violent than their predecessors. These characters don't have many positive messages for boys. They don't teach them about nuance and self-control, or about different approaches to difficult issues.

> Long before they reach school, many boys are introduced to violent toys, at a time when little girls are generally surrounded by dolls and soft toys.

These fictional heroes are even less helpful to boys because the way they behave is at odds with how society now operates. Our young boys, however, are still drawn to these characters because they are everything the boys are not: strong, invincible and adored, and in control of their lives and the lives of others.

Parenting is no easy task. And certainly most parents try hard to provide the best environment they can for their boys, but this is increasingly hard to achieve in a rapidly changing world, where yesterday's toys and games are already old hat. Even when parents do not buy violent toys and games, it is difficult to shield their boys from violence, because it is now present in everything from sport to the nightly news. One study of children and television violence indicated that while one-third of the children interviewed were upset by movie violence, two-thirds were affected by news violence.[2]

On average, Australian children spend 21 to 22 hours each week watching television – this is a lot of television by any standards. It's hard to gauge the full impact this steady diet of viewing – which frequently contains violent episodes – has on young boys. What indications we do have are not encouraging. Studies show that even on Saturday morning children's television shows, there are between 20 and 25 acts of violence.[3] It is chilling to note that by the time an American child reaches 11, it is estimated that they will have observed around 8000 murders.[4] Girls also see films and watch television, but overall boys are more attracted to violence in games and movies, and are in turn more likely to act out the violence they witness.

WHEN THINGS GET VIOLENT

Most boys are not as resilient as many of us like to think. Continual exposure to violence does de-sensitise them to the feelings of others, and skews their view of life. Recently I was asked to judge a writing competition for children aged 7 to 12, and I was shocked at how violent the boys' stories were, especially those written by the younger boys. Most of the stories contained explicit accounts of terrorism or intergalactic violence.

This preoccupation with violence can have serious outcomes. Numerous studies show that regular exposure to violence can give boys a misguided sense of their own invulnerability and the invulnerability of others. That's when boys hurt themselves and those around them, because they haven't fully understood the consequences of their actions. Basically, when we allow violence to be regarded as entertainment, boys will view it this way.

> *While parents may not tolerate screen violence, often they end up promoting violence, or subjecting their son to violence in less obvious ways.*

In *Boys Will Be Boys* Myriam Miedzian relates a conversation she had with a teacher friend, who was disturbed to find a serious discussion about the alleged cannibalism that had taken place in Jamestown greeted by her male students with *excitement*, and an eagerness to know all the gory details.[5] While this might seem like an isolated incident, violence is now so much a part of boys' lives that increasingly they accept it as the norm. We only have to think about the boys we know to see how addictive many of these violent games are, and how much a part of boys' lives they have become. Whether they are on a bus or a train, or relaxing at home, often they prefer to spend time with their Game Boy than do anything else, particularly interact with their family.

We can dismiss this as being alarmist, or we can start to face up to the very real consequences all this violence has on the way boys think and act. When Jim Garbarino, professor of human development at Cornell University, asked a 9-year-old boy from a violent neighbourhood what would make him feel safer, the boy's response was immediate: he said his life would be so much better if he had his own gun.[6] While we are not yet experiencing this level of violence in Australian schools, when you talk with teachers it is clear that more and more boys are bringing weapons to school and/or behaving violently at school. The more attuned boys are to violence the less safe they feel, so what are they to do? They know they are expected to be able to handle themselves. Yet unless they receive *positive* support from adults about how to deal with potentially threatening or uncomfortable situations, can we blame them for protecting themselves in the way they've seen their heroes do? This is a significant issue, because it is almost always boys who are the perpetrators of extreme violence outside school.

'My teenage years were a nightmare. I had the shit kicked out of me so many times. It's really hard for guys who are not violent. It took until I was twenty-five to feel safe.' *Ryan, 50*

Violence manifests itself in a boy's life in many ways. While his parents may not tolerate screen violence, often they end up promoting violence, or subjecting their son to violence in less obvious ways. Often fathers encourage their sons to be aggressive as a way of solving differences of opinion or asserting their rights, instead of encouraging them to talk things through.

'I was bullied very badly at school. The advice was: just punch them back. Then people wonder why boys get into violence. It's bred into them.' *Lawrence, 33*

Most children are punished, but the ways boys are punished often have an element of violence. The kinds of punishment boys are subjected to are often more intense, simply because they are boys. Some boys are hit at home for misbehaving, and frequently frustrated parents resort to humiliation or verbal abuse in an attempt to get their message across. Again, because boys are not likely to give any indication of how wounding these forms of punishment can be, it's assumed that no harm is done, but this is just not the case. We are all aware that some little boys are out of control, but violent responses are not the answer.

'I remember we had this one guy at school – he was the roughest boy – but we never knew why. Then one of my friends went to stay at his place. His dad was in the army and a bit crazy, and would lose the plot with his kids.' *Joel, 20*

'My father was angry all the time. He'd stand and shout at me, like, two or three inches from my face, just shouting. I remember wanting to kill him big time. We had a two-storey house and there was a big drop down two storeys. He used to sit on the rail at the top of the stairs. I used to think that I could just rush him and push him in the chest. He'd go down on his head onto the concrete and that would be the end of it. I never did, but that's what I wanted to do. I now avoid anywhere there is conflict.' *Doug, 52*

When boys get to school

A WHOLE NEW BALL GAME

Once boys reach school age, they face a whole new set of challenges. School does offer boys many wonderful things. There are new friendships and activities to immerse themselves in; they have the opportunity to stretch themselves, and to start to embrace a much wider world. All these things are what parents hope for their boys during their school years. What many parents are not aware of is just how confronting, if not terrifying, school can be for boys on a number of levels.

> 'There's a lot of anxiety at school. I don't think there's a lot parents can do, except allow kids to talk to them. You don't talk about certain stuff. You just soldier on.' *Nathan, 19, who attended a boys' school*

> 'It was pretty savage at school. Other boys would beat us until we couldn't stand up. We used to band together in groups, to protect each other. We had lunch together and left school together to try to stay safe.' *Craig, 58, who attended a co-educational school*

Bullying and schoolyard violence is something most boys have to deal with on a regular basis. Girls also face these challenges, but for most it is less physically violent. There's also no doubt that many boys do love to be physically active – horseplay, teasing and jokes are all ways they get to know each other and become friends.[1] Sometimes this play is harmless, sometimes it is aggressive. Boys need to learn early what is acceptable play, and what is not.

'In Year 7 I went to a new school where I didn't know anybody. I sort of had to prove myself because some of the bigger guys picked on me. It wasn't too bad or anything, but it got rough. It was my problem to deal with. You don't want to talk about stuff at that age. You're introduced to a new part of society with new rules.' *Joel, 20*

The difficulty for boys is that many adults are ambivalent about the behaviour they expect from them. Often parents try to impose one type of behaviour, while popular culture encourages a completely different approach. Until society and parents are clear on what is acceptable and unacceptable behaviour, boys will remain vulnerable. Too often they are left to figure it out on their own, and they end up following a pack mentality of survival-of-the-fittest.

One of the factors that complicates what boys see as acceptable is that violence at school is on the rise, forcing boys to be constantly vigilant against attack. It is also important we recognise that schoolyard violence doesn't only happen in underprivileged schools; it also takes place in the most prestigious ones.

Terrible things can and do happen
to boys at school.

Tragically, many boys endure their school days rather than enjoy them, because terrible things can and do happen to boys at school. Many boys are so shamed by the cruelty and humiliation they experience at school, they will never talk about these things, not even to those who are close. They also keep quiet because they don't want to let down those they love by admitting they're not coping.

In order to survive, boys are often driven to do things they wouldn't otherwise do, and can end up becoming part of the cycle of violence they seek to avoid. Sometimes they are the victim, and sometimes they victimise others. 'Often a bully is someone who is afraid of being bullied themselves,' points out Dean Francis, director of the film *Boys Grammar*. 'The easiest way to avoid it is to bully others. This comes from a deep insecurity within the bully, and this is sad. Bullies see themselves as superior to their victims, but this is all in their minds.'[2]

> 'I don't know what causes the cruelty at school – I suffered it. I was very depressed. You think you are alone with it.' *Nathan, 19*

In an effort to appear strong or to survive, boys may end up betraying close friends. Even boys who witness the terrible things that take place at school tend to keep quiet, because they are too frightened or embarrassed to do otherwise, and so this cruelty is perpetuated.

> 'You're very aware of how you look next to other people; not so much physical image, just your image. It started to hit me after primary school. People start to grow up around you, and you start to see weaknesses and strengths, particularly among the boys. That's when you start to realise there's a kind of pecking order. You get a place.

There's somewhere you should be amongst the other boys, where you stand. It does create anxiety, because people are always trying to move up, and there's also a bit of a fear of failure that comes with that, because you don't want to be down the bottom. You don't want to compete, because the person above you might put you in your place.' *Sean, 20*

This situation is complicated by the fact that the overwhelming majority of teachers are now women. Because of this, those boys who are in desperate need of positive adult male role models miss out on spending time with men they can look up to. The problem is further aggravated by the fact that not all male teachers are ideal – some can be real bullies. It was sobering to talk to a number of boys who had attended a boys' school, to get their side of the story. I had assumed it would be a largely positive experience, but many found it alienating and brutalising because of male teachers who were 'out of control'.

Even boys who didn't go to boys' schools often had bad experiences with male teachers, as Lawrence told me. 'Bullying started from the moment I arrived at school until I was sixteen. Around the age of twelve and thirteen was worst – it's a really helpless time for boys. There was a real fear. It can really affect people's lives. It's horrible. You can see why school kids commit suicide. I experienced teachers, mainly men, who encouraged bullying. The male teachers who taught footy and those kinds of macho things were worst. They would laugh at us when things happened. When I tried to appeal for help, they'd either say bullying was good for me, or that I shouldn't encourage bullies.'

When boys are in crisis they need to be around men who know how to establish firm boundaries, and to *actively* demonstrate how a man can handle a tricky situation, without obliterating a boy's sense of self. I think we all recognise how difficult it is being a teacher today, and that teachers need more support. Teachers also need to know the difference they can make to boys when they do provide this leadership. 'What I find is, in the schools where I worked, where the level of adult supervision was very high and the protections are great, how grateful boys are after there has been a threatening incident and adults have stepped in,' explains psychologist Michael Thompson.[3]

> *The combative world boys face at school often means there are few places they can relax and feel safe.*

WHEN TEACHERS DON'T ACT

It is up to *all* teachers to create the appropriate environment for boys at school. Some do this well. Others let boys down, because they don't understand the impact their actions can have on boys. For example, when teachers learn of schoolyard incidents, too often they fail to respond, or they respond inappropriately, because they are overworked or because they genuinely don't know what to do. Or they simply dismiss the latest drama as 'boys being boys'. Other teachers prefer to steer clear of combative situations, because they want to be popular with their students. Many teachers don't realise just how important appropriate intervention is.

Jim Garbarino tells the tragic story of a 16-year-old boy he interviewed in prison, whose life of violence began at 8 when his friend was attacked by a group of boys at school. Their teacher saw exactly what happened, but walked away. From then on this boy felt he was on his own, and acted accordingly. Studies show that when teachers are firm but humane, and have the skills to get difficult boys under control, they help prevent aggressive peer groups forming.[4]

Boys welcome boundaries. When they are able to operate in a structured environment that takes account of their needs, they feel less threatened and are more able to relax and enjoy the moment. Where there are no boundaries and safeguards, they feel compelled to take charge of their own safety, and they form peer groups to do so.

'You are either intimidated by teachers, or you have to sit back and watch other boys being favoured. It makes you feel rebellious. I think women teachers are better at being even-handed.' *Nathan, 19*

WHAT BULLYING CAN CREATE

The combative world boys face at school often means there are few places they can relax and feel safe. Bullying has become so prevalent that boys feel they need to be constantly on guard. According to Professor Ken Rigby, an expert on bullying, approximately one in six students is bullied on a weekly basis.[5] As boys are unlikely to let parents and teachers know how bad things are, adults need to be aware of the warning signs, and take action by making it clear that bullying is not to be tolerated, and by teaching kids conflict-resolution skills. If a boy has lost interest in school, if his marks have declined, if he is fearful or unwilling to attend school, if he has become a loner or seems down, he may need help.

'There were plenty of fights at school. When I was at primary school I enjoyed fighting, because the worst thing that could happen to you was losing a baby tooth or getting a cut. There wasn't the strength to do real damage. Bullying was very different as a teenager. It had a real psychological element to it. You couldn't just forget about it.' *Jason, 22*

Boys do need to learn to stand up for themselves, but they need help to do so. It takes a strong sense of self for adults to stand their ground in a trying situation, so how much harder must it be for a kid? Many boys struggle through school simply trying their best to survive. Some make it, some don't. Some of those who are losing the battle decide to take matters into their own hands. For some boys this means suicide, while others work on getting even.

In one of the most tragic cases of bullying I have heard, 15-year-old Andy Williams took a gun to Santana High School, where he killed two students and wounded an additional eleven students and two adults. Described as a skinny, baby-faced boy, Andy had been repeatedly bullied and called names at school. Even though his life had become unbearable, Andy didn't talk to his teachers, nor did classmates who witnessed this bullying speak up. So, in a desperate attempt to end his pain, this seemingly mild-mannered teenager killed two classmates and was sentenced to fifty-years-to-life. Andy later admitted that just before the shootings he considered whether he should go ahead. But when he realised that if he didn't, the bullying would continue, he felt he had no choice. Andy knew he would either be shot or end up incarcerated, but as awful as it may seem, he saw these outcomes as preferable to what he was dealing with.[6] We are yet to experience a school massacre; let's hope we can protect our boys so they don't feel compelled to resort to such extreme measures.

Schools are now working hard to combat bullying, but it is a difficult issue, because bullying is on the increase and continues to take on new forms. Ironically, the Andy Williams incident happened at a school that had already implemented an anti-bullying campaign. It had even made anonymous sign-in sheets available for students to report bullying, but still the culture of cruelty and violence at school won out. This cruelty can and does follow boys into adulthood, and so the cycle is perpetuated.

> 'Bullying is a pecking order based on physicality. It's an animal thing, a very jungle thing. Some men never ever let up. They take it right on. They bully their way through their careers, bully their families.'
> *Doug, 52*

> 'I don't think the bullying stops at school. I used to work for some people who all went to the same private boys' school. They were the worst mental bullies I've ever met. They would find a person's weakness and just go for it. There was one staff member who was short, and they honed in on that and just wouldn't let up. It was horrible.'
> *Lawrence, 33*

One of Sydney's most prestigious schools was in the limelight in 2001 when two students pleaded guilty to indecently assaulting a fellow student with a dildo made in woodwork class. It was alleged this boy had been assaulted by two schoolmates on approximately twenty-five occasions.[7] When the boy's parents first heard of the assault through doctors, they assumed the doctors had the wrong boy. What is shocking is that not only did these two boys strip the student to his boxer shorts, tie him up and assault him as other students watched, the boys who did this were regarded as 'good mates' of the victim. They had stayed in his home a number of times, and had been taken on various outings by his parents. Clearly no-one had picked up on this bullying. In his findings the public prosecutor noted that, 'The culture of rumbling and bullying seemingly went unchecked by school officials.'[8]

'Basically I feel that if the peer group says bullying is in, it's in. And if the peer group says it's out, it's out. It's really important for schools to work not only with the victims, the bullies, the parents, with teachers, but with the peer group. The peer group have incredible power.'
Psychologist Evelyn Field[9]

Prompted by these events, Dean Francis directed a short film, *Boys Grammar*. 'The school system perpetuates bullying,' he explained. 'When we worked on the film, we asked all the cast and crew whether they had experienced bullying, and all of them had in some way. They all had some horrible stories to tell.' Dean believes that it is the unwillingness of schools to tackle the issue that helps perpetuate these situations. 'At the moment, schools tend to create an environment where bullying is not talked about, or quietly condoned. By not talking about it, victims feel that they can't express their suffering, and are then unable to find a solution to their problem.'

As we have already noted, teachers have an important role to play, not purely in terms of discipline, but in being aware of the effect of their actions. Dean agrees. 'Teachers often don't realise that the way they treat students impacts the way those students are treated by the rest of their peer group. A good example is a kid who is not good at sport. I remember being criticised in front of the class for not being able to run fast enough. I remember that criticism flowing over into lunchtime and the next lunchtime. It was painful.'[10] Parents and teachers need to know more about the dynamics of peer groups, so they can influence them positively.

'In my primary school the bulk of the boys were in a sort of gang, and they did this thing called scragging, which was where they ran after you [and] pulled your pants down. Out of all the boys in my year, there were only two or three of us that made sure we never got scragged. They'd even scrag each other. If they couldn't get one of the weaker ones, then they'd turn on each other. To me it would have been a majorly humiliating thing had it happened to me, so all the time in the playground, we didn't go over near where the mob was, and we ate our lunch slightly separately, and we were on guard all the time. *Lord of the Flies* made a lot of sense when I read it. It's very real.' *Doug, 52*

LEARNING DIFFICULTIES

It's not only cruelty boys have to deal with at school; many struggle with their studies because of learning difficulties. Studies show that boys are three times more likely than girls to end up in remedial reading classes, and four to five times more likely to have language disorders and disabilities. They are five times more likely to stutter and to experience extreme difficulty in learning to talk, and four times more likely to suffer from autism.[11]

We know that boys are under-performing at school, but what we don't fully realise is what this lack of success *feels* like for these boys. Many of them aren't exaggerating when they say they hate school and see it as irrelevant or uninviting. Of all the students who are suspended or expelled from school, the vast majority are boys.

For many boys, school is a place of containment and punishment where they are bullied by peers, and misunderstood or mistreated by teachers. And because these boys don't feel their teachers engage them in meaningful ways, they assume their teachers don't care.[12] Perceptions are not necessarily the same as reality, but as we all know, they are a potent factor in the way we experience the world. Most teachers do try hard to draw the kids into their classes. However, as linguist Deborah Tannen points out, still girls tend to get most of the praise and positive attention at school.[13]

> 'Boys need a comfort zone. The majority of boys don't feel comfortable at school.' *Nathan, 19*

Most educationalists now realise that more appropriate ways are needed to encourage boys to learn. Part of the current evaluation of school curricula and teaching styles recognises that boys need plenty of activity *during* the school day, and that subjects and teaching styles must be more conducive to boys, just as the requirements of girls and special-needs children are now more to the fore. A number of good initiatives are already underway, where boys are allowed to be more lively in the classroom; where they are being actively encouraged to study subjects not traditionally considered 'male' subjects; and where their emotional needs and concerns are addressed. Yet, as most of these and other programs are still in their infancy, for the majority of boys the experience of school remains largely unchanged. And when faced with big classes and heavy workloads, it can be extremely hard for teachers to find positive ways to reach difficult boys, so they have little option other than to try to keep them under control, and this usually means punishing them. The end result is that for many boys at school there is little opportunity to be listened to, let alone catered for.

WHAT CAN HAPPEN TO HIGH ACHIEVERS

I was concerned to discover that it's not cool to succeed at school. Even academically bright boys now tend to be more worried about how their peers view them than how well they do at school. Often boys will act up or under-perform so they don't get singled out by the bullies, who are often the less academically able boys. The boys I spoke with were quite open about their concern not to outshine their peers in case of paybacks. For those who did come under this scrutiny, it's not something they forget. It's hard to imagine the amount of pressure boys must be under to compromise themselves in this way. Unless these boys get effective help, they will continue to feel they have no choice, other than to do what their peers expect.

'There is some sort of desire . . . not to outdo your peers, by not being too good at anything.' *Sean, 20*

While this pressure doesn't simply apply to boys, often the pressure to conform is more acute for them because the ways in which they can express their masculinity can be very narrow. In their struggle to fit in with peers and succeed in the workplace, boys tend to steer clear of the humanities and social sciences, opting for maths and science instead. 'That is where the money is, and status resides in the rational–technical culture of a macho, male-dominated workplace,' academic Don Edgar points out. 'The paradox is, it won't be for long, as productivity comes to depend more and more on creativity, and interpersonal skills.'[14]

It was clear from my interviews that boys are very aware of the vocational expectations peers and teachers have of them. And while it is seen as desirable for boys to have more choices in the subjects they take, they are aware from very early on of the need to be a good provider and to make their way in the world. So they are more likely to study computing, business or science subjects than arts, social sciences or languages.

'We learnt about maths and science, and English and stuff, but I always found it strange we were never taught about emotions and how to interact with people. It was almost like if you can't put a mark to it, then why bother.' *Robert, 30*

WHAT DO WE WANT FROM BOYS?

Sadly, too few adults understand what it's like for boys at school today, and when they are faced with problems, their responses lack consistency. 'We expect too much of boys – and we don't expect enough,' one teacher told Dan Kindlon. 'On the one hand, we expect them to do things they're developmentally not ready to do, and to be tough "little men" when they're really just little boys who need goodbye hugs and affection. On the other hand, when they behave in cruel and thoughtless ways, we say, "Oh, boys will be boys." We let them off the hook over issues of respect and consideration for others.'[15]

As we have seen, appearances can be deceptive. Most boys are not nearly as tough as they appear. As Olga Silverstein points out, too often we're happy to take boys at face value, not realising how shut-down many are inside. 'Male children in adolescence are assumed to be well functioning when they are athletic, do reasonably well in school, and show signs of leadership qualities and bravado, while remaining basically attentive to authority. That they may also be detached, uncommunicative and emotionally sealed off is seldom perceived as a problem,' she explains. 'But twenty years of looking at the results in the therapist's consulting room have convinced me that the costs are too high.'[16]

Birth of a hero

LEARNING TO BE GOOD SPORTS

Boys long to be loved and respected by their family, especially their dad. Generally, one way boys can gain this acceptance is by excelling at sport. Sport can be good for boys, because it challenges them and helps teach them discipline. It also gives them the opportunity to immerse themselves in something they love, to experience winning and losing, and being part of a team. Many boys find sport exhilarating, but for those who aren't athletically inclined, the fierce competition and pressure many sports demand can prove hard to take. Few of these boys will admit to how they *really* feel about sport, because they are all too aware of parental and peer expectations. And as most adults are unaware of the anxiety boys can experience around sport, they don't even think to question whether their boy really loves his sport or not.

A friend of mine confessed recently that she was worried about her son's preoccupation with the performance of his cricket team. Her son was attending a school with a strong sporting reputation, and he had just missed out on making a higher grade team. Each week this boy was becoming increasingly anxious about the game. It wasn't until his mother spoke to him about it that she discovered he was ashamed to be in a team that wasn't very good. He was also worried that his prospects to progress to a better team were less and less promising as his team continued to lose. No-one wants to feel like a failure, but this is what prevailing attitudes towards participation in school sport often create.

> *Few boys will admit to how they really feel about sport, because they are all too aware of parental and peer expectations.*

When we dig a little deeper we discover that the pressures boys face in sport aren't confined to the football field or basketball court. Boys also have to learn how to handle the locker room. For many boys the locker room is an intimate and exhilarating space of sweat and tears, exhaustion and injury. It's the place they retire to, to reflect on their victories and defeats. This confined space is one of the few places where boys can show their emotions, and celebrate being male. But for any boy who doesn't measure up, the locker room can be a terrifying place. Here boys are often singled out: because they are new to the team, because they are slight, or because their performance is lacking. Or they may simply be in the wrong place at the wrong time. For those of us who have never been in a locker room after a game, it is shocking to discover that this is where boys can and do intimidate, hurt or humiliate – where they force each other into cruel, degrading or crude behaviour. It is here boys are set on, taunted, isolated, ignored. The awful thing is that most boys simply accept what is happening to them, and try to survive the best they can.

'We institutionalise <u>violence and make it okay.</u> Look at rugby and the way they take each other's heads off.' *Ryan, 50*

WHO GETS TO BE HERO?

For those <u>boys lucky enough to excel at sports,</u> their experience is quite different – <u>they become heroes.</u> They are heaped with praise and given a lot of encouragement, because they represent all that society regards as intrinsically male. Often these kids become so pumped up that, as far as their peers are concerned, they can do no wrong. Too often <u>this elitism creates new levels of dysfunction in</u> boys and men. In her *New York Times* article 'Bad Sports', elite athlete Maria Burton Nelson details a number of disturbing rituals that have crept into American sport, including 'pig parties', at which the footballer who brings the ugliest partner wins a trophy. There is nothing heroic about this kind of behaviour, but these and other demeaning rituals are becoming more and more prevalent in male sports at all levels, because no-one challenges them.[1]

'I was okay because I played soccer. It's rugby that's the kind of gritted-teeth sport. Those boys were a bit of an elite group, and that's a worry. It doesn't help those boys, because their ego builds up.' *Nathan, 19*

It is these <u>cultures that encourage athletic boys to believe they</u> <u>have the right to sexually assault girls,</u> attack others and <u>trash hotel</u> <u>rooms.</u> One of the most notorious high school sports scandals was the Spur Posse in Lakewood, California, in the 1980s, where a group of high school jocks competed with each other as to who could sleep with the most girls. Some girls slept with these boys willingly, others did so because they were intimidated or forced. When asked why they behaved this way, one boy said, 'They're not really girls to me. They're just points.'[2] When challenged about this behaviour, the father of one of the boys said, 'Nothing my boy did was anything that any red-blooded American boy wouldn't do at his age.'[3] What these boys did *was* inexcusable, and adults defending this behaviour doesn't help change it.

> A recent study into male intimidation and violence in high school athletics revealed that violence and intimidation were not only prevalent in school sport, but were regarded by some athletes as a legitimate way to help them win.

Now sport has become big business, sporting heroes are gaining even greater profiles. As sponsorship dollars are poured into sport, the ambitions of schools, parents and coaches continue to increase. A South African friend of mine described recently how boys in his former school's rugby team are treated like royalty. They are feted everywhere they go, and are now accompanied to matches by a whole range of back-up, including a physiotherapist. When these boys are singled out for this level of attention, they are allowed to believe they can do whatever they like, on and off the field.

This willingness to turn a blind eye encourages unacceptable, even violent behaviour that can and does follow these boys into adulthood. A number of Australian football fans were so concerned about the number of alleged sexual assaults by players, they formed Football Fans Against Sexual Assault. They have documented more than twenty allegations of sexual assault by Australian footballers that were covered or revisited in the media: in 2004 alone, these alleged incidents included an assault on a 19-year-old woman by Cronulla Sharks players at a motel in Riccarton, New Zealand; another on a woman in her 20s by a Brisbane Lions player in a London motel room; and an alleged gang rape of a Los Angeles woman by a Hawthorn Hawks official and at least two players in a motel room in Hawaii.[4]

WHAT IT TAKES TO WIN

Solid figures about cheating in local sport are hard to come by, but a recent study into male intimidation and violence in high school athletics in North Carolina gives some indication of the nature of the problem. This study revealed that intimidation and violence were not only prevalent in American school sport, but were regarded by some athletes as a legitimate way to help them win. Even players who disliked violence and intimidation admitted to being drawn into these tactics to help maintain or improve their position on the team. A number of players believed they were evaluated not only on their ability to be good at their chosen sport, but also their willingness to be aggressive on the field. Over half the athletic directors who took part in this study said that verbal intimidation was a 'very serious' or 'a somewhat serious' problem in school sport.[5]

> *Over half the male respondents in one study believed it was acceptable to deliberately inflict pain in football and to intimidate an opponent.*

In its 2004 Sportsmanship Survey of 4200 high school athletes, the Josephson Institute of Ethics in America revealed that 58 per cent of the male respondents believed it was acceptable to deliberately inflict pain in football and to intimidate an opponent; 40 per cent felt it was fine to keep quiet when an official declared the wrong score in favour of their team; 39 per cent thought it was okay to fake injury to get extra time out; and 37 per cent believed that it was more important to win than be a good sport.'[6]

While these figures are American, they clearly demonstrate how the values boys are exposed to in sport can have a dramatic effect, not only on the field, but in the rest of their lives. If we allow boys to cheat and to emasculate each other to win at sport, they cannot be blamed for believing this behaviour will be acceptable in their social and working lives once they grow up.

In this same study, 30 per cent of those surveyed believed people who break rules in sport are more likely to succeed, while 56 per cent agreed that in the real world people who break the rules are more likely to get ahead.[7] Perhaps it's time to refine our definition of success in sport. A number of boys I spoke to had fathers who were successful sportsmen – in almost every case the boys had a hellish home life, because of the pressures and values they were exposed to.

'There is a lot of pressure on boys. There is an expected image to live up to – to succeed, to be good at sport.' *Jason, 22*

WHEN THE PRESSURE GETS TOO MUCH

Some boys are naturally aggressive on the field, but aggression is also learned. How teachers and coaches conduct themselves is crucial to boys learning appropriate behaviour both on and off the sports field. There's no doubt that what some coaches say officially bears no resemblance to what they demand of their players. Many coaches do provide boys with excellent coaching, but others are clearly in the game to win at all costs, and encourage boys to take this approach by motivating or intimidating them. Sporting groups in Britain have become so concerned about the many pressures kids now face in sport, they have set up the Child Protection in Sport Unit to minimise abuse in sport by focusing on bullying, over-rigorous training and lack of attention to the developmental needs of young people in sport.[8]

> 'You get these hard teachers. I remember one saying to me, "You only break the rules twice if you play football: once if your opponent does so first, and second if you're losing." Winning's important. If you have to break a few heads, then that's what you have to do. I guess this translates into the playground where you learn to play tough, be hard, be mean.' *Robert, 30*

To date there is little research on what the pressure to win does to boys involved in sport. Part of the deal in playing sport is learning how to handle the pressure and the pain. Coaches are there to apply pressure, but the question needs to be asked: how much pressure is reasonable? Coaches themselves are now under far more pressure from parents, schools and sporting bodies, which makes their job even harder.

A recent *Woman's Day* article reported that Australian sport had lost 70 000 coaches and 116 000 referees and umpires across all sports between 2000 and 2005. It also revealed that some parents were paying up to $70 000 per year in coaching fees for such sports as tennis, in the hope their kids might become professional players.[9] Parents are pivotal to a boy's positive experience of sport. In recent years their behaviour on the sidelines has deteriorated to the point where some parents have been banned from attending games. If parents are behaving badly in public, it's hard to imagine the pressure their kids are under at home.

> *Too often adults assume boys can deal with situations when they can't.*

According to academic Peter West, the emphasis schools now place on sport helps create a defective male image that is arrogant, elitist and violent.[10] There's little doubt that for those not good at sport, school can be a gruelling experience. 'The way sport is taught at school can be very humiliating,' Lawrence, now 33, told me. 'There was no choice about participating until I was sixteen and able to assert myself, and say I didn't want to take part. There's a lot of bullying in contact sport — it happens out on the field. The teachers humiliate the non-athletic kids in front of everyone else.' Most kids don't forget this kind of fear and humiliation. It came back to haunt Lawrence when he was in corporate life. 'We had a team-building day at the company I was with. It was very competitive. I felt a violent reaction against it.'

'I was a little bit lucky as I was a pretty sporty kid. I played soccer, so as far as other people were concerned I was okay. The geeky, dorky people wouldn't participate unless they had to. Some of them got picked on and pushed to the ground, their pants pulled down — that sort of thing. You can't really justify it, but people were doing it to make an example, to impress their friends. It wasn't really outright violent anger or anything, just people trying to be cool, that sort of stuff.' *Sean, 20*

Even if a boy is a talented artist, a maths genius or a fine musician, he will receive far less kudos than if he were good at sport. By excelling in a non-sporting area he is likely to be subjected to cruelty and humiliation by his peers. One of Doug's most enduring memories of school was of being bullied and left out. Although Doug is now an artist and landscape gardener, he has never forgotten the terrible sense of isolation he felt at not being able to take part in outdoor activities after school, due to his fair complexion.

Too often adults assume boys can deal with situations, when they can't. Boys need tangible encouragement from those around them, as much as they need boundaries. For Lee, now a 48-year-old IT professional, the support his teachers gave him was one of the main reasons he enjoyed school, and why he chose the career he did. 'My geeky and technical friends and I had fun; passing exams was quite easy. The teachers liked us a lot. I think teachers being supportive and kind to me and my friends helped us.'

Clearly, good teachers can make all the difference and, along with the support of parents, they can help protect and nurture boys as they attempt to find their way. Every boy has the right to be respected and acknowledged. But whenever the system singles out a handful of boys for special attention, the rest come to believe they are failures, long before they have had a chance to prove themselves out in the world.

Angry young men

STANDING ON SHAKY GROUND

When boys reach their teenage years, often they become angry and uncommunicative. It can be a bewildering time for them, as their hormone levels change and their bodies seem to grow almost daily. Not only do they have their complexion to deal with, there's their hair and wardrobe to worry about, and the constant concern over whether or not they look cool. Their attitude towards sex, girls and male peers is also confused, as they begin to experience emotions they were previously unaware of.

Often it can feel as if they are swimming against the tide. While their parents continually remind them they are not yet grown up, teenage boys are acutely aware their adult lives are just around the corner. Long before manhood they start to worry about what they are going to do with their life, and whether they'll be successful. Now more than ever they are aware of the need to be materially successful, because they believe that if they're not, much will be denied to them.

'Anger is the first emotion that comes up. If you feel sad, the first emotion is anger. It's very rarely pure anger for young men. If you're feeling guilty or hurt or weak, then you express it with anger, because if you're angry, you're a man. It has to be aggressive anger, not latent anger, otherwise that's seen as girly.' *Tony, 26*

Today teenage boys also need to come to terms with the changing roles of men. 'Boys are now aware of the new identities emerging for men, and the many expectations that come with this,' says teacher John Lee. He quotes Patrick, a Year 11 student talking about what counts: 'If you go on what men say [you're meant] to be the big tough sort of person, a big football star, if you go on what the women say it is to be more emotional, softer sort of people.'[1] Patrick is fortunate to have some sense of how to be tough *and* caring. 'You can be both; you can be the big tough sort of guy in the home, to your girlfriend; you can be [a] softer, more emotional sort of person, do things around the house, clean for her, cook for her.'[2] Most boys are not so clear about how they can be macho and considerate at the same time. Like many grown men, they struggle with how to meet these seemingly conflicting social expectations.

> *Teenage boys are acutely aware their adult lives are just around the corner.*

PEER PRESSURE

Not only are teenage boys trying to establish their own identity and win the respect of their parents, they also have their peers to worry about. The approval of peers is crucial to teenage boys. The problem for most boys during these years is that their peers' values often differ greatly from those of their parents. Unless parents can be open about their *own* teen struggles with peer pressure, the conflict many boys face around peers will remain undiscussed.

Often boys try to solve this conflict by being one person with their friends, and another, quite different person at home. Sensing this, some parents come down heavily on their sons to protect them from what they consider to be unhelpful influences. What many parents don't realise is that this approach simply intensifies the already considerable pressure their boys are under. Other parents ignore the difficulties their boys are facing, hoping they will resolve themselves.

'My friends and my parents were fine. Then all of a sudden I started wanting more and more and more. I'd made a new . . . group of friends. That was when we started going out drinking and smoking dope, and breaking the law, and that sort of thing. I couldn't please both, so I chose my friends. Basically I told my parents to get stuffed. It wasn't peer pressure that drove me to do that. I was very conscious what I wanted. I didn't want to be home with my parents. You have a fight with your parents and you get a bit angry, then you go out with your friends and you have a great time.' *Sean, 20*

Teenage life has probably never been easy, but parents need to realise that the competing pressures teenage boys face can be intense. It is easy to discount how pressured boys feel to measure up to peer and parental expectations. These pressures have probably always been there, but they are more acute than generations ago, because of teenagers' access to money and freedom, and the prevalence of working households.

Often these pressures surface in unexpected ways. For psychotherapist Roger Horrocks, who grew up on the wrong side of the tracks, his main challenge as an adolescent was to deal with the divide between social classes. Roger was bright and ended up in a private school. He dealt with this by developing a 'posh' accent at school, which he would then drop when he was at home or out with neighbourhood friends. 'I had to live like an actor, remembering which costume, which identity to put on, depending on which setting I was in.'[3]

> *Every boy needs to discover how to be a man.*

Not only do teen boys have peers and parents to contend with, there are girls to come to terms with as well. This isn't easy, because as well as outstripping boys academically, girls are way ahead in emotional maturity. Far more is now expected emotionally of men and boys. Yet while it is more acceptable for men to express their emotions than it was a few decades ago, as teacher John Lee points out, 'teenage boys are still bound by a very narrow definition of masculinity, which gives them relatively little freedom to express their many feelings.'[4] It's a big ask to expect boys who have never been encouraged to express their emotions appropriately to be emotionally at ease during their turbulent teens. With all these issues weighing on them, it's no surprise that teen boys often explode or retreat, preferring to spend long periods of time alone in their room or with friends.

WILL THEY *EVER* GROW UP?

Today there is childhood and adulthood, and what to most boys can seem like an excruciatingly long time in between. Far too many boys face years of uncertainty and confusion as they struggle to live up to what is expected of them by parents and peers. With the increase in single-parent households run by overworked mothers, and the absence of meaningful rites of passage that help boys make the transition from boyhood to manhood, often their teen years are far more difficult for boys than they need be.

'I drank and smoked, but when my friends got into drugs I walked away. I never discussed it with my parents. I was too afraid to discuss these things with them, in case they rubbished me. It was really hard, because I had all these conflicting emotions.' *Robert, 30*

Every boy needs to discover how to be a man. But to do so they need to be around men. When boys lack this help, they set about creating their own rites of passage, often taking their cues from the largely violent, dysfunctional representations of men they see in movies and video games, and on television. In a desperate attempt to prove they are heroes, they begin to drive too fast, drink too much, get involved in fights and use drugs. The number of young men who die on the roads is cause for concern, but they cannot be held totally responsible when almost every film they see has elaborate car chases and other death-defying stunts.

Not all teenage boys get drawn into extreme behaviour, but they can still be challenging to their parents, teachers and community. While parents and teachers complain constantly about dealing with disaffected teenage boys, they also tend to assume this is how teen boys are meant to be. But as psychologist Dan Kindlon points out, it is tragic that society has come to accept dysfunctional teenage boys as the norm.[5]

'The whole concept of masculinity involves the concept of toughness, and being a fighter is very much a part of that. The trick is to become a warrior, not a thug. It's important to give boys some purpose, some direction for their energies. That's what happens when you get them fighting in a competitive sense. All of a sudden the aggressive tendencies take on a meaningful dimension; that's significant. The other thing you're trying to do with boys is to give them a sense of belonging, that has a rationale beyond themselves. At Fight Club they feel part of a team. There is the framework of the group, of younger and older men that we're trying to initiate them into. The value is that we are offering them a positive male role model.' *Father Dave Smith, Fight Club*[6]

'Boys need to understand there is no stereotype they must follow,' said Craig, 58. 'I had an uncle who was only two years older than me, and he took me under his wing. He broke with the family mould and went into the theatre. He exposed me to a different environment to what I grew up in, [which] broadened my options on what life was.' This uncle proved a lifesaver for Craig, who grew up in a tough working-class household. According to Craig, one of the best things about his uncle was that he was honest about himself. 'Knowing his faults helped me acknowledge and accept mine,' he explained.

For John Day, a long-time educationalist and headmaster for fifteen years, the influence of good male teachers in schools remains central. 'Young men are being stereotyped and tamed. The result is underachievement, frustration and aggression.'

Again and again the strong sense of isolation many boys feel surfaced during my interviews. 'I never really felt like I expected my parents to help me. It wouldn't occur to me to ask my parents for help,' reflected Sean, 20, who as a teenager experienced problems with drinking and drugs sparked by peer pressure and a friend's father who made marijuana freely available to these boys, allowing them to smoke in his home whenever they chose. Lawrence, 33, felt the same way: 'I was a very sensitive child – I felt everything. I had drug problems and mental health problems, and I also attempted suicide.' His teenage years were extremely painful. More than once he asked for help from parents and teachers, only to be told it was up to him to handle whatever he was dealing with. 'So I moved away from home as soon as I could.'

MAKING THE CONFUSION AND LONELINESS GO AWAY

Once we can appreciate how adolescent boys feel about themselves and their world, it is less of a surprise that so many of them turn to drugs and alcohol as a way out. All the boys I interviewed talked openly about how much alcohol did for them. They enjoyed drinking because of the comfort it brought. 'You want to fit in and have the image of being rebellious,' explained Nathan, 19. 'Alcohol becomes a good excuse. It makes you feel you can get away with anything. It does make socialising much easier.'

> 'I got into alcohol and drugs at thirteen. I was attracted to the [allure] of it. It was supposed to be good and it was. I started pinching alcohol out of my parents' cupboards. When I took alcohol and drugs I just felt relaxed and comfortable. Things that normally bothered me, didn't. I introduced my friends to it. I worked out a level where I could drink and smoke and still handle it.' *Jason, 22*

The struggle our teen boys currently face in making a successful transition from childhood to manhood comes at a time when there are more movies in which men are drinking and using drugs, and also more alcohol ads. Marketers do their homework; they know how to get teenage boys to respond to these ads because they make it their business to know their vulnerabilities. Boys respond. Naïvely they assume their responses are their own.

'I had a bit of a block when I was sixteen. Underage drinking was a big thing for me. I would go to a few park parties. The fun part about that was that everyone was there, everyone you knew from school, except that you're out there doing this forbidden thing – drinking and smoking. Everyone was basically out there for the same thing. They just wanted to have fun. It's pretty much the fascination with meeting lots of people. You just embrace it, and often you go over the top.' *Sean, 20*

Drinking is attractive to boys because they believe, as ads constantly suggest, this is what *real* men do. While teen boys are drinking, for a few short hours they are able to feel how they most long to feel – like men. The same is true of their drug-taking – it relaxes them and makes them feel good. It's interesting that while they regarded these activities as macho, when asked if they would be happy for a sibling to be drinking and using drugs, they were all protective of younger brothers, and sisters in particular, and said they would do what they could to prevent them from going down this same route.

'I took a lot of drugs. I started young and finished young. I started smoking around eleven. By thirteen or fourteen I was smoking marijuana. I took a lot of LSD at school. The drugs allowed things. They made you feel closer to other people, and it gave you the chance to be emotional, because you could always blame it on the drugs. There was definitely a yearning to try new things. You basically didn't want a drug out there you hadn't tried. It was an outlet.' *Tony, 26*

'Drugs for me were huge. When I left high school, I did say no to drugs. But then the first time I took ecstasy it was wonderful. Everything was so fabulous. I felt I'd been lied to. The campaigns should concentrate on what happens to you when you take drugs – peeing your pants, vomiting.' *Lawrence, 33*

Not only are alcohol and drugs addictive, they impair a boy's ability to make good judgement calls, which is why so many teen boys get into fights, get attacked, get behind the wheel of a car and end up dead. We need to understand *their* perspective before we can find workable solutions.

'I am drinking and smoking more marijuana now. It is affecting my academic ability, and it's the same for a large portion of my friends. Life is just happening for me. I find it hard to have ambition. It's hard to be positive.' *Jason, 22*

LOOKING BEHIND THE MASK

Now more than ever it is crucial that adults don't take the confidence of teen boys at face value. Parents and other adults who come into daily contact with adolescent boys need to learn to look behind the mask. Then they will see the anger, sadness and fear that lies behind the bravado. While boys are maturing earlier than previous generations – because of better diets and education, and more freedom – what many adults fail to realise is that these boys still have to catch up emotionally. Society continues to assume teenage boys can cope with their teenage years, so it tends to focus its attention on the vulnerability of teenage girls instead.

Teen girls do need good support, but they are already ahead of boys in this regard. Not only do many of them talk to each other about their issues, they have magazines, sitcoms and soaps to discuss everything from their emotions and aspirations, to make-up and the intricacies of their bodies. All these things help educate and entertain girls, and nurture their sense of self. Boys don't have these outlets to the same extent, so their doubts and frustrations remain locked inside, or surface in inappropriate ways. By assuming only girls are vulnerable during their teenage years, society continues to ignore the needs of teen boys. We need to learn a great deal more about what makes boys tick, then find positive ways to support boys and girls to the same level.

> *Today many boys have few men in their lives.*

In the many interviews I conducted, I was surprised to discover how readily grown men recalled the loneliness and frustration they felt as teenagers. 'Thank Christ that's over. No-one was helping me work it out,' reflected Rowan, 41. Craig, 58, agreed: 'My recollections are of sexual confusion and innocence, and the insecurity of not knowing my path in life.' Neil, 34, admitted that he 'had barnies with everyone . . . I had a filthy temper and would react to almost any provocation – a tad insecure, I think.'

Without meaning to, we pass over teenage boys in all kinds of ways. Even the most loving parents are more inclined to celebrate their teen daughter's milestones than those of their teen son, because they know girls need nurturing and encouragement. Teenage boys have many significant moments in their lives that are worthy of celebration, from their first shave and first date, to getting their licence or securing an after-school or holiday job. There are many ways adolescent boys can be nurtured. Academic Peter West encourages parents to support their sons by talking about their own past mistakes and vulnerabilities, by encouraging boys to talk, by actively rewarding good behaviour, and by ensuring the family home is somewhere they want to bring friends.[7]

> 'Today we don't have community. We need to wake up. When I was growing up I was parented by almost everyone in my community. Now we're too afraid to approach kids who look like they need help.'
> Ray Lenton, family group counsellor [8]

WHERE ARE THE MEN?

While boys might not always say so, their family and community are extremely important to them. In the past boys had an extended family of uncles, grandparents and older male cousins to look up to. They were also able to benefit from the wisdom of older men and from greater access to apprenticeships and on-the-job training. Today many boys have few men in their lives. Those who do have access to a wider community seem to fare better during their childhood and teens than those who don't.

This was clearly the case for Mark, 32, who was born in Iraq but spent most of his early years in the West. When Mark returned to Iraq at 10, he had to learn a whole new language, but he thrived on the support he received there. 'Not only were the men around more, there was more opportunity to spend more time with each other. The country was full of tea houses, where you could spend hours with male friends playing dominoes and backgammon and chess. It was easier to learn how to *be* a boy or young man, or an older man, because you had many examples around you all the time.'

When I spoke to Michael, 50, he told me he found growing up

in the Jewish faith helpful. 'In Judaism you actually have a formal, ritualised rite of passage in the form of a bar mitzvah for boys at the age of thirteen. You go through this whole process where you have to study for a couple of years to do some quite difficult things, like publicly reading out parts of the Biblical text in classical Hebrew. On your bar mitzvah you are the centre of attention. The sense that you have had to do something quite difficult in a public context, then get lauded for it, is a pretty significant thing at the age of thirteen. I don't think anyone who has been through it would ever forget it.'

'I was pretty lucky in my childhood and teens to have a strong family base and a close group of friends. I would imagine without these two things I would have turned out quite differently. Knowing this makes it a little easier to understand that when people don't have this, they can sometimes go off the rails.' *Tim, 25*

'The influence from my family was amazing – especially the strong bonds between my uncles. I remember when I was in the middle of my darker period and I went to one of these family things, I just had this sense of an unspoken bond – the understanding between these three brothers in their fifties. I really wanted to be a part of that. It made me rethink just how strong and amazing [my] family was. Being part of the family was a similar feeling to the security I felt with my mates. It made me feel like I was a part of something bigger than me.' *Sean, 20*

Walking on the wild side

VIOLENCE AS ENTERTAINMENT

In talking with men and boys I was shocked to discover how many felt lonely, confused and cast adrift during their teenage years. Their very real feelings of isolation are made all the more intense because there are few facilities for teenage boys in the community. And what facilities do exist, apart from parks and sporting facilities, are often questionable at best. All too frequently the only other outlets for boys are shopping centres and movie theatres. So, yet again boys are left to their own devices. In Kay Donovan's documentary *Tagged*, set in Sydney's outer west, one teenager confessed that he and his friends spent a lot of their summer holidays sitting on the railway platform.[1] The depressing thing is that these boys aren't isolated cases. Far too many boys have nothing else to do in their spare time except roam the streets at night and weekends.

> 'What is there for boys to do? You can play sport, hang around in big groups with other boys, and take drugs. That's sort of the extent of it. You can go to the movies, but that novelty soon wears off. Hanging

around for me was, like, I felt like the street was my suburb. You hang around with other guys your age. You're hanging around or doing drugs, because there's not much else to do.' *Sean, 20*

Where they can, boys will congregate in and around game arcades, because they provide the action and excitement boys long for. Even the kids who don't frequent game arcades often have access to violent games at home. One study into the effects of violent video games indicates that, while in the early days of these games the graphics were relatively unrealistic, when Nintendo was introduced in the mid 1980s the games became far more realistic and violent.[2] Not enough parents vet the games their boys have access to, so most have no idea of just how violent the content can be.

Studies show that a boy's school performance suffers from exposure to these games. These boys start to see the world as a hostile place, and respond accordingly. I was disturbed to learn that aggressive *and* non-aggressive boys display more aggression after frequent exposure to these games.[3] Studies also indicate that violent programs not only desensitise boys, they excite them, encouraging them to imitate the behaviour they see on screen.[4] It is easy to forget that for teenage boys these games are not just entertainment; they can be a detailed, if distorted, representation of life and how to behave.

Because boys tend to be more overtly angry and physically aggressive than girls, society needs positive ways to deal with this. I caught up with Anglican minister Father Dave Smith, who runs his own fight club in Sydney's inner west. He teaches boys to box to help them deal with their aggression. 'This has always been a traditional approach. Teach boys to fight, to make them less aggressive. We've lost that. We try to repress and dismiss and overlook a fundamental dimension of masculinity. Boxing is cathartic. Hitting something gets things out of the system. Any strong physical activity is a release. I think our guys do it pretty naturally. Even if you're carrying a lot of anger, I don't think other guys take it out on each other in the ring, I really don't. I guess that's because of the relationships they have here of mutual respect.

'If a boy has issues, then he doesn't do well in the ring. Self-control is the key. The more agro you get, the slower you get – you lose your focus. I say to the guys, "If you can get to the stage where someone is trying to take your head off, and yet you can stay in control and focused, and can make your own decisions, instead of just responding to the pressures, then you can do anything." Then when their mates say, "Let's do a break-in or take a hit," they're in a position to say they're not interested. They're able to make their own decisions while being put under an enormous amount of pressure. I think that's why we find the guys have such a good record once they get into a disciplined training regime. They're not getting into trouble with the law. They're not getting into trouble with school. All those symptoms start to disappear.'

Teenage boys need help to find positive ways to express their desire for action and excitement.

WHAT BOYS GET OUT OF GANGS

Teenage boys need help to find positive ways to express their desire for action and excitement. When they don't get this at home, at school or in their community, they make their own entertainment. This may mean nothing more than a couple or handful of boys hanging out together, or it may mean joining a gang. Youth gangs aren't new. Shakespeare's *Romeo and Juliet* opens with a violent clash between the Montagues and the Capulets, part of an ongoing feud that blights the lives of everyone concerned. The more central gang membership is to a boy, the more dangerous his involvement can become. When a boy's identity is first and foremost with his gang, he's in trouble. As he loses his ability to make good, independent decisions, often he gets drawn into a cycle of violence that can culminate in the kind of warfare that was witnessed in the 1984 Milperra Massacre, in which a 14-year-old girl and six bikies died after a showdown between the Comancheros and Bandidos.

'The way I turned out was a lot different from others in the group. They always called me the sensible one. They were heavily into alcohol and drugs, and were always getting into trouble with the police. One boy suicided. That was a big shock. One got sent away to work on a country property. He was into trouble with gangs. He was living out in the bush, shacked up in a dismal little cottage by himself. Somehow he survived. He still smokes marijuana, but he's much better. Another mate is finding it hard to quit the booze and marijuana. He was working to fund his habit. His situation is a direct consequence of his parents' divorce. He's slowly getting there.' *Nathan, 19*

While gang culture differs from country to country, and suburb to suburb, the reasons boys are drawn into gangs are largely the same. Boys are attracted to gangs because they feel bored, isolated and ignored. A recent report on Australian gangs indicates that often gangs are little more than loose groupings of kids drawn to each other for social contact, and what crimes these kids do commit tend to be low-level crimes that are often opportunistic. While there is no excuse for criminal behaviour, research suggests that the negative attitudes that commercial managers and police have towards these kids congregating in public spaces causes them to feel even more isolated from the rest of society, which can in turn spark criminal activity.[5]

'There were people I just met in my area – kids my age. We started hanging around, drinking and roaming the streets late at night. One of the parents would let us smoke dope in the house, so we would just go around and smoke a joint. That was fun. We were all very similar, with similar interests. That was the best part of the day, getting home from school. The whole group mentality is good fun. You're out there. You feel powerful as well when you're in a gang of blokes. You have the confidence . . . Your testosterone goes through the roof. Basically you feel more empowered as a man, and you do find yourself being more witty, a bit quicker, much more sociable, much more able to make friends and meet people, as opposed to just being by yourself.'
Sean, 20

While figures on gangs are hard to come by, few would question that gangs are on the increase as more and more kids are left to their own devices. There were an estimated 2000 gangs in America in 1980; by 1996 this had grown to 31 000 gangs with around 846 000 members.[6] Traditionally the boys attracted to gangs have tended to grow up in poor, often unsafe communities with few social and economic resources. These boys often lack adult male role models, have already experienced violence or deprivation, failed school, and hold few expectations for themselves. Tough, aggressive boys in need of excitement are the most likely candidates for gang membership, as are boys seeking protection from other boys and/or because they live in an unsafe neighbourhood.[7] In the absence of little if any positive support from adults, boys turn to peers for acknowledgement and protection. As one boy explained to Jim Garbarino, professor of human development at Cornell University, 'If I join a gang I'm 50 per cent safe, if I don't join a gang I am 0 per cent safe.'[8]

Much of the information we have on local gangs is based on

anecdote and the media. What we do know is that kids often congregate according to shared values and experiences – ethnicity;
similar tastes in fashion, music, activities and culture; and low socio-
economic status.[9] Not all boys are from poor homes. Justin, now 43,
was from a solid middle-class family. 'My mother died when I was
still sixteen. It was the same day I bought my first leather jacket. By
this stage I had gone from being top of the class to being more of
a chain-smoking dropout. I got a job working at Woolworths on a
casual basis, and this funded my drinking binges and my smoking.
By age seventeen I had purchased my own motorbike, and the image
was complete. I had a girl. I had a bike. I had the leather jacket. I carried a knife and looked tough, even though I was more show than go.
I remember being angry and abusive much of the time, even to those I
cared about. I was the lead singer of a punk band by this stage, and
was linking in with a punk gang that hung around our area. I enjoyed
the feelings of power that I got when I was with the group.'

Moving beyond their often-overwhelming sense of powerlessness can be a key motivation for the boys drawn into gangs. We
might assume these boys join gangs because they have no concern
for authority, but linguist Deborah Tannen has a different view. She
suggests that far from being *unaware* of authority, these boys are
in fact well aware of authority to the point that they are *oversensi-
tive* to it[10] – it is this oversensitivity that causes them to rebel. Again
this points to the difficulties boys face when they grow up without
proper support. Unless they have a clear understanding of why certain behaviour is not acceptable, then as they struggle to make sense
of the world around them they are left with few, if any, resources to
deal positively with the many challenges they are confronted with.

Boys do long for boundaries and to feel safe.

We need to understand far more about gangs. Headlines about gang activities in our newspapers are frequently misleading and unhelpful, because they often suggest more violence on the part of gangs than actually happens. This in turn serves only to further alienate these boys from the community, and allow them to feel like heroes for the wrong reasons. We cannot afford to be complacent about boys in gangs, and it's important we understand why boys are driven to gangs in the first place.

'There were a fair few gangs in my area. Essentially it's a family – a kind of brotherhood–type atmosphere, where you take on responsibility, you're part of something, you can make a difference.' *Joel, 20*

Gang violence is taking on new forms. According to investigative journalist Dan Korem, gangs are no longer the preserve of underprivileged kids. In his book *Suburban Violence: The Affluent Rebels*, he details the emergence of gangs from well-heeled neighbourhoods across America and Europe.[11] He indicates that in 2004 a bomb went off in an affluent community somewhere in the United States almost every week. 'Some were built by youths acting on their own, but many were built by youths in affluent gangs,' he explains. 'There are many at-risk youths, who might not have the physical constitution to engage in physical assaults, but they do have the money, mobility and connectivity through computer terminals to cause widespread destruction.'[12]

'I drifted into a gang. I was looking for a sense of belonging. The gang scene was racist and violent. It was attractive and revolting at the same time. There was a freedom and an attitude, and a rejection of stuff – there was an honesty about it. There was a lack of real concern for other people. I do remember a sense of power, being with a group of tough guys.' *Justin, 43*

BOYS *NEED* BOUNDARIES

While it may seem otherwise to desperate parents and teachers, boys *do* long for boundaries and to feel safe. They need to understand how society works, and how they can be an integral and valuable member of their community. This idea is backed up by those I have spoken with who work with at-risk boys. They see part of the process in rehabilitating these boys as helping them see in concrete terms what *their* role in life might be. It is easy to underestimate just how much boys need to know this.

One of my friends, who is involved in the men's movement, took a group of at-risk boys out into the bush for a weekend with some Aboriginal tribal elders. During their time together, the boys' issues began to emerge. Then one of the boys broke down. 'But what are men supposed to *do*?' he asked. When we understand our place in society, we begin to understand the structures and respect them. How are we helping boys to do this?

'The irony was that when I was a teenager I rejected all authority, except my fight club, and that had more discipline than anything. I realise my issue wasn't authority, as much as the authority I could respect.' *Father Dave Smith, Fight Club*[13]

The reason boys often gravitate towards gangs is to gain a sense of belonging, direction, safety and importance. The tragedy is that once they are inside the gang, they have to learn a whole new set of rules that isolates them even more from their families and community.

Frequently their desire to belong comes at a huge cost to themselves and others, as they descend into a life of crime, or even lose their life.

KEEPING THEIR FEELINGS TO THEMSELVES

During their teens, boys face many dilemmas on their journey to manhood. Some become extremely sensitive to anything regarded as feminine, including emotions, because they see this as standing in the way of them being strong and invulnerable. By the time they reach adolescence, boys have learned to mistrust their feelings. They work hard to suppress them or push them aside, because they are desperate to embrace their masculinity. If they don't make the grade, they become outsiders and are branded by their peers as losers.

Many boys also worry about their sexuality. As their emotions rage, few know what to do with the unfamiliar feelings they are experiencing, because they have had little opportunity to explore or express emotions. Many still care about their male friends, but because they are terrified any gestures they make may label them as weak or gay, they keep some distance between themselves and their peers, competing with them instead. These boys are therefore constantly on guard, and their keen sense of isolation grows.

This fear of the feminine can even inspire boys to harass or bash boys they know or suspect to be gay. When a teenage boy is afraid of being abandoned or ridiculed by his peers, behaving in a violent or uncaring manner can seem the perfect way to prove he's got what it takes. This kind of behaviour is destructive for everyone involved, especially for those boys who *are* gay. Its devastating effects were highlighted to me by a gay male friend of mine – seeing gay kids at school victimised was enough to stop him in his tracks. Another gay boy at his school wasn't so lucky – he ended up committing suicide because of the bullying he received. My friend got a very clear message about being honest about his sexuality, and didn't find the courage to come out until he was in his 40s, when he was married with kids. Even today life can be incredibly hard for gay teenagers. My friend is now working to help these kids find their way.

HANDLING SEX

Even though teenage boys may work hard to mask their emotions, few can ignore their emerging sexuality, whatever its orientation, especially when their penis seems to have a mind of its own. Some boys are fascinated by their penis; others fear it or try to ignore it. Either way, most teen boys remain pre-occupied with sex, and with wondering whether girls find them sexually attractive. For gay boys life is even more complicated, because often they try to convince themselves they are straight.

One of the hardest things for teenage boys is figuring out how to handle their sexual impulses. When they don't have the opportunity to read or talk openly about sex, they are unable to deal with their sexuality in a mature and satisfying way. Instead they are likely to become even more obsessed and furtive about sex, especially if they are constantly told sex is wrong. Boys don't talk honestly to each other about sex because they naturally assume that everyone else is 'doing it' when they are not, or are doing it better than they are, and so yet again they are left to sort things out for themselves.

'What happens is that a boy thinks: "This girl is kissing me, she likes me, so she wants sex." Then when the girl says no, he feels a terrible sense of rejection. Part of hanging around with the boys is talking about your victories. If you don't have a victory, then what do you do?' *Tony, 26*

It can be very confusing for boys to grow up in a world in which sexually explicit material is so readily available, but where good advice on how to express themselves appropriately is in relatively short supply. Almost daily, teenage boys see provocative images of women's bodies. Everywhere they look, sex is seen as exhilarating. And in the movies, magazines and soaps, teen characters are depicted as leading complex sexual, emotional and social lives that would be difficult to handle even as an assured adult. With little if any preparation for the emotional complexities demanded in these situations, teenage boys are extremely vulnerable. And as girls appear to have more confidence, and enjoy greater physical and sexual freedom than in previous generations, it is easy for teenage boys to misread the cues.

'I think there's an enormous disrespect for male sexuality. I feel for teenage boys, especially these days. I don't think most girls have a clue about how much dressing provocatively affects boys. I don't think they realise how much a boy's total sexual obsession takes over their whole lives. Girls need to be made aware of their effect on other people.' *Father Dave Smith, Fight Club*[14]

GETTING CLOSE AND PERSONAL

After years of being encouraged to ignore their emotions, it's a big ask to suddenly expect teen boys to be empathic towards girls, and to approach sex with the emotional maturity that true intimacy demands. Genuine intimacy requires boys to understand their *own* emotional needs and those of others, and how to fulfil these needs. Popular culture has created huge expectations around sex that can be a minefield for teenage boys and girls. Girls can be very hurt by the cavalier attitudes teenage boys show towards sex. Equally, the boys I spoke with admitted to being devastated to learn that not all girls are caring and loyal. Many boys are torn between the desire for love and affection they can get from girls, and the terrible fear they may get hurt. Underlying this is the strong sense boys have that girls have more power.

'Boys don't know that girls don't know what they want. Also boys don't have much choice, because they have to be the initiator. But because a girl is more likely to say no to you, she has the power over you. It's like girls have this power that you want, but they won't give it to you.' *Tony, 26*

Boys mask this vulnerability by appearing indifferent towards girls – by criticising them, or treating them like 'one of the boys'. Because we expect boys to appear strong and be capable, and to keep their emotions to themselves, it doesn't leave them anywhere to go.

'I saw some friends who I was with at primary school, who were such gentle boys, change when they went to a boys' school for secondary. They were horrible. I remember I was at a party and met one of them. He'd have been about fourteen. He told me about this girl he wanted to have sex with. She said no. His response was, "So I slapped the slut." I was so shocked by his attitude and how much he'd changed.' *Mitchell, 26*

When boys allow themselves to be vulnerable enough to get close to a girl, they are risking a great deal. Few teenage girls have any idea how hard it is for teen boys to let down their guard and express their interest in and/or feelings for a girl. It's not just the emotional land-scape and the mechanics of sex teen boys need to be aware of, it's also the social nuances. Girls are way ahead of boys in emotional maturity and social niceties, because they have been raised to understand and express these things. As boys lack this level of sophistication, rela-tionships can be extremely perplexing for them.

> 'Teen relationships are very confusing. One of my friends had his first serious girlfriend when he was seventeen. They had been going out four or five months when it was Valentine's Day, so he got her a really nice present. She freaked out and said they hadn't been going out that long, and that it wasn't that serious. So, when her birthday came around shortly afterwards, he didn't get her a present, and he got his arse whipped.' *Mitchell, 26*

THE PRICE OF LOOKING GOOD

The complexity of teenage years is due in no small part to the increasing effectiveness of the marketing campaigns directed at teen-agers, telling them what's hot and what's not. As the gap between what's cool and what is way off the mark continues to narrow, kids need to be constantly vigilant to ensure they don't get left behind. These multi-million-dollar campaigns actively work on the fear teen-agers have of being considered unlovable, and their strong desire to be accepted. These campaigns are extremely effective; never before have teenagers been so consumption-oriented. Even when kids do have the money to buy the 'right' clothes, still the competition to stay on top is intense.

For kids from poorer backgrounds, teenage life is not only hard, it is endlessly disappointing, as they struggle to look cool with what

little they have. Some go further, resorting to theft and street violence to get what they want. Sometimes the price of looking good can
be inordinately high. This desperation to 'join the club' has sparked
a growth in attacks on teenage boys by other teenagers. Some boys
have even been murdered purely for their mobile phone or their run-
ners. It is alarming to see how often young men are set upon. As the
pressure to consume intensifies, teenagers become more and more
sensitive to having the right look, especially when they are led to
believe this is the price of acceptance.

When boys suicide

WALKING ON THIN ICE

Clinical psychologist William Pollack isn't exaggerating when he claims that adolescence is the most perilous and confusing time of a boy's life.[1] Of course not all teenage life is bad. Many boys come through these years relatively unscathed. What concerns me is the increasing number of boys who are choosing to kill themselves before they reach manhood. While we are all know this is happening, it's too easy to see boys in this situation purely as statistics.

After what seemed like a positive childhood, Gareth, now 35, descended into depression during high school. Although he excelled in a number of areas including sport, increasingly he felt as if he didn't belong. He became addicted to risk-taking, which culminated in a number of suicide attempts. 'I got into bikes. I became an adrenalin junkie, and thought those that weren't were uncool. I used adrenalin to push away the boredom, so I could feel I was alive and was achieving. My fear of life was greater than my fear of death. The thought of living fifty, sixty, seventy years was too overwhelming.' No-one understood what was going on, so it took Gareth until his 30s to turn his life around.

It is important we understand what creates this level of despair in boys. Internationally renowned expert on suicide Edwin Shneidman defines suicide as, 'when the psychache is deemed by that person to be unbearable'. He explains that suicide is a person's response to unmet or frustrated needs — the need for acceptance, achievement, dignity or self-esteem. Those who commit suicide take their lives in order to achieve 'freedom from pain, freedom from guilt, freedom from shame, freedom from rejection, and aloneness'.[2]

The more I researched the suicide of boys, the more I asked myself: what unmet needs, what unbearable pain do so many teen boys have that causes them to take their own lives? When you look at the figures, some concerning trends emerge. Suicide rates for young men in Australia were steady over much of the twentieth century, until 1963 when they started to increase. Between 1973 and 1987 the rate of young men committing suicide increased by 66 per cent in Australia, and by a staggering 127 per cent in New Zealand.[3] By 1996 Australia had the third-highest suicide rate in the developed world.[4] By 2001 four times as many teenage boys were committing suicide than teenage girls.[5] I suspect we have become so distracted by the difficulties we have in relating to teenage boys, that we have stopped asking ourselves why it is that whole generations of boys are so susceptible to suicide.

When we further analyse the suicide rates, we discover that boys in rural and remote areas are most at risk[6] — approximately 50 per cent more Australian male youth suicides take place in country areas than in cities.[7] The very real tragedies behind these statistics affect us all. At the time of writing this chapter, my friends were mourning the loss of their young son who ended his life. Just a fortnight before his funeral, another boy from his school also suicided. Hardly a year ago saw the loss of our neighbour's son. And so the story goes on.

What unmet needs, what unbearable pain do so many teen boys have,
that causes them to take their own lives?

'The suicidal mind is very narrow and focused on anxiety and depression,' explains Australian psychologist Bill O'Hehir. 'They can't be reasoned with. That's why it's important they get professional help. People often say there are no warning signs, but if you know what to look for, there are plenty of signs. Suicide is never just for attention. From the point of view of that individual, everything else has failed.'[8] Suicide is often sparked by a number of factors, such as parental separation and divorce, a family history of suicide, physical or sexual abuse, relationship breakdown, or failure or unhappiness at school. We often don't realise that factors such as unemployment can also trigger suicide attempts, because without a job or income boys are more likely to live on the fringes of society, enjoying fewer chances of forming long-term romantic relationships, or of being independent.

Too often we fail to recognise the cries for help. When boys are being difficult we focus more on managing the situation – keeping them under control – rather than tackling the very real angst many are feeling. We need to help boys to be more articulate – to allow them to talk about their anxieties and shortcomings without fearing that we will see them as weak. Too many of our young men die when they have a great deal to live for.

Parents also need help so they can be aware of the warning signs. According to Bill O'Hehir, these signs can include a deteriorating record at school, depression, dropping out of school, previous suicide attempts and loss of interest in friends, clothes and hair. Physical symptoms of depression can include headaches, poor appetite, poor concentration, broken sleep patterns and lack of interest in work, family and hobbies.[9] What we do know is that depression in teenage boys is now happening earlier than in previous generations, and can persist or recur in adult life. It's important to note that depression often appears *alongside* anxiety, disruptive behaviour, substance abuse or serious illness and these behaviours and conditions can often mask the depression.

One of the difficulties for parents, teachers and doctors is recognising that teen boys may be suffering from depression when they appear simply to be having problems at school or to be sullen, snappy or down. Too often these symptoms are dismissed as teenage angst, so the depression goes undetected.[10] Experts also warn that sudden lifts in mood might not be as positive as they seem: a boy may have moved beyond his dejection, but he may also have decided on suicide as a way out. What is crucial is that we learn to read boys more accurately, and not assume they are fine just because they say or appear so. If parents have concerns it is critical they seek professional guidance from their child's school or their doctor.

COPYCAT SUICIDES

While some teenagers are more at risk of suicide than others, schools and health advocates have become increasingly aware of how suggestible a teenager's peers are. A number of studies indicate how dangerous coverage of suicides can be, regardless of whether this coverage is in a film, documentary or news report. Such coverage is unhelpful because it helps lessen the taboo around suicide by making it appear a 'normal' response to difficulties or depression.[11] After one German television station aired a program depicting a teenager jumping under a train, the number of male teenage suicide victims aged between 15 and 19 increased 17.5 per cent.[12]

I was talking with a hospital chaplain recently who has seen this same trend. He told me that there had been a spate of teenagers self-immolating. One of the most tragic aspects of these cases was that most of the teenagers hadn't realised that they wouldn't necessarily die when they set themselves alight – that they might just become horribly burned. The coverage of teen suicides is now handled with extreme care, so these copycat or cluster suicides don't result. Attempts have also been made by the media not to focus on undue details of suicide, in order to avoid glorifying or sensationalising the act.[13]

> 'For me a fully alive boy is one who has genuine and powerful aggressive, intellectual and emotional drives, and is able to control those, with the help of his peers and older mentors. When he can channel these drives creatively, it is a magnificent thing. The first thing is respecting the drives that are there. Then we need to build a community that will help boys to use these drives positively. Boys need to be part of a community that cares, that gives a damn.' *Father Dave Smith, Fight Club*[14]

BOYS NEED TO KNOW THEY HAVE *REAL* CHOICES

As I spoke with men and boys, it became clear that teen boys need a real understanding of the many wonderful aspects there are to adult male life. They need to be *actively* encouraged to explore and embrace what it means to be a man. Without good information and positive reinforcement, teenage boys will have little sense of the choices available to them, and will continue to be locked into destructive stereotypes. To achieve this, boys must receive proper guidance, so they know the difference between healthy and unhealthy ways to assert themselves, how to handle their feelings appropriately and how to deal with sex.

Teenage boys also need to know they are not alone in the many issues they struggle with. One of the key factors in helping them feel good about themselves is in encouraging them to form positive goals, and to have supportive adults around them to help underpin these goals, without taking away their sense of self. If no-one else believes in these kids at home or at school, then why should they?

> *The best way to learn about being a successful man is to spend time around one.*

Schools and the community need to give teenage boys more attention and back-up, by providing programs and activities that are not only relevant to boys, but that inspire them to embrace being a boy and growing into a man. In *Boy Troubles* Jennifer Buckingham also emphasises the huge influence the home environment and family experiences have on boys – during their adolescent years, and in becoming healthy adults.[15] We cannot ignore the importance of good men in boys' lives. The best way to learn about being a successful man is to spend time around one. Boys can't go it alone; nor should they start their journey towards adulthood feeling they have to apologise for being male.

Sons and their mothers

HELPING BOYS THRIVE

It goes without saying that a boy's relationship with his mother is very different from the relationship he shares with his father. While mothers know this, in theory at least, often they have no sense of how many special qualities they can bring to their son's life. A boy's mother can do so much to help create a safe space in which her boy can thrive. The relationship a mother shares with her son is very intimate from the beginning. Not only is a boy conceived in his mother's womb, it is his first home. And when he is born, it is her body that first nourishes him. For most boys, their mother is the focal point of their earliest years.

Most mothers do work hard at nurturing their sons. And while their little boys may not say much, the many tasks their mothers perform – from preparing meals and washing clothes, to dispensing kisses and cuddles, and reading bedtime stories – are deeply nurturing for boys. This doesn't mean mothers should be chained to the kitchen sink, but it is important they realise how much their sons are nourished by these things. For too long we have failed to understand the impact nourishment has on boys. Now that fathers are taking on a more nurturing role in parenting than in the past, boys have the potential for even more nourishment.

In my interviews with men I was surprised at how warmly many men spoke about the nurturing they received from their mothers when they were little. One of the significant areas of nourishment for them was food. Doug, 52, recalled his mother baking cakes for him and his brothers on her one day off, as a gift to them for when she wasn't around. Morris, 61, also remembered his mother's baking: 'Her sponges and cream puffs would never reach the table before they were leapt on.' I was also interested in the number of men who spoke with great fondness of the many friends and family who visited the family home. They recollected the talk and laughter over shared meals, attributing the welcoming atmosphere and the hospitality to the warmth of their mothers.

WHEN THERE IS NO NURTURING

What was also apparent during my interviews was how often boys picked up on whether or not their mothers were *genuinely* nurturing. Where this nurturing was lacking, they talked openly about their feelings of sadness, loneliness and alienation. It was clear that I was one of the few people, if not the only person, they had ever talked to about such things. These and other stories are all the more poignant because these men have kept their feelings to themselves.

'Mum took ten years off work to be at home with us. She was there physically, but she was emotionally absent. She provided, but she wasn't comfortable in the role.' *Cameron, 32*

'My mother was a very emotionally cold person. Once we were down playing in a creek and a kid threw a rock at me. It split my lip. I was scared because I was bleeding profusely, so I ran home to Mum. She just slapped me around the face for "misbehaving".' *Lawrence, 33*

'My mother never showed any affection. I always loved my mother, but she always seemed like an unassailable fortress, where you could never see inside the walls.' *Craig, 58*

'I can never remember being hugged or touched by my mother. The only time I can remember being touched was when I was a little boy going to school, and I would ask her to do up my shoes.' *Morris, 61*

For some women the role of mother doesn't come easily, which shouldn't be a surprise, because motherhood can be extremely demanding. It is only recently that we have started to recognise this and allow women not to feel guilty about it. Bringing up sons can be even harder, especially for mothers who have little experience of boys, because boys seem so different to girls. Boys do tend to be more lively, and enjoy taking risks more than girls. Often they find it difficult to sit still for any length of time, or to be neat and tidy. Many love belching and farting, and aren't always interested in staying clean. Yet even though boys are energetic and enjoy pushing the boundaries, they still need a strong, loving base. Providing this firm base is one of the most significant contributions mothers can make to their sons' lives.

'My mother is everything to me, and I can vouch that's the same for all my friends. She's been there whenever I've had problems – not solving them for me, but giving me guidance. Mothers carve the way for a young boy to grow.' *Lance, 23*

WHEN BOYS ARE CUT LOOSE

Even though they may have very real misgivings, all too often mothers end up deferring to family, friends and partners about how their son should be raised; this often means stepping back from their son's life. They can become nervous about showing and receiving affection from their son, and worry about what to do if their boy is emotional or doesn't seem to be coping, fearful lest they 'taint' their boy. That's when they allow their sons to be pressured into taking part in sport, or proving themselves academically, even when this pulls against the boy's natural abilities and inclinations. Or they let go and allow their boys to 'be boys', in the hope that by indulging larrikin behaviour, it will help 'make them a man'. Mothers who distance themselves from their sons have no idea how abandoned these boys feel, or how much they ache for their mother's warmth and input. Why would they, when women have been raised to see men and boys as naturally strong and self-reliant?

> 'I remember one day getting beat[en] up by a gang, so I ran home. I was crying because they'd shoved a chilli down my throat. When my mum saw me crying she locked the door and said I couldn't come in until I'd challenged one of the boys. I said there were three of them, and one of me, but it made no difference. I had to go back and find one, and fight him. It didn't matter what the circumstances were. You couldn't show any sign of weakness; you had to show you were a man.' *Craig, 58*

I remember when I was about 7 my parents talking with close friends who had sent their boys off to boarding school. The youngest boy was about my age and was so desperately unhappy he kept running away from school, only to be sent back because the place had a fine reputation. At this school the boys were made to take cold showers all year round, and harsh penalties were handed out for the slightest infringement. This poor boy had been forced to run numerous laps of the playing field in an English winter for touching his brother's hand as they passed in church. It is chilling to think that a young boy's attempt simply to reach out for the comfort of his brother's touch would have such painful consequences. It was no doubt a bitter lesson, and one he is unlikely to forget.

I remember thinking I'd die if I were subjected to such a harsh environment. It never occurred to me that this was how so many boys feel. Often we place boys in the most terrible positions because we genuinely believe it will be the making of them, not realising how much of them we might be destroying in the process. It was perhaps this desire to do the right thing by her only son that prompted Rowan's mother, a single parent, to send him off to military trade school at 16. 'I don't know what my mother was thinking,' Rowan, now 41, admitted. Rowan didn't disappoint his mother; he rose to the challenge and joined the elite ranks of the SAS. Now that he has left his military career behind, he has had to seek professional help to deal with the toll this career exacted.

HE'S *MY* BOY

Some mothers take the opposite approach when bringing up their sons, by trying to be everything to them. This is often the case with solo mothers and mothers whose partners are too busy or too distant to take an active role in parenting. In these cases mothers do not help their sons by overcompensating for the lack of men in their boy's life. Boys naturally want to remain close to their mother, but they need to do so on their *own* terms. No matter how much a boy loves his mother, if he gets too close to her he will feel suffocated.

After bringing a boy into the world and nurturing him through his early years, some mothers find it hard to give their sons more space. Allowing boys room to experience life for themselves is very different from abandoning them. Some mothers try to stage-manage their son's life, because they feel responsible for them or because they don't receive adequate support from the boy's father. It is becoming increasingly clear to educators and health professionals that mothers cannot and should not be expected to parent their boys on their own. If the father is absent, women need the support of a variety of good men.

'The mistake I made with my son was not only walking on the bridge with my son, but to stand in the middle and direct the traffic . . . The sadness I now feel is that I should have been looking sideways, instead of lamenting my son's father's absence as he reached adolescence. I had two good men – platonic friends, who would have helped me if I had asked. But I thought I had to be in control and be super-woman. I thought any involvement would make me a lesser parent.'[1] Celia Lashlie, author and single mother

Virtually all the men I interviewed agreed that boys do need their mothers, but they also emphasised that boys need good *male* role models to teach the intricacies of what it means to be a man.

'Learning masculinity is not easy. Some lessons are clear, but there are doubts about some things. The more important lessons about life need to be explained and demonstrated by older men. I believe that most men carry scars with them from the very acts of learning their own maleness.' Kieran, 58

SETTING CLEAR BOUNDARIES

Having men around does help boys understand the concept of boundaries, and supports mothers in their crucial role. Often mothers are the ones left to discipline their sons, especially when their boys are young. Overburdened mothers can become frustrated by this and resort to punishment to try to keep their boys under control, because they don't understand the wider dynamics behind these issues. For some boys this works; for others it simply encourages them to rebel, making their mother's job harder still.

When disciplining boys, mothers need to be aware of just how sensitive boys are, although they may never show it. Girls are also punished, but because they are encouraged to be more expressive about how they feel, their feelings are more likely to be taken into account. Even when boys are young men, they can prove surprisingly tender. Kieran, now 58, was kicked out of home as a young adult by his mother. Although he doesn't blame her, looking back decades later, he recollected the real sense of trauma he felt at having to make it on his own at 19.

> *To be their mother's 'little man' is an unbearable emotional pressure for any boy.*

When under pressure, some mothers overreact, because they cannot understand what life is like for boys. Others can be abusive. 'I always see men presented as child abusers, but where I grew up it was always the women,' said Lawrence, 33, who described his mother as cruel, overbearing and sadistic. 'The fathers stood back and watched while mothers screamed at and beat their children. This is what I still notice on the streets and on public transport. I think that society needs desperately to face up to this.'

Parents do not need to resort to such measures to be good disciplinarians. When they get the discipline right, they preserve their son's sense of security and self, while at the same time encouraging him to mature. 'Mum played a more serious role, because Dad was a bit of a softy,' explained Matthew, 27. 'Yet no matter how serious Mum was with us, she always showed us love and affection and support.'

BEING MUMMY'S 'LITTLE MAN'

When fathers are absent from their sons' lives, greater pressure is placed on boys and their mothers. Often when relationships collapse or partners die, mothers turn to their sons for comfort, because even though they are young and vulnerable, boys are meant to be strong. To be their mother's 'little man' is an unbearable emotional pressure for any boy. While he might not show it, a boy will struggle with the overwhelming sense of responsibility and helplessness he inevitably feels in this situation. Aware of his mother's expectations, a boy will do his best to help compensate for his mother's loneliness, for her pain. The greater the distress a mother experiences, the more compelled her son will feel to try to make things right, unless it is made clear this is not what is expected of him.

'Most women who are single parents are not getting enough support, so the unmet needs of the mother get projected onto the boy,' said Rowan, whose parents split up when he was very young. 'Basically at five I was "married" to my mother in every way, except sexually. She took me into her heart, and would cuddle me. I was getting all the warmth and affection from my mother, which was great, and which made her feel better. Women then think, "I don't need another man, because I have my son." My mother remarried when I was twelve, and suddenly all the affection was cut off, and a boy's heart is broken. It's too much pressure to deal with.' Rowan doesn't blame his mother, but as an adult, he's aware of the fallout. 'It's eight years since Mum died, and I've been doing some research into the family. Mum clearly had issues with other men in the family. I now realise that for years I've been compensating for the "sins" of my father and grandfather.'

Soren, 56, is adamant that while some women try to compensate for their sense of loss through their sons, boys should not have to carry this burden. 'I was nine years old when Dad committed suicide. There was no way I could escape my mother.' He remembers his mother as a harsh, unrelenting woman. 'Basically I brought myself up. I lived with the pain and learnt how to survive.'

> *A boy's mother is the first woman he loves, and it is from his mother that a boy first learns about women.*

A mother may not ask her son directly for help, but when she draws him into her problems and shares her feelings of despair, her son naturally assumes she is seeking his assistance. The younger a boy is, the more helpless he is likely to feel, because he does not have the resources to deal with such complex personal issues. It will help him immensely if his mother can free him from these fears. I spoke with 10-year-old Emil, who recently lost his father to cancer. Seeing his mother's terrible sense of loss, he tried to comfort her by telling her he loved her so much he would never get married. While Emil's mother was touched by this gesture, she was wise enough to release him from the burden of her grief, by telling him that one day he would meet someone wonderful, and that she was looking forward to seeing him in love and having children of his own.

'Dad had an affair when I was little. Mum packed up and left. One minute Dad was there and the next he was gone. I can't remember saying goodbye to my friends or anyone. Mum was . . . a mess. I can remember going into the kitchen and seeing Mum cry. I put my arms around her. There was a whole lot of sadness going on. You carry that sadness inside, and also bitterness. It's devastating for a young boy. I didn't have [the] skills to work it out. I just wanted Mum to be happy.' *Robert, 30*

WHEN MOTHERS ENTER NEW RELATIONSHIPS

Dealing with his mother's sexuality can also be a very hard thing for a boy when his father is no longer present. It can be difficult for mothers to appreciate how confusing and alienating it can be for their sons to witness a string of relationships, or to come to terms with someone who is to take the place of their father. Certainly Justin, 43, didn't find it easy. 'My teenage life was confused by having one too many men around the place. I think my mother took a number of partners, some more discreetly than others. The indiscretions were more upsetting at the time. It was unhealthy, looking back. I just wanted to escape the situation.' Justin also had to deal with the knowledge that his mother had been raped. 'She was raped by our landlord. I remember her telling me about this. I was all of fourteen, and didn't have a clue what to do.' Naturally Justin felt overwhelmed and helpless, because he didn't have the skills or experience to know how to help his mother. What boy would? Such dynamics can end up being tragic for all concerned.

FIRST LOVE

A boy's mother is the first woman he loves, and it is from his mother that a boy first learns about women. If this is a healthy relationship, a boy can learn many good things from his mother that will help him in adult life. Through kisses and cuddles and other meaningful gestures, boys are able to explore the sheer delight of physical contact, long before they learn to express themselves sexually. This warmth enables a boy to discover for himself the nuances of touch, and the warmth and fun of being physically close to someone you love. Touch is important for *all* human beings, and it is especially so for children.

The supportive space a mother can provide for her son has many layers, and it should include a safe *emotional* space, because boys need to know there is somewhere they can be tender, confused, vulnerable. By creating a safe environment for their sons to open up in, mothers enable them to develop their *own* emotional repertoire. Without this, often the only emotion boys are likely to express is anger. Allowing a boy to learn how to best express his different emotions isn't just necessary to help him feel good – it is an essential life skill, because without emotional intelligence boys do not cope well in our rapidly changing world.

> One of the great dilemmas mothers face is that while they want to be there for their sons, they fear that allowing boys an emotional life will make them weak.

When mothers aren't emotionally available for their sons, when they ignore their son's feelings or try to tell him how he should be feeling, they deny an essential part of who their son is. When this happens boys can feel abandoned and unworthy. This behaviour can continue to impact these boys as they reach manhood. Although now 32 and a parent, Cameron is still dealing with the emotional absence of his mother. He openly admitted it has left him with a fear of women. 'I find it hard to trust women. I don't understand how they operate. I find their lack of directness and covertness hard. And also the neediness – that's *really* hard.'

Mothers who lack emotional maturity can hold their family to ransom; abiding by her wishes is the only way the family knows how to avoid her displeasure. 'Mother called the shots,' recalled Morris, 61. 'My father would plead with me to "not upset your mother".' This left Morris with a lifelong dislike of authority figures, and an ongoing struggle with his own passivity.

Often a boy will share his fears and concerns only with his mother. If she is emotionally available to him and handles these moments well, she helps to teach her son how to deal positively with life's daily challenges. When mothers can provide this level of emotional respect and support for their sons, it can help sustain them throughout their adult life. 'I actually felt more comfortable talking to Mum about what I was thinking,' admitted Tim, now 25. 'I still have a relationship with Mum whereby I know that if something is bothering me I can talk to her about it.'

> *While boys need their mother's love, they also need space.*

One of the great dilemmas mothers face is that while they want to be there for their sons, they fear that allowing boys an emotional life will make them weak. It's not only mothers who have this fear. During a recent radio interview, a father whose 5-year-old son had been badly mauled by a dog was asked how his 8-year-old son – who had witnessed the attack – was faring. With some reluctance the father admitted his older boy was feeling 'a little bit emotional'. Why are we so unwilling to admit a boy of 8 could be feeling vulnerable after being involved in such a frightening situation? This man was clearly a very loving dad, but his son's vulnerability worried him. He didn't want to admit to his son's feelings, yet had this been a little girl, there would be no question of the emotional trauma she had experienced. Who wouldn't be emotional after witnessing an incident like that?

In *Raising Cane*, psychologist Dan Kindlon says that it is the boys who lack emotional intelligence who fare worst in life, because they have little to draw on in tough situations.[2] It is time to recognise how important the emotional development of boys is, and that this *isn't* the sole responsibility of mothers. Regardless of whether or not a boy's parents have separated, he needs the men in his life to display empathy, and to paint a realistic view of life. Boys need to know that sometimes they will succeed, and sometimes they won't.

'At the beginning of adolescence Mum told me what adolescence would be like. She said that sometimes you'll feel awkward and embarrassed, and sometimes you'll make mistakes in public, but you don't worry about it, these things happen. That was a brilliant, brilliant thing for her to tell me.' *Doug, 52*

BREATHING SPACE

While boys need their mother's love, they also need space. When boys don't get space, whatever love they do get from their mothers quickly becomes oppressive. 'I never doubted my mother loved me. Looking back, however, I'm sure this love was always conditional,' admitted Nigel, 72. Oppressive love manifests in different ways. Some mothers use emotional pressure to keep their sons close, while others try to control their son's lives, by literally telling them how they should look, think and behave.

'Quite often I'll hear about what's not right about me – it really hurts. Mothers need to be careful of their words. If they're trying to push you around, it's hard to feel fulfilled. Sometimes it really hurts, even as an adult. They can really destroy the day.' *Robert, 30*

In the searing novel *The Naked Husband*, Mark recalls his mother's behaviour the day he left for university. 'I remember how she sobbed on my shoulder at the train station. It was like disengaging from an octopus.'[3] Family therapist Michael Gurian describes this behaviour as mothers devouring their son's soul.[4] The only way a boy can survive in a relationship of this intensity is to try to be a good boy, or to keep his distance and withhold his feelings from his mother. These latter boys grow up to be men who cannot commit, or who are emotionally unavailable. Many spend the rest of their lives trying to make it up to their mother, never challenging her, no matter how difficult or invasive her behaviour.

UNDERSTANDING A BOY'S NEEDS

It is good that boys are now raised to understand and respect the needs of women. However, if a boy is drawn too far into a woman's view of the world he can lose his own identity. Boys need to make their own way in life, to understand who *they* are and what *they* want to achieve. This is a complex process for a boy. As a son he needs to separate from his mother, while at the same time trying to win her approval by being the kind of man she wants him to be. How often do boys jettison who they want to be in favour of what their mother wants, because they assume she knows best?

When a mother tries to turn her son into her ideal man, she robs him of essential parts of who *he* is, as Joe Tanenbaum, author of *Male and Female Realities*, points out: 'I have observed in my workshops and in private consulting that boys brought up predominantly by women (women-trained males) learn to adapt their behaviour to accommodate women. On the way, however, they usually suppress some very normal male behaviour that is frowned upon by women. As a result these boys grow into men who tend to know how to please women but seem unable to discover what it takes to please themselves. They also have difficulty in relating to other men and usually lack close male friends.'[5]

> *When a mother tries to turn her son into her ideal man, she robs him of essential parts of who he is.*

This is compounded by the fact that when a mother clings to her son, he can have little chance of developing a real relationship with his father, so father and son miss out. Some mothers who behave this way don't even realise they are cutting their son off from his father. Others set about winning over their son with fierce determination. Having given up on their husband as their ideal man, these women turn their attention to their son, as a way of dealing with their own relationship disappointments. While their boys may enjoy being treated like princes, by not being prepared for the *real* world, rarely do these boys experience any lasting satisfaction when they do grow up. Unless a boy can break free from the stranglehold such a mother has over him, even as a grown man with a wife and family, he will always yearn for the blind devotion he received from his mother.

STORIES THAT MAKE AND BREAK

Over their formative years, there are many ways boys learn about what is expected of men and how they are viewed. These messages have a direct impact on how boys see themselves and their role in life. One of the more interesting developments in psychology is the examination

94

of the family narrative. When viewed through an expert's eye, the way families talk about themselves can reveal a lot about a family – from how it views family members and the family as a whole, to how it sees its place in the world. Stories that families relate about themselves and each other tell family members how safe the world is. These stories indicate who can be trusted, and what to expect from life. They also inform the family about relationship dynamics.[6]

Mothers play a central role in the family narrative, because they are generally the main storytellers. Through the stories they relate, and through off-hand comments they make, their boys get a sense of the expectations their mothers have of them, and how their mothers view those around them. For example, if a boy is constantly told his father is hopeless or a disappointment, it is hard for him to then develop his own appreciation of his father, because he can only relate to his father through the eyes and expectations of his mother. A healthy family narrative helps boys prepare for life in an unpredictable world, while unhealthy narratives keep boys from learning about themselves and life.

If boys are constantly told that men are abusers and not to be trusted, they can grow up with a strong sense of shame at being a male, and have little desire to explore their own masculinity.

Once they grow up, often boys see things quite differently, and can end up feeling very cheated by what their mothers have told them. Rowan, 41, recalled how his mother always portrayed his father as absent and an 'evildoer'. As a grown man he feels deeply saddened by this now he has developed a relationship with his father. Kieran, 58, had a very similar experience. His parents divorced just before he turned 5, and he grew up almost exclusively with his mother.

'I definitely missed out on the wonderful influence that my father could (should) have had on me,' he admitted. 'I also missed out on seeing early the compassion that my father held for others. His generosity of spirit was only revealed during a short time before his death from cancer when he was fifty-nine and I was twenty-three.'

Sometimes the unhelpful stories are about men in general. If boys are constantly told that men are abusers and not to be trusted, they can grow up with a strong sense of shame at being a male, and have little desire to explore their own masculinity. Instead, they can spend their time trying to compensate, or become angry and confused, and rebel. Not all negative messages about men come from mothers. A friend of mine was alarmed recently to hear her young son saying he didn't like being a boy. When she explored this with him, she discovered that he had seen several news clips of the atrocities committed by soldiers during the Iraq war, and was so appalled by them, he felt guilty by association. My friend was then able to explain that being a boy was a wonderful thing, and that like everything in life, there are good and bad men. This left her son free to continue to explore what being a boy is all about without the hang-ups.

Mothers also need to be aware of the unconscious scripts they can slip into at home that promote negative attitudes towards women. Those mothers who permit themselves to be dominated or treated disrespectfully allow their sons to believe this is how women are to be treated. This not only affects these boys, but the women they meet as adults, who can end up receiving the same treatment. There is great power in stories. Positive stories inspire and empower everyone concerned; mothers can use them to great effect. There are so many wonderful ways mothers can help teach their sons about being a man. It is good for boys to hear mothers talking openly about the men they love, and why they love them. This helps build a constructive image of men that boys can consider as they start to think about the kind of man they'd like to be.

WHEN MOTHERS ARE THERE FOR THEIR SONS

Mothers have many special qualities to share with their sons, which can help liberate and encourage them to be who they are meant to be. When a son begins to push beyond the confines of the family and no longer feels comfortable with physical intimacy during early adolescence, he will still need love and support. Even boys who seem emotionally self-assured are also very tender and in need of reassurance. Mothers who understand this can continue to be there for their sons as they develop.

'If I had a bad day at school, just hearing my mother's voice or feeling her presence was very comforting.' *James, 19*

What boys need in adolescence is for their mother to be there for them in less obvious ways – by making their favourite meal or simply doing something their *sons* enjoy. While their sons may not say much, they will appreciate it when their mother continues to listen to them and to share their concerns, because they still need to know she believes in them. Most boys find it hard to sit down and talk face to face, but they will often open up during shared activities. It helps when mothers are aware that time for joint activities can be good talking time.

'My mum had a big influence on me. She took on quite a large role in my life. She always had something to do with whatever I was doing. Like, I started playing baseball, and she took on being scorer, then a manager, then she was coaching for a bit, and things like that. She took a huge interest in my life. I think I would have dealt with it if she hadn't, but at that age I don't think I realised what kind of an effect that her being a part of my life would have. What I really appreciated my mum doing was basically taking that initiative.' *Sean, 20*

Most mothers will never know how much they have enriched their son's life, or how important a buffer they have provided from the harsher aspects of life. The important thing is that mothers help shield their boys, without smothering them. Even though his father was an angry, distant man, Doug, 52, recalls his mother as 'noble, loving and busy'. It was her warmth that saved him from what might otherwise have been an impossible childhood. When Nick, 53, thinks of his mother, he remembers how she opened him up to a more spiritual view of life and to the world of art, both of which have been major influences in his adult life and his career as a film-maker. When Neil, 34, looks back he appreciates the way his mother always supported his creativity, which has helped balance his working life in the financial sector. These men showed me that mothers who understand the nuances of boys' lives not only help support their sons to be who they most long to be, they can take pleasure in sharing their journey.

'When it came to puberty, my mother went out of her way to take me out to theatre groups and things. I think she saw it as this European idea of introducing me to society. I thought it was a bloody brilliant idea – stretching me, introducing me to adults. Often I was too embarrassed to say anything, but it was a great thing that she did. I don't remember my father being around when that happened. I thought that was a fantastic thing to do.' *Doug, 52*

In search of the perfect body

WHAT MAKES A *REAL* MAN?

One of the ways boys seek to gain love and approval from those they care about is by acting like a man. Hungry to be grown up, boys seize on anything they can to help them understand what it's like to be a real man. Many boys turn to popular culture for their cues – to the good, bad and indifferent images they see of men in magazines and movies, in games and on television. Increasingly grown men are also being influenced by advertising, films and reality television. Now most aspects of a man's life – from his work and his wardrobe, to his sex life – are in the hands of advertisers, scriptwriters and fashion gurus. It is these individuals who dictate how a man should *present* himself to the world if he wants to be taken seriously.

In previous generations it was a man's strength that was valued, because it enabled him to serve his family and community. It was his commitment to these ideals that earned a man respect. In many ways, it was a more straightforward path for men. Now far more is expected. Strength is still part of the equation, except that now it's the *appearance* of strength that matters. As academic Peter West points out, muscularity has become the new definition of masculinity.[1] Many of the younger men I spoke with were very aware of these expectations. Mitchell, 26, admitted to feeling intimidated by the need to have the right look. 'We all have to be physically big and musclebound, plus our dicks have to be large. This is how masculinity is presented. If you do not have the body, you simply are not a man.'

> 'There is some pressure to present yourself a certain way. There are two reasons why guys push that V shape, big muscles, and all that – to look good for girls, or to look stronger around other blokes. I'm fairly comfortable with how I am, although I'd like to be a bit stronger. There's a confidence and a security that comes with that. It's an image thing. Being strong is a big thing to do with masculinity.' *Sean, 20*

We live in a world where good muscle tone is important for men to achieve the right image and attract attention. It suggests someone who is powerful and in control of his destiny, while those who lack tone and definition are to be pitied. These perceptions are reinforced time and again in such television shows as *Extreme Makeover* and *The Biggest Loser*. These shows leave viewers in little doubt as to what is and is not acceptable in terms of body image. *Queer Eye for the Straight Guy* goes into great detail about how men should look, and how their homes, wardrobes and diets need to change if they hope to be accepted by family, friends and society. It's no coincidence that the show features the friends and partner of the man under the microscope, because the whole focus of the show is on how to gain greater love and appreciation.

Some men I spoke with find their way through this maze of expectations with ease, and enjoy their daily grooming rituals. 'Quite a few men I know, like myself, do have good jobs, earn well and are quite polished. We wear a suit that actually fits, wear polished shoes from England, have clean hands and fingernails, and occasionally can have a pedicure, and can fix most things like the car and computers, even if we haven't encountered the problem before. Largely we move through life with confidence in our abilities. It all comes down to a basic belief or confidence in oneself,' said Lee, 48, an IT professional. The difficulty is that increasing numbers of men lack this confidence. They see flaws in themselves that don't exist, or become totally fixated on what flaws they do have.

> 'I think this image thing exists – it affects how well you do socially. I was always a pretty skinny guy. In Year 7, I had to stand up for myself. Those who picked on me were more obese – the weight gave them an advantage. After that I tried to put on more body fat to give me protection. *Joel, 20*

GETTING THE RIGHT LOOK

Everywhere boys look there are messages about the ideal male body shape. Even the toy figures they now play with emphasise the kind of body a hero is meant to have. Just as girls have Barbie dolls, boys now have Wolverine action figures. As the authors of *The Adonis Complex* point out, in the last couple of decades the body shapes of action hero toys have changed to reflect this new ideal male body. Even the *Star Wars* hero Han Solo, released in toy form in the late 1970s, has gone from looking like a well-proportioned man to a superhuman figure with bulging biceps and a narrow waist.[2] At first glance this might seem harmless enough. Not so, according to Dr Harrison G. Pope, chief of biological psychiatry, McLean Hospital, Belmont, Massachusetts: 'Boys are exposed to these figures while they are still very young – long before they are old enough to form an independent opinion about what a realistic man's body should look like.'[3]

> 'In the west we live in advanced capitalist societies where the creation of desire and need is a key driver in the socioeconomic system. But in order to create a sense of need, capitalism must also create a sense of dissatisfaction. Mass media, modern marketing and other agencies construct and promote an ever-changing ideal of physical perfection.'
> Associate Professor Wendy Seymour [4]

This heightened focus on the male body in the media is now impacting the lives of men and boys. In a recent *Sydney Morning Herald* article, beauty therapist Dee Davies agreed that men are now under more pressure than ever to look good, and that there had been a significant increase in male clientele at her beauty salon since *Queer Eye for the Straight Guy* was first aired in 2003. Alarmingly, her youngest male client is 13.[5] Outside the beauty salon, male cosmetics and toiletries are now an increasingly important part of cosmetic sales worldwide; between 1997 and 2003 global sales of male products rose by 48 per cent.[6]

Men and boys have as much right as women to be informed about fashion and grooming, but is this where the sudden spotlight on men ends? A recent study looked at whether various types of magazines – sports, health/fitness and fashion – made teenage boys dissatisfied with their bodies. It revealed that health/fitness magazines caused boys the most body dissatisfaction, because of their emphasis on muscularity and body shape. While not all boys were affected by health/fitness magazines, the study demonstrated that boys who read these magazines on a regular basis are more likely to be dissatisfied with their body image, and to want to take pills and artificial supplements to enhance their body shape, if they don't already do so.[7]

'We hear so much about women and eating disorders in the media. It's important that these issues are covered for women, but it's not the complete story. Even though I've done many interviews, I still get looks of total surprise from journalists when I talk about eating disorders in men and boys. For most people it's still a "girl issue".
Dr Murray Drummond [8]

The consequence is that, like girls, boys are now suffering from eating disorders. There has been very little coverage of eating disorders in boys. Few parents pick up on these disorders, because they are not aware their sons are at risk, and because, unlike girls who want to be thin, many boys are doing everything they can to bulk up. Amid growing concerns about obesity, parents — not realising what is actually going on — are often relieved to see their boys exercising and eating well. Parents need to know that an inordinate interest in fitness magazines, or sudden changes in their son's diet and weight might not be such a good thing. They also need to be aware of more extreme measures sports coaches might suggest to achieve weight loss, and be willing to question these measures. [9]

> *Unlike girls who want to be thin, many boys are doing everything they can to bulk up.*

WHEN MEN HATE THE WAY THEY LOOK

Eating disorders that are not picked up during adolescence can follow boys into adulthood. There are many more men than we realise suffering from eating disorders. Far fewer men than women talk about eating difficulties or seek help. Currently around 1 million men in the United States suffer from eating disorders, [10] and in Australia men and boys make up around 10 per cent of people suffering from eating disorders. According to Dr Murray Drummond – an expert on men, body image and eating disorders – these figures don't represent an accurate picture of the men and boys suffering from these disorders, because these figures are only based on those who are currently in the medical system receiving help.[11]

The disorders men and boys are suffering from include anorexia, bulimia, situational eating and binge eating. Perhaps most disturbing is the emergence of muscle dysmorphia (muscle dysmorphic disorder), also known as reverse anorexia or bigorexia – the obsessive need to appear lean and muscular. Men suffering muscle dysmorphia often go to extreme lengths to achieve the classic V-shaped body through a rigorous exercise regime and strict diet. Even when sufferers have achieved the 'perfect body', they still feel ashamed and inadequate. When they look in the mirror, they do not see their narrow waist and bulging biceps; they see a person whose body lacks tone and definition. Far from flaunting their super-sized bodies, often these men go to great lengths to hide their perceived lack of muscle by wearing loose-fitting or layered clothing, even in hot weather. Many end up taking steroids and other hazardous body-building drugs, and exercising eight or so hours a day to maintain their super-sized body.

'In a lot of cases I've seen people give up their jobs, and not . . . take leaps and bounds in their career, because they figure it'll interfere with their body-building. I've seen it consume people to the point where there is nothing else.' *Tony Doherty, weights coach and body builder*[12]

Muscle dysmorphia is almost exclusively a male phenomenon. 'I think the fact that muscle dysmorphia is primarily a condition that afflicts men is very, very important in the sense that muscles are a symbol of masculinity,'[13] explains psychologist Precilla Choi. Not everyone who is into body building is at risk, but they are more aware of their body than most. Weights coach and body builder Tony Doherty recounted his desire to achieve the classic v shape, which began in childhood and was consolidated during his teens. 'I remember I was about fourteen or thirteen and I saw Arnie on the *Mike Walsh Show* or something back then. I remember just looking at this guy's body and I suddenly knew what I wanted to do with my life.' Although Tony is committed to his sport, he doesn't believe he is ruled by it, although he has seen many who are.[14]

Even when these men are suffering from injury, they will keep to their rigorous exercise regime for fear of losing ground. Frequently their work, relationships and social life come under threat as their excessive attention to diet and exercise takes over their lives. More extreme sufferers have been known to leave their jobs and relationships for fear of compromising their stringent exercise regime. Many avoid eating in restaurants in case they don't serve the 'right foods'. One study of men from twenty-three Boston gymnasiums revealed that those suffering from muscle dysmorphia were not only unhappy with their bodies, they considered themselves less healthy than did those not suffering from this disorder.[15] Diagnosing muscle dysmorphia can be especially difficult because sufferers look healthy and have hearty appetites, and are seen to be doing 'what men do'. To address this problem we need more public education, so that teachers, parents and family are aware of the symptoms and of the help available.

'What we need to be concerning ourselves with as a culture is that increasingly boys are being controlled by how they look. Often it's not even an eating disorder they're suffering from, but an attitude towards themselves that has a huge impact on how they see themselves and what they do.' *Dr Murray Drummond* [16]

MAKING THEMSELVES ATTRACTIVE TO WOMEN

Not all men and boys are driven to extremes, but many are unhappy about the way they look, and have completely unrealistic views about what women find attractive in men. A recent study of men in Austria, France and the United States revealed that men are now seeking a leaner, more muscular look. In all three countries men thought the ideal male body was around 12.7 kilograms more muscular than they were. These men also believed women preferred men to be around 13.6 kilograms more muscular than they were. Yet when women were canvassed, they were clearly attracted to men with *ordinary* physiques, and confessed they found the classic body-builder physique distinctively unattractive. [17]

'A strong link is made between the classic V-shaped look and sexual appeal. You've only got to look at *Men's Health* magazine. The guy on the cover is muscular and athletic. He is appealing to heterosexual and gay men. First there'll be a statement about having big pecs or whatever, and the next statement is about sex. It's all about the body being able to perform.' *Dr Murray Drummond* [18]

In spite of the fact that most women prefer men with 'normal' physiques, the preoccupation with the 'perfect male physique' remains strong. The chance for men to achieve this look is supported by a multi-billion-dollar 'fitness' industry, which manufactures everything from dietary supplements to home gym equipment. Then there's the fashion end of the market, which produces sports and leisure wear, so punters have the right 'look' when they turn up to the gym.

The constant stream of ads and editorials on body image also makes it clear that men can't get their dream body by themselves – they need *professional* help. This means having a personal trainer, or access to professionals at a gym. There is nothing wrong with wanting to exercise and keep in shape, as long as these activities don't heighten a person's vulnerabilities.

MEN IN SPORT

With the massive sponsorship money being poured into sport, it too is now big business. Top athletes are no longer just elite sportspeople, they are celebrities with glamorous lifestyles. Doors are now open for them to the top ranks of business. Off the field they mix with politicians and movie stars, dominate the news and are frequently featured on the covers of newspapers and magazines. Sportsmanship is no longer just about being a world-class athlete, it's about being an icon. Aware of this, athletes are often drawn into drastic dieting and to using a whole cocktail of drugs to ensure they maintain 'the look'.

Many of the eating disorders, sparked by interest in sport, start early. Linda Smolak, professor of psychology at Kenyon College, Ohio, believes one of the reasons boys are currently facing eating disorders is because they take up sports that are not compatible with their natural body type.[19] Others, however, deliberately choose to pursue sports as a means of weight loss;[20] in sports such as rowing, body building, running, wrestling, dancing, swimming, gymnastics and horse racing, a minimum body weight is required.[21]

On the surface this might not seem like such a big deal, except that in a two-month period in 1997 alone, three college wrestlers from schools in North Carolina, Michigan and Wisconsin died from losing too much weight too quickly.[22] Each of these young men took extreme weight-loss measures and ended up with cardio-respiratory arrest. Again the pressure men feel to be seen as masculine can prove far more destructive than most imagine. 'Common for many men is the perception that enduring physical pain is part of what it means to be a man,' says Dr Murray Drummond. 'Therefore involvement in endurance sports is viewed as being masculine.'[23] The tragedy is that men and boys are literally dying in pursuit of these masculine goals.

> *Some of the more overtly masculine professions, such as the armed forces, now have to deal with eating disorders.*

In some sports, players are under the opposite pressure: they need to bulk up. Some players end up literally force-feeding themselves to achieve their desired weight, consuming meals of up to 10 000 calories at a time. This rapid weight gain can strain muscles, joints and vital organs, especially the heart.[24] Sporting history is littered with those who have pushed the boat out too far. Many of the East German swimmers at the 1976 and 1980 Olympic Games were given pills and supplements to enhance their physique, and thus their performance. Twenty or so years on they are now suffering from pancreatic cancer, liver tumours and heart disease, and many of their children have birth defects.[25]

It is no surprise that some of the more overtly masculine professions, such as the armed forces, now have to deal with eating disorders. In a 1997 study, just under half of the 4800 US Navy men in active duty surveyed had symptoms of eating disorders: 2.5 per cent suffered from anorexia, 6.8 per cent from bulimia, and a further 40.8 per cent from eating disorders not otherwise specified.

This study also revealed how these men suffered profound anxiety about their weight and overall body tone prior to height, weight and fitness measurements.[26]

One American military weight-management group reported that their servicemen engaged in bulimic weight-loss behaviours two to five times more often than the comparison civilian weight-management group, and that their men resorted to vomiting, strenuous exercise or the use of a sauna four times as often as the civilian group.[27] All these excessive behaviours put the body under undue pressure and can cause a whole range of disorders, from stress fractures and poor judgement, to irreversible heart or kidney damage.

'The way men are raised doesn't help with eating disorders. We just don't expect ourselves to be problematic, so we don't get help, because that's not what men do. The interesting thing I've found is that the majority of men who do get help with their eating disorder do so because there's a significant female in their lives – a mother, sister or partner – who goes to a clinic to seek assistance.' *Dr Murray Drummond*[28]

GOING TO EXTREMES

When boys and men become desperate about the way they look, they are more likely to resort to extreme measures to achieve the perfect figure. The 1993 National Drug Strategy household survey revealed that approximately 44 000 Australians aged 14 and over had used anabolic steroids for non-medical purposes,[29] while another study of four New South Wales private schools indicated that one-third of their male students aged between 16 and 18 considered taking steroids in the future.[30] It appears that the majority of users are young, and that by 17 they have already used steroids.[31]

While men and boys who take steroids do so because they are focused on their looks, when I spoke to expert Dr Murray Drummond he suggested the problem went a lot deeper: 'What I find with teenage boys is a lack of understanding about masculinity. They see it as strength, power and dominance, because they don't know how to be masculine in their own way. They think if you look big and strong, then you'll get by. They become fixated with dominating "weaker" people – gays, women and weaker boys.'[32]

Not only can inappropriate steroid use endanger physical health, it can also have serious psychological effects. Strong links have been made between users and the escalation of violence and paranoia in their behaviour. Harrison G. Pope and colleagues have documented a number of cases of men with no history of psychiatric illness or criminal behaviour who have become violent after taking steroids. These include a 32-year-old prison officer who shot a shop assistant in the spine; a 24-year-old teacher who broke off his engagement and then planted a bomb under his fiancée's car; and a 23-year-old construction worker who murdered a hitchhiker.[33] The problem of 'roid rage' is sufficiently widespread for a group of British women to set up the Steroid Abusers' Wives Association.

> In one survey 17 per cent of the men said they would trade three years of their life to reach their desired weight.

In the 1997 *Psychology Today* national survey of body satisfaction, 43 per cent of men said they were dissatisfied with the way they looked, compared with 15 per cent of respondents in 1972.[34] In another study, when men were asked, 'How many years of your life would you trade to achieve your weight goals?', 17 per cent said they would trade three years of their life to reach their desired weight, while an additional 11 per cent said they would be willing to trade five years of their life.[35]

When I asked the men in my survey whether they felt any pressure to present themselves in a certain way, those under the age of 50 were clearly the most vulnerable to this pressure. Even those under 50 who claimed *not* to be under any pressure stressed the importance of looking good at work and when out socially. As Daryl pointed out, nobody wants to be noticed for the wrong reason. The single men I spoke with were the most aware of the importance of being attractive to women. Those in relationships also felt it was important to maintain their looks – to show they are appealing and successful. Regardless of their age, the biggest concern among the men I interviewed was their stomach, followed by the size of their penis, their hair and their chest.

> 'Successful is what my fiancée wants me to portray to everyone – I believe to prove she has made the right choice in choosing me.'
> Evan, 27

MEN WITH EATING DISORDERS

Dr Murray Drummond believes that male eating disorders are on the increase. 'We are now developing a have and have not mentality about the body. It is elite to have a lean body, and it is considered failure to carry extra weight,'[36] he explains. According to the *Better Health Channel* around 17 per cent of Australian men diet, 4 per cent are bulimic, and 3 per cent are binge eaters, while 10 per cent of anorexics are men.[37] The full scale of the problem is hard to gauge, because men are much better than women at disguising their problems, and society is less practised at picking up problems in men.

It also appears that men find these disorders harder to beat. 'Even though there is a smaller percentage of men with eating disorders, compared to females, the prognosis is not as promising for men as it is for women. It has been suggested that only 20 per cent of males, as compared with 50 per cent of females, have a good outcome,'[38] says Helen Fawkner, a Melbourne University PhD student researching body image.

In recent years eating disorders have claimed some high-profile male victims. Elton John has suffered from bulimia,[39] and Daniel Johns, former lead singer of Silverchair, suffered from ano-rexia.[40] Champion Australian Rules footballer Mark Harvey was a bulimia sufferer during his playing career. 'It initially started when I got to the football club. I had a bit of puppy fat and players, team-mates would actually just joke about it, and I think it scarred me a little bit,' he explains. His disorder started when he put on several kilos while recovering from a broken leg. One night after a heavy drinking session he felt ill, so he made himself sick. The following morning, when Mark weighed himself, he discovered he was 1–2 kilograms lighter. By accident Mark had found an effective way to control his weight.

Mark's obsession with his weight grew, inspiring him to run while wearing a plastic garbage bag, even in 30-degree temperatures, and to do sit-ups in front of the heater in order to shed kilos. For Mark, his desire to please fans became uppermost. 'When I ran out in front of 80 000 people I just wanted to look good, and I thought subconsciously, once again, that if I wasn't a certain weight when I ran out on the ground, I wasn't going to play well.'[41] It wasn't until Mark had blood coming out of his throat and anus that he sought help. Having fully recovered, Mark now encourages men not to feel awkward about suffering a disease that was once regarded as a woman's complaint. Like so many sufferers, Mark didn't realise he had a problem. The more information there is available about the eating disorders men and boys face, the easier it will be for them to get help.

When men have weight problems or don't like the way they look, rather than seek professional guidance they tend to opt for tortuous exercise regimes, and are now also choosing cosmetic surgery. We have tended to assume cosmetic surgery is a woman's domain, but this is no longer so. While Australian statistics on cosmetic surgery are hard to come by, there is no doubt the numbers of Australian men opting for cosmetic surgery procedures are growing. It has been suggested that there is one man to every nine women seeking cosmetic surgery in Australia each year.[42]

According to Sydney plastic surgeon Alf Lewis, the type of procedure men go for is dependent on age. In his experience the most common procedures for men under 35 are breast and nose reductions, while those aged 35 to 55 tend to be concerned about enhancing their eyelids and general body shape – particularly their 'beer gut'. Older men also opt for breast reductions, facelifts and eyelid reductions. The reasons men seek cosmetic surgery vary, from changing or enhancing some aspect of their body, or moving ahead after a marriage or relationship breakdown, to achieving a look they can't attain through a healthy diet and exercise.[43] As the workplace becomes more competitive and youth-focused, cosmetic surgery is providing an attractive option for men determined to maintain their career prospects.

When men have weight problems or don't like the way they look, rather than seek professional guidance they tend to opt for tortuous exercise regimes, and are now also choosing cosmetic surgery.

The beauty of the male body has been contemplated, admired and desired in art, literature and sport, from ancient Greece and Rome to the Renaissance and beyond. Yet while the male figure was idealised and often represented as a god in human form, at least that body shape was attainable. Now, even though the ideal male body is getting further and further out of reach, men are led to believe this kind of body is not only possible, but highly desirable. Like women's bodies, the male body has now become *decorative*. It is used to sell everything from jeans to jocks. The magazine industry talks openly of male models as 'eye candy'. Younger and younger male models are now being featured in magazines to help sustain the interest of women readers, and keep circulation figures up.

The body building industry also helps to promote this one-dimensional view of men. As academic Peter West points out, body building magazines talk of men's bodies in terms of their hardness – of rock-hard muscles, and of becoming an iron man. 'Yet men's bodies – rather like women's bodies – are not hard. Flesh is soft however pumped-up it becomes . . . The rhetoric flies in the face of reality.'[44]

'Things are changing rapidly. Men's bodies are being commodified and commercialised in the way women's bodies have been, and it's having a real effect. More and more men and boys are wanting to look muscular and athletic, but the classic V shape is hard to achieve without control. Boys are spending more and more time on their bodies, but it's for looks, not for health.' *Dr Murray Drummond*[45]

When men are regarded as objects, they begin to see themselves in this way. This trend is increasingly apparent to a theatre director friend of mine. In recent years she has noticed how young male actors cluster around her, wearing clothes that highlight their every contour, in the hope it will give them the edge.

At the heart of men's issues with body image is the desire to feel worthwhile and be valued. The marketplace has seized on this need, exploited it and used it to diminish and dehumanise men. 'The old model of masculinity showed men how to be part of a larger social system; it gave them a context and promised them that their social contributions were the price of admission to the realm of adult manhood,' says Susan Faloudi. 'Ornamental culture has no such counterparts. Constructed around celebrity and image, glamour and entertainment, marketing and consumerism, it is a ceremonial gateway to nowhere.'[46]

When men are vulnerable

LETTING WELL ALONE

How men appear and how they experience life are frequently not
the same thing. Yet still we continue to assume men are never anything other than strong and capable, regardless of what life throws
at them. In *Joe Cinque's Consolation* Helen Garner told the story of
how in October 1997 Canberra law student Anu Singh planned to
murder her partner Joe Cinque after a Friday night dinner party at
their house. Even though some of the dinner guests had heard talk of
murder, none of them spoke to Joe about this. After the guests left,
Anu laced Joe's coffee with Rohypnol and then while he was unconscious she administered what should have been a lethal hit of heroin.
Joe didn't die. He woke up on Saturday and stumbled around the
house. Again Anu laced his coffee with a large quantity of Rohypnol
and then when Joe passed out she injected him with more heroin.
Somehow Joe Cinque survived Saturday night and the following
morning. During this time Madhavi Rao, Anu's best friend, saw Joe
lying unconscious on his bed, but did nothing, even though she knew
his body was full of Rohypnol and heroin.

It wasn't until around midday Sunday, when large quantities of black vomit were pouring from Joe's mouth, that Anu Singh rang the paramedics, giving a false name and evading questions about Joe's location. When finally the paramedics arrived, they were too late to save Joe.[1] The horror of this story isn't just that Joe Cinque suffered a protracted and unnecessary death, but that even though a number of people knew of the plan to kill him, they did nothing – and Joe Cinque lost his life. If Joe Cinque had been threatening to kill his girlfriend, would friends and acquaintances have left him to it? Why didn't anyone talk to him? Was it because they were embarrassed, or because they just didn't care, or was it because Joe was expected to look after himself because he was a man?

THEY CAN HANDLE IT

Men often find themselves alone facing potentially dangerous situations – from street attacks to personal emergencies – because it is assumed they can handle whatever situation they are in. As a result some men are needlessly harmed, while those less fortunate end up dead. Many of us feel uncomfortable about seeing men vulnerable, because it challenges everything we have been led to believe about men being strong and able to cope. Yet to realise men too can be vulnerable in certain situations doesn't compromise their strength and capabilities; it simply acknowledges that they too are human.

Men are capable of great acts of courage, but there are times when they need help and protection. So much of how we react towards men is based on our perceptions of how society wants them to be, rather than how life is for them. The men I spoke with talked repeatedly about the strain of having to appear strong all the time. Stan Dale tells of a cross-dresser friend whose car broke down. His friend was dressed in drag when this happened, and to his relief, two men went out of their way to help him with his car. A month later Stan's friend had more car troubles. This time he was dressed as a man. No-one came to his aid, so he rang a motoring organisation for help. On hearing a male voice, the man who answered yelled down the phone that this wasn't a garage.[2]

WHAT YOU DON'T KNOW CAN HARM YOU

Like it or not, men aren't always able to handle themselves in every situation. Apart from sexual assault, men are far more likely than women to be victims of violent crime. If they're young they are at even greater risk. In 2003, 67 per cent of Australian homicide victims were male. Those aged 15 to 24 were most vulnerable to assault and armed robbery, while men aged 25 to 44 were most at risk of homicide. While women are most likely to face attack from someone they know in residential premises, 46 per cent of male assault victims were attacked by strangers, and 70 per cent of these assaults took place in non-residential locations.[3]

> 'What we realise about violence is that most of it is perpetrated against men.' *Ray Lenton, family group counsellor*[4]

As you think about all the young men you know or read about in the papers, you start to realise just how many young men get hurt, for no other reason than they were in the wrong place at the wrong time. My nephew was mugged coming home from college; he is now dealing with a fractured skull and other injuries. At the time of writing this chapter a young man in his early 20s was attacked by a group of men outside a city restaurant. A crowd gathered to watch him being punched and kicked. No-one lifted a hand to help, even when he was unconscious. Four days later he died of his injuries. He was to have been married later in the year.[5]

While most male homicides and serious assaults do come to the public's attention, the majority of lesser assaults and sexual violence against men do not. Many men don't even report these incidents, because they think they're expected to get on with life, so male victims continue to be under-represented in crime figures. Only now are we beginning to understand how vulnerable men and boys can be to assault, including sexual assault. In the late 1970s while working in London I interviewed a promising young professional for a job. Everything about this candidate was impressive, apart from the fact that he was extremely evasive about why he had left his last job. Finally he admitted he had been raped by his boss. I can still remember my shock at realising men were also vulnerable to rape.

'When men are raped we don't take any notice. We don't want to know that men are physically, mentally and emotionally vulnerable. From a boy you're taught not to be overpowering towards girls, but there's nothing about the vulnerability of men – you've just got to get on with it.' *Tony, 26*

In Australia in the twelve months prior to April 2002 there were 4800 reported adult male victims of sexual assault, but we see little-to-nothing about this in the media.[6] Society's ignorance of the extent of men's vulnerability keeps men vulnerable. Men aren't encouraged to consider their safety, nor do they know what to do if they are harmed. Unless we provide men with appropriate help for the many types of assault they face, including sexual assault, they will continue to conceal the terrible things that happen to them. In a recent survey in Ireland of 3000 randomly selected adults, 3 per cent of the men reported having been raped, while 28 per cent said they had been sexually assaulted or abused. Of the ninety-eight men who revealed they had been sexually assaulted as adults, only one had reported the incident to authorities.[7]

'There seems to be a lack of understanding that men can be the victims of all the things women can. I think all too often men are tarred with the same stereotypical brush – initiators of sex, initiators of violence, strong, in control and most certainly more capable of looking out for themselves than women.' *Mairi Eadie, law graduate*[8]

While some countries do recognise that men as well as women can be raped, Scotland doesn't. 'A stigma is firmly attached to male rape victims in Scotland, brushing the crime under the carpet and discouraging victims from coming forward,' says Glasgow-based law graduate Mairi Eadie, who has conducted extensive research into the impact of this out-of-date law, which does not recognise that a man may be raped by another man. 'Many people I contacted for my survey felt that it was worse for a man to be raped, because of the lack of understanding they would face, along with the challenges to their sexual identity.' She went on to tell of a victim who had been drugged and raped by someone he knew. When this man went to report the crime, the local police suggested he leave town, or take personal revenge. This man made the decision to get on with his life – what other choice did he realistically have?[9]

This is hardly the kind of situation any victim would want. 'Some men may well be able to cope with violent attacks, as no doubt some women can,' says Mairi, 'but other men will be unable to defend themselves through size or fear. Some will be unable to deal emotionally with what has happened to them, and some will feel ashamed and degraded. The only difference is that women will mostly face sympathy and support, whereas men will all too often face assumptions, accusations and sometimes plain disbelief.'[10]

HOME TRUTHS

It's not only out on the streets that men are vulnerable; many men experience violence at home. A recent *Times* article indicated that the number of male victims of domestic violence had grown by nearly one-third in recent years, to around 150000, and it now accounts for 34 per cent of all the reported cases of domestic violence in Britain.[11] One of the difficulties in trying to gauge the full extent of domestic violence is that it takes place behind closed doors. And, like many women in this situation, men who have been abused can be reluctant to speak out. Unlike most women, however, when a man does speak out, there is a good chance he won't be believed, or even that he will be ridiculed.

If a man does call the police, he is likely to find himself subject to scrutiny. A *Dispatches* television program aired in Britain in January 1999 revealed that 25 per cent of the 100 male victims of domestic abuse interviewed had been arrested while seeking police help (because when police arrived on the scene they presumed it was the man who had perpetrated the abuse), and 89 per cent felt the police had failed to take their situation seriously.[12] Things are slowly changing. In Australia some police stations now have dedicated domestic violence liaison officers who have the skills to deal more appropriately with this situation.

'Abused men often downplay the seriousness of abuse and consider it not worth talking about, let alone reporting to the authorities. This is more so for abused husbands with a long history of domestic violence, such as having been abused by their wives for a long period of time, and/or having witnessed and/or sustained violence at home, at school or in the community as children.' *Adjunct Professor Sotirios Sarantakos*[13]

While generally men are stronger and bigger than women, size and strength don't matter where domestic violence is concerned. Women compensate for their lack of physical strength by using weapons, or by attacking men when they are most vulnerable: while resting or asleep. Their choice of weapon includes domestic utensils such as knives, hammers and pans. Men also report being scratched, punched, kicked and bitten, having their face slapped and their hair pulled out. More extreme cases include men being stabbed, drenched with boiling water, threatened with an axe or having glass placed in their food. Others talk of having their most treasured possessions destroyed and their clothes trashed. Some men are badly hurt during these incidents, others lose their lives.

Every day men are being harmed in their homes.

It seems inconceivable that every day men are being harmed in their homes. 'The vast majority of people view this problem with disbelief and are reluctant to admit it exists. Even in modern societies, standards and norms indicate that men are strong and women weak. Such standards and principles are inconsistent with the notion that women abuse their husbands. Firstly, women are weaker and cannot assault strong men. And secondly, how can a woman be violent against her husband, who loves and protects her to death, if necessary,' says Sotirios Sarantakos, adjunct professor, School of Humanities and Social Sciences, Charles Sturt University. 'People find it difficult to believe that even weak spouses can assault their partner if they hold the power. And they find it difficult to accept that there are other types of abuse, such as psychological, social etc., which require no physical strength, and which often are as painful and harmful as physical abuse.'[14]

'The violence was there when I met my wife. There was a sad history of violence and attempted suicide in her family. She wanted to escape, and wanted to be loved. Maybe she or I saw myself as a knight in shining armour that would take her away from her dysfunctional family. She had a lot of emotion and anger in her, and I always wanted to understand why, so I could help. I put off having kids as long as possible due to my wife's inability to cope with life. Over the years my father-in-law and I started to share more of our stories of frustration in living with such abusive women. Our stories were almost identical. These conversations became more frequent over the years. He and I endured impossible marriages out of a sense of loyalty and our strong Catholic religious beliefs. You see, marriage is supposed to be forever.'
Andre

Domestic abuse is no respecter of gender or position. Its more notable victims have included Abraham Lincoln, John Wayne and Humphrey Bogart.[15] Responding to battered men's need for help, the British organisation ManKind was set up to provide counselling support for men. It has also established two men's refuges to give battered men somewhere safe and supportive to get help. In a recent interview, national organiser Stephen Fitzgerald said that the men who seek help from ManKind have suffered an average of six years of mental and psychological abuse in their home.[16] Mike Kenny, a British businessman in his 30s who was in an abusive relationship, has now set up It Does Happen, to help victims of abuse. In its first fortnight more than 20 000 men visited the website.[17]

It is hard to pinpoint the extent of this abuse. A number of studies, including that by Associate Professor Bruce Headey of the University of Melbourne, state that men are equally likely to be victims of domestic violence as women, and to suffer injury and pain in such situations. After examining domestic violence studies and victims' reports from Britain and America since 1972, Professor John Archer, president of the International Society on the Research of Aggression, stated that 40 per cent of these victims were men. Other studies, including those by Dr Michael Flood of the Australian National University, dispute that the incidences of domestic violence towards men are this high.

'There has been a lot of resistance to domestic violence in general; it's always seen as someone else's problem to deal with. Until recently it was a no-go zone, because it was assumed that men don't get clobbered, and that the only victims are women. Male victims of domestic violence do exist and are rarely given a fair go. I'd like to see the statistics for the number of men who apply for and are subsequently refused interim orders, placing them at considerable risk. Justice demands that each case must be treated on its own merits, regardless of gender.' *Vaughan (who has worked in the courts)*

What is evident is that domestic violence towards men exists, and that the actual numbers of men experiencing domestic violence are greater than those represented in crime statistics. Male victims are not only reluctant to admit there's a problem; they fear they will not receive adequate help and/or empathy should they pursue their claim. Domestic violence services in Australia do provide support and accommodation assistance to men in need, as part of their overall service. The difficulty is that until we recognise that this form of abuse exists, and let male victims know they can receive assistance, men will continue to keep this abuse to themselves.

'My wife always wanted someone, anyone, to blame when things went wrong. My wife and her sisters had been taught very well by their mother to hate men – to blame them for everything that went wrong in their lives, to never accept responsibility for their own actions. I had to be on tap for her all the time. I've never been against women's rights, but any relationship between partners has to be based on mutual respect. I persisted stoically for over twenty years. It is very humiliating to admit you have a problem. No-one wants to air their dirty linen in public. We went out with each other for nearly four years before the marriage, but it wasn't the same as living with her. For years I've been locked out of the house, plus physically and verbally abused. She would wake me in the middle of the night, beating and thumping me on the back with her fists.' *Andre*

Violence towards men isn't confined to a specific age group. It can happen to relatively young men, who are not in strictly domestic situations. A recent study of male university students revealed that 40 per cent had experienced physical aggression from their girlfriends; 29 per cent described this abuse as serious.[18] Violence doesn't just affect the men concerned, it spills over into their families and friendships, affecting the lives of those around them. In Australia, since Reg and Sue Price founded the Men's Rights Agency in the early 1990s, one-third of all the calls they have received have come from mothers, sisters, new partners of male victims, or from concerned colleagues.[19]

Violence doesn't just affect the men concerned, it spills over into their families and friendships, affecting the lives of those around them.

WHY MEN CHOOSE TO STAY

The reasons why men stay in abusive relationships are similar to the reasons why women do so. Many of these men still love their partner and hope to turn things around. Others stay because their self-esteem has been crushed, or they have nowhere to go, while others stay for the kids. Until writing this book I had no real knowledge of domestic violence towards men. But then as friends opened up, I learned of one woman who regularly beats her partner; of another male friend who finally found the courage to leave a physically violent marriage; and of a girlfriend's brother who remains in a violent marriage because he fears for the safety of his kids. I was shocked to find this was happening so close to home, and to experience the very real angst that family and friends felt. The overwhelming feeling was one of helplessness, because this subject is still largely taboo.

One of the reasons many people don't take domestic violence towards men seriously is because they assume women only harm men in self-defence, but research indicates otherwise. In one Canadian study, for example, 62 per cent of the women resorting to minor domestic violence – which included throwing things, pushing, grabbing, shoving and spanking – confirmed they were not acting in self-defence.[20] Abusive women admit they harm men out of anger or hurt, to dominate or control, or because they are jealous or can't handle a communication breakdown. By their own admission more female abusers than men initiate violence.[21] 'Abused men still living with their abusive wives are powerless and traumatised, and therefore do not have the courage to address the problem logically and constructively, and to look for solutions. This often encourages abusive wives to intensify and consolidate further systems of abuse,' says Sotirios Sarantakos.[22]

'One of the worst cases I saw was a man who had been forced to live outside in primitive conditions in a sleep-out in the backyard. He had to obtain his wife's permission first before entering the house to cook, wash, shower, even to use the toilet.' *Vaughan (who has worked in the courts)*

This violence hurts men psychologically as well as physically, often making it hard for them to be effective at home or at work. Others suffer a breakdown in health. One victim of domestic violence I spoke with hasn't been able to work for more than three years due to years of abuse. In one study almost 40 per cent of those surveyed talked of the emotional hurt, while nearly 35 per cent reported sadness or depression.[23] 'You had to be in it, inside the violence, either delivering it or receiving it, to understand it. For it to be real,' says Luke, the central character in Matt Condon's brave novel *The Pillow Fight*, which explores the brutal reality of domestic violence from a male victim's perspective: 'Whatever he did for Charlotte was never enough. No matter how hard he tried she kept raising the crossbar. He had become exhausted, and wanted to know if raising the crossbar would ever end.'[24]

'I had no qualms about going to a counsellor, but my wife was paranoid about it. It was the control stuff all over again . . . The counsellor suggested I keep a diary of the abuse, but I would too often forgive her and not record many incidents. It did help, because I could then look back and see clearly what was happening. After three years I could see it was getting worse – the violence was escalating. I was never against women's lib, but there has to be mutual respect. We lasted over twenty years.' *Andre*

One of the reasons many people don't take domestic violence towards men seriously is because they assume women only harm men in self-defence.

MIND GAMES

Not all domestic abuse by women is physical. Some women resort to psychological abuse. They constantly put their partner down, damage his property, misuse money, control his contact with family and friends, use sex as a weapon, treat him as if he were a boarder, lock him in or out of the house, or make false allegations of violence against him. Some of the men I spoke with were forbidden to see friends and family, effectively cutting them off from wider support. One of the greatest weapons abusive women have are their children. Threats to harm or take away the children can be an extremely effective way to get men to toe the line. 'Abusive wives are reported to threaten their husband that if he left the relationship or reported abuse to the authorities, "the children will suffer",' Sotirios Sarantakos explains.[25]

> 'I think we underestimate the violence of words. I think that psychological pain is much more painful than physical pain. Often women say things, but the guy finds himself unable to respond. I do find the verbal stuff difficult.' *Justin, 43*

Again, since putting together this book, a number of friends have confided in me the ways in which friends and siblings are being psychologically abused in relationships: by becoming a virtual slave at home, by being subjected to profligate spending and constant abuse, or being barred from using joint possessions. 'Abused men do not report their problems to the authorities and do not feel comfortable talking about it to others. Instead they stay in the relationship for as long as they can endure violence, until they gain some independence, and until their children are old enough to withstand the effects of the abusive mother, or – better – until they leave home,' says Sotirios Sarantakos.[26]

To some outsiders these situations may seem highly unlikely or even laughable, but for those inside these relationships, it can be a living nightmare. Once these men have been sufficiently ground down, they no longer have the emotional energy to assert themselves. They live in constant fear of what is going to happen next, and frequently start to believe all the terrible things they are accused of.[27] The sooner we recognise the many ways in which men can be vulnerable, the sooner we can put in place provisions to minimise this vulnerability.

'One day, after recently being belted again by my wife, at the conclusion of the visit from my father-in-law I just looked at this frail, old, but highly intelligent and decent gentleman who I loved, and told him honestly that I could not take much more. My marriage to his daughter would not last much longer. We both had tears in our eyes as he pleaded with me. You see, I had come to the realisation that I did not want to end up like him. I could not let myself end up like him.' *Andre*

HOW MEN SEE THEMSELVES

When we characterise men as dangerous and not to be trusted, they feel compelled to go to great lengths to ensure no-one else thinks of them in this light. I heard recently on a radio talkback show of a young man who was leaving the local library at a busy time of the day when he saw a distressed toddler who had been separated from his mother. This young man didn't feel he could go back into the library, in case the child disappeared while he was gone, but he didn't feel he could approach the child either. So he stood by helpless, watching and waiting, until a woman took charge.

When we fear men, it's hard for us to celebrate them, and for them to feel genuinely good about themselves, Doug, 52, explained to me. 'I hate that thing of men as predators; it's a loathsome, loathsome, wicked thing. It's like the tar baby thing: once you're thrown onto that tarry hedge, no matter how much you struggle you'll only get deeper into it, so you just shut up and you don't express how you're feeling. You internalise it. You have to wear it, and it's not a good thing.' The difficulty for many people, including men, is that it has become normal to regard themselves and each other as dangerous or potentially dangerous, which colours their whole way of looking at life.

'That I might be perceived as predatory is always upmost in my mind whenever I am alone with a woman in a public place, regardless of the time of day or night, whether it is in a lift, walking down the street or a corridor in a building. I will never walk behind a woman. I will slow my pace or divert my route, or maybe if possible burst ahead. In a lift or similar situation I feel I dare not initiate any conversation, or make an expression, in case it is misinterpreted. I will, however, respond in a friendly way if any comment is made. I have no idea whether women actually feel threatened in any of these circumstances, but I feel the need to minimise any possibility they might.' *Allan, 54*

THE SUICIDE GENERATION

As we start to come to terms with the many vulnerabilities men face, we can begin to see why male suicide needs greater attention. Men are not only vulnerable to external forces, increasingly they are falling victim to their own demons. While Finland tops the male suicide rates in industrialised countries, New Zealand, Australia and Canada aren't far behind.[28] Men aged between 25 and 44 give particular cause for concern, because they now represent almost half of all Australian suicides.[29] In the 1980s and early 1990s when these men were teenagers, male teen suicide figures took off. Now these men are in their 30s, they are continuing to commit suicide in larger numbers than previous generations, earning them the tag of 'the suicide generation'. According to Dr Harrison, co-author of a recent report into suicides in Australia, the year a man is born seems to make a difference to his chances of suicide. 'What is disturbing is that it seems the later you were born, the more likely you are to commit suicide, and the more likely you are to commit suicide earlier in life.'[30]

> The year a man is born seems to make a difference to his chances of suicide.

Experts suggest that the spike in suicides in this age group could be due to a combination of factors, including an increase in substance abuse, fewer job opportunities and more relationship breakdowns. Another possible factor is that depression wasn't picked up in these men while they were teenagers, so it has remained with them into their 30s. The issues men face with suicide and depression are even more problematic because men don't tend to seek help. Many turn to alcohol and drugs instead, to numb their pain.

There is a strong link between depression and suicide in men.

Acknowledging that men can also be vulnerable to depression is the first step to recognising that they have significant needs that are not being met. When men remain depressed they are at risk. Men also have a responsibility in this regard – they need help to recognise when they might be suffering from depression. They also need to know it's okay to articulate their pain.

'Most of us go about our day-to-day lives hoping nobody will notice. We think if we just keep up the appearance of having it all together, we'll be okay – lives of quiet desperation.' *Rowan, 41*

In a recent *Sydney Morning Herald* article Richard Jinman shared his own struggle with depression. 'When I was 29, Dad lost a one-sided fight with cancer and I began to lose the plot. There were outbursts of irrational anger and a paralysing sense of despair, which made it hard to leave the house or pick up the phone. I became an enthusiastic binge drinker and thought about, but never attempted suicide . . . After three rollercoaster years it took an ultimatum from a desperate girlfriend to finally force me to seek help.'[31] We need more men like Richard to help remove the stigma around this problem.

'I read somewhere recently that seventy per cent of the suicide generation are men. It doesn't surprise me. It loops back into confidence that you've got, and how comfortable you are in your skin. There's a lot of men who are not comfortable in their skin, because their niche has been eroded, or it's not nearly so clear. You used to be able to click right into it, and it was a perfect fit, it was secure. Nowadays it's not a given. Certainly the most challenging thing for me, and I think it is probably the most challenging thing for all men,

is: What is the definition of enough? Or when you can say, "Right, I should be content with being successful or not."' *Alex, 35*

Often it is the inability to seek help that places this group of men at high risk of suicide. If these men are abusing drugs and alcohol, their reluctance to admit there is a problem can be complicated by the fact that when they seek help, the drugs and alcohol mask the depression, so it remains untreated. 'We are extraordinarily bad at recognising depression in men,' claims Graham Martin, the national chairman of Suicide Prevention Australia. 'Men don't go to doctors, and when they do, they are often patted on the shoulder and told, "Don't worry, mate." Men don't tell anyone at work their problems. Instead, they might start drinking, get violent or do something impulsive like suicide.'[32] The bottom line is that too many men die unnecessarily. Most of these men had the capacity to lead rich and fulfilling lives. When they die, so much dies with them.

The truth about relationships

WHAT MEN WANT

Relationships can confound the best of us. What surprised me when I spoke to men about their relationships was the tenderness with which they spoke. Many women see men as strong and unemotional, and don't realise that, like women, they long for meaningful relationships. And that, like women, often they end up feeling hurt, confused or betrayed by the relationships they do have. Even though there is far more sexual and personal freedom than in previous generations, a level of frustration and disappointment remains between the sexes. Now more than ever we are aware of our needs; fulfilling them, however, is a different story. Magazines and newspapers are full of articles about women – not just their achievements, but what they love and aspire to, and the long list of things they do and don't want from men.

We know that women want to be valued, nurtured and understood by men, but what do men want from women? We are told men enjoy sex, and that many are obsessed by it, but is this *really* the full picture? When I asked men what they wanted in relationships, none of them talked just about sex. They talked of wanting to be 'supported and held', to have 'somebody to share things with', 'encouragement', 'trust, honesty and a friend', 'loyalty, affection and love', 'forgiveness, admiration', 'shared goals, ambitions, hopes and values', 'a friend, soulmate, guide, partner and bed mate', 'a companion and a lover'.

> *Frequently women are also unaware of the depth of men's need for tenderness.*

These responses are very different from the stereotypes generally held of men. Even though they may not admit it, most men yearn for tenderness and shared experiences. 'The reality is that males, like females, desperately need affection,' says psychologist Bill O'Hehir. 'They need to be able to communicate their anxieties and fears.'[1] Because men keep their emotions well hidden, their feelings rarely get taken into account. Frequently women are also unaware of the depth of men's need for tenderness. This then impacts their relationships in many ways. When women disagree with the men in their lives, they tend to treat them very differently than they would a girlfriend. While most women are careful not to hurt their girlfriend's feelings, they are often far more forthright with men, because they don't consider a man's feelings nearly as much. What the men I spoke with did appreciate was *gentleness* in women. They were not talking of compliance, so much as a kinder, less combative approach to differences of opinion.

'It's kind of nice being around someone where you have to be respectful.' *Jason, 22*

TENDERNESS WITHOUT STRINGS ATTACHED

This is not to say that women are never tender towards men. Women are capable of great tenderness, but the way women express this tenderness is often suffocating to men. 'There is a deep conflict at the heart of men's relations with women,' explains psychotherapist Roger Horrocks. 'There is the wish to be intimate with a woman, to become one with her, and also the dread of being enveloped again.'[2] While they rarely talk about it, many men feel the tenderness women give frequently comes with conditions. The men I interviewed spoke repeatedly about how much they longed to be understood, to be met where *they* were at. 'Women never want men to stay the way they were when they got together,' Evan, 27, reflected.

> 'Funnily enough women are usually attracted to men by the very thing they then try to beat out of you over the next 20 years – be it your sense of humour or an odd way of dressing.' *Adam, 44*

When I asked how women can show men they care, men talked of 'being listened to', 'encouraged', 'accepted', about having *their* needs, *their* feelings, who *they* are taken into account. Perhaps the most perceptive comment came from Rowan, 41, who felt that women need to love themselves first, so they can give generously to those around them, because neediness is never a good basis for a relationship.

> 'The women I've been around pay way too much attention to my emotions, worrying about how I'm feeling, where we're going. They need to be more free and easy, and not worry so much.' *Jason, 22*

REACHING NEW LEVELS OF UNDERSTANDING

With society's emphasis on how *women* view the world, it is tempting for women to want men to fit *their* ideals, rather than comprehending and celebrating men, and finding meaningful ways to bridge their differences. To ask women to take a more inclusive approach does challenge current thinking, especially as most things masculine now have negative connotations attached to them – even the word 'male' is often used in a derogatory way. Asking women to take a more open approach towards men is really no different from the approach women now ask of men. Almost all the men I interviewed, regardless of age, education or income, respected the fact that attitudes towards women needed to change, and that women have the right to be treated equally and enjoy the same range of opportunities as men. The question is whether society has progressed far enough for women to do this for men. Author Warren Farrell agrees. 'The challenge to women will be to be as open to the man's experience of powerlessness as you would to the woman's.'[3]

> *With society's emphasis on how women view the world, it is tempting for women to want men to fit their ideals, rather than comprehending and celebrating men, and finding meaningful ways to bridge their differences.*

The many freedoms that feminism has brought women are to be celebrated, not only for what has already been achieved, but because these choices can be more far-reaching than most women might imagine. If we can further extend these freedoms, we have the capacity to liberate men as well. The implications of this are enormous, because when men have more ways to express themselves, this cannot help but impact *positively* on their relationships, and on their conduct in society.

To achieve this we need to move beyond our fixation with the differences *between* sexes, so we can start to fully enjoy and understand what men and women have to offer each other and society. As writer Helen Garner points out, one of the difficulties with contemporary relationships is that we have lost the ability to express our appreciation for each other in ways that are not only appropriate, but inspiring and affirming.[4] Perhaps it's time for us to create a new language to express the depth of our admiration and love for each other, by allowing ourselves to be more open and imaginative in the way we construct and experience our relationships.

ARE MEN *REALLY* ALL THE SAME?

When relationship topics emerge, many women complain that men are all the same, but while it may be convenient for the media and advertising to categorise men as spunks, Gordon Gekkos or dopes, there is far more to men than popular culture allows. When society portrays men in this narrow, often demeaning way, everyone misses out on the many nuances that become apparent when men feel free to be more open, to be appreciated for themselves. Almost every man I approached for an interview prefaced his comments by saying he wasn't a typical man. It wasn't until I had heard this comment a number of times that I realised these men were asking to be treated as *individuals*. When they understood this was my approach, they were amazingly frank and articulate. I marvelled at their openness, the richness of their life experiences and the depth of their emotions.

CONFUSED SIGNALS

Much of the current dissatisfaction women have with men is based on their belief that men don't understand what women want. Many men wholeheartedly agree with women about this. However, if women are totally honest, many would admit they are not clear about their *own* needs, apart from the fact that they want a good man to fill those parts of their lives that seem empty. Many men yearn to be this person. They want to be someone's hero, but they don't know how to do this anymore, because heroes seem almost irrelevant and out of date.

As the signals between the sexes become more confused, men are less able to be there for women in meaningful ways. Rowan, 41, felt that much of the unhappiness experienced by both sexes is due to the many expectations people now have of relationships. Tim, 25, suspects that communication is still a big issue. Kieran, 58, agreed: 'Quite often men are left to figure things out for themselves or they simply assume that what they like will agree with a woman, which is seldom the case.'

> *As the signals between the sexes become more confused, men are less able to be there for women in meaningful ways.*

The challenges men now face in relationships are not purely a result of gender. Today we have become very focused on our *own* needs. Unrealistic though they may be, a fulfilling relationship is now about finding someone who can magically fulfil *our* needs. We feel that once we find Mr or Ms Right, we'll be fine. But in a recent article in *Psychology Today*, psychiatrists and marital advocates suggest otherwise. They argue there is no such thing as true compatibility. 'A real relationship is the collision of my humanity and yours, in all its joy and limitations,' says psychotherapist Terrence Real.[5] Does this mean the expectations men and women currently hold of each other are too high? Psychologist Frank Pittman believes they are. 'Nothing has produced more unhappiness than the concept of the soulmate.'[6]

ARE *ANYONE'S* NEEDS BEING MET?

When one's needs are neglected or ignored in a relationship, unhappiness creeps in. Women are often quite vocal about how many of their needs are unmet. What many women might not realise is that a lot of men feel exactly the same way. The problem is that men just don't have the skills to articulate it. Time and again the men I interviewed spoke of how women don't understand them or their needs.

> 'Just as men stereotype women, women stereotype men.'
> *Matthew, 27*

> 'Women need to listen and to understand men more, and concentrate on what they are, not how they present.' *Lance, 23*

While many men admit to not having a clue what women want, some women presume they know all about men, and men are very aware of this. 'The majority of women do not know exactly what it feels like to have the thoughts and emotions of a man – the thrill of competition, mateship, etc.,' Evan, 27, told me. Edward, 71, pointed out, 'My wife of forty-eight years thinks she knows all about me, but she cannot know how my mind works.' Assumptions about who men are and how they think and feel can be damaging to any relationship. In *Men, Mateship and Marriage*, Don Edgar agrees: 'We can only respond appropriately to other people if we have some insight into how they feel, what they are thinking.'[7]

As we have seen, when boys are not brought up to listen to

their feelings or to read the feelings of others, they lack emotional intelligence and are ill-equipped to then deal with the demands of a committed relationship. This lack of understanding works both ways. When girls are raised with a purely feminine outlook on life, it doesn't help them appreciate and celebrate the differences *between* the sexes, let alone find meaningful ways to bridge these differences.

> *Women talk frequently about how hard they work at their relationships, getting very little in return. What many don't appreciate is that men feel this same pressure.*

BUT WHAT ABOUT *ME*?

With the desire for limitless happiness in relationships has come a growing obsession with *self*-fulfilment. If this is taken to extremes, having one's needs met not only becomes central, it can end up being the *only* item on the agenda. The problem is that when someone is focused on themselves, there is little room to accommodate the needs of their partner. As a person's expectations grow, there is more pressure on their partner to provide them with all the parts of themselves that are missing. This dynamic then places huge pressures on *both* parties.

Women talk frequently about how hard they work at their relationships, getting very little in return. What many don't appreciate is that men feel this same pressure. They too work hard in their own way to fulfil their partner's expectations, and are well aware of how often their efforts fall short. There's a world of difference between being there for someone, and having to keep them happy 100 per cent of the time. Women frequently cast themselves in the latter role. What is interesting is that many of the men I spoke with admitted to doing the same thing, even though they may not always succeed.

It is exhausting to be in a relationship where everything is constantly up for discussion.

THE SEARCH FOR FULFILMENT

Now that both partners come into a relationship with their own bank accounts, interests, identities, jobs and aspirations, relationships have become 'continuously negotiable', according to Don Edgar. 'Maintaining separate identities, instead of being submerged in the partner's status, offers greater satisfaction but also greater fragility,' he cautions.[8] It is exhausting to be in a relationship where everything is constantly up for discussion. Our determination to lead the 'perfect life' can place a huge strain on everyone concerned. It's easy to forget that the belief that we can be totally fulfilled in a relationship is a recent concept.

'Honestly, the girls who are caught up in *Cosmopolitan* and all that bullshit – they live in their own little world. They don't behave like they really are – they're all trying to be like Britney Spears. I think they're looking for something, but they don't know what it really is.' *Joel, 20*

The older men I spoke with talked frequently of the high expectations their children had, and how often they seemed disappointed with their lives. Previously relationships were more about children, family and community, about contributing to ideals *outside* oneself. As we have become more self-obsessed we have also become less inclined to consider the needs of others. One of the less-helpful aspects of the gender debate is the preoccupation with whose pain is greatest. This obsession prevents many individuals from moving beyond their own often overwhelming sense of self-interest.

> *When image is everything, there's little room for tenderness, respect or understanding.*

When our focus turns inwards, we start to view everything and everyone we meet in terms of how they reflect on *us*. Sitcoms, reality television and magazines constantly emphasise the importance of measuring up. But when image is everything, there's little room for tenderness, respect or understanding. Part of gaining approval now lies in our ability to present ourselves well. And it's not just women who are expected to package themselves in a certain way — now men also have major expectations placed on them.

'If you start to think about it, you have to be this Renaissance man. The contemporary version is *Sex and the City's* Mr Big, who is very male, but at the same time is very nicely finished. He's got plenty of polish, but it's not that realistic. There aren't really that many men who are well read, can play an instrument, be strong as an ox, but that's the sort of standard. The expectations around men now have lots of elements to them. They need to have a job paying ten times more than most, be incredibly chiselled, and you can't possibly be losing your hair. It's just not realistic that you can be Conan the Barbarian one minute, and incredibly sensible and considerate the next.' *Alex, 35*

BUYING HAPPINESS

Not only do we seek fulfilment in relationships, we have come to believe that part of being with someone means we can 'have it all'. The deluge of information on everything from the lives of celebrities, to house and garden makeovers and reality television, can place additional pressure on men and women in relationships, as they strive to live out these larger-than-life fantasies. While men rarely admit to this pressure, they feel it keenly. 'The modern condition suggests you can have everything, and if you don't, you're a failure. It's like, if in five years we don't have a second storey and all the other bizarre things we think we want, then we've failed,' said Alex, 35. 'What's the corner we've got ourselves into? Now you can have it all, then you suddenly realise, "Why did I want that?"'

> The clash of values in current relationships is more acute than in previous generations, because so much more is now possible.

The growth of material ambitions is compromising meaningful relationships. In the past it tended to be women who complained about getting swept along by their partner's aspirations. Now men are feeling the pressure. After a hectic career Lloyd, 42, wanted to pull back a bit, but he felt unable to do so because his wife, also a busy professional, refused to modify any aspect of their lifestyle. Lloyd is not alone. A significant number of men spoke to me of being caught up in their partner's aspirations. Jack, 41, ended up going for a promotion because his wife had set her heart on new carpets and curtains. He didn't particularly want this step up, but he did want to make his wife happy, so he did what was expected of him. The clash of values in current relationships is more acute than in previous generations, because so much more is now possible. What should men do? Some people would regard Jack and Lloyd as weak for caving in to their wives. Yet if the tables were turned, most people would feel sorry for a woman caught up in her husband's aspirations.

'All the stuff they read in magazines and papers really affects their lifestyle – and they listen to their girlfriends too much.' Lance, 23

What happened to the chemistry?

DON'T GET ALL EMOTIONAL ON ME

Emotional issues are one of the main sources of frustration in relationships. Frequently women despair of having meaningful conversations with the men in their lives. But what is going on here? Is it really that men can't be bothered to nurture their relationship? A number of men spoke to me of the despair they felt in their relationships because *their* emotions were rarely taken seriously. At the same time many felt overwhelmed by the emotional life of their partner.

'Women's feelings are more dominant. It's the basis of relationships these days – it's all about *her* feelings.' *Joel, 20*

'Growing up in a household that wouldn't allow any sort of weakness affected the first few years of my marriage. I found it very hard to show affection, because I thought that was normal.' *Craig, 58*

Men who are raised to suppress their feelings are hardly in the best position to deal with the many emotions that surface in relationships.

Most women don't realise this. Nor do they realise how alarming their emotional outbursts can be for men. But this doesn't mean these men don't love them. Recently I overheard a conversation between two men in their early 20s. One man was clearly madly in love with his girlfriend, and was telling his friend all about her. Then he paused, and added, 'The only thing is, how would you like to be told by your girl-friend she loves you every half hour?' In that brief exchange we get a sense of how suffocated men sometimes feel around women.

Unless women know that as boys many men have been progressively and deliberately shut down, they cannot help but take personally a man's lack of response to their emotions. Women do become hurt and frustrated by men's inability to cope with their emotions; they then see men as unfeeling or as emotional cripples. 'Men are notorious for having delayed or misplaced emotions,' says clinical psychologist Alon Gratch. 'When men feel shame they try to minimise it by not communicating (silence), by communicating the opposite (lying), or by communicating indirectly (evasion).'[1] As few women understand these dynamics, all they see is that men lie, that men always seem to be silent and evasive, and everyone ends up filled with despair.

'I think that sometimes men can't win in the eyes of women. If you don't show emotion you don't care. If you do, you're told to grow up. If you don't take care of yourself you're a slob. If you do, then you're seen as girly.' *Mitchell, 26*

'Friendship is the main thing in a good relationship, and not being around each other all the time – but that's the expectation. If your girlfriend is studying and you go out with mates she tells you off for not ringing, but if you ring you're in trouble for interrupting her while she studies – you can't win.' *Lance, 23*

The bottom line is that women inhabit a complex emotional landscape, and men do not. As most men have never had the luxury of exploring their emotions, these subtleties are genuinely confusing to them. So when women cry, men panic, because they do not know that for a woman to express her emotions is perfectly natural. From her early years a woman has been encouraged to be aware of her feelings, and the feelings of others. Sharing feelings is *her* way of creating intimacy. How much easier it would be for men if women understood what it feels like for them when they get emotional. 'I have always wilted in the face of her sorrow,' admits Mark in *The Naked Husband*.[2] Many men do wilt when women are upset, because they are aware of their own helplessness in dealing with emotional moments. There are few things more concerning for a man than being with someone they love in a situation they can't fix.

> *Every time a man fails to read his partner, yet again she is left feeling upset and misunderstood.*

WHY MEN TRY TO FIX THINGS

When men do respond to the emotional outpourings of women, more often than not they try to rectify the situation. They don't realise that because a woman is feeling down at work doesn't mean she wants to leave, or that just because her mother constantly criticises her, it isn't the same thing as wanting to give her mother the flick. Women *feel* better talking things over. But as men are raised to *fix* things, it is *action,* not talk that counts. '[Men] can't understand why women would want to stay in a place of discomfort,' explains relationship psychologist Toby Green. 'The challenge is for men to realise they're not being impotent or unmanly by being with a woman's feelings.'[3] Every time a man fails to read his partner, yet again she is left feeling upset and misunderstood. Often women then assume this must mean the man in their life doesn't love them.

'Women seem to thrive on conversations about themselves, and they seem to delight in sharing and interpreting each other's inner feelings. I find it very hard to participate in this.' *Nigel, 72*

Once everyone can step back a bit, they can start to get a clearer picture. 'When those close to us respond differently to events than do we . . . the ground on which we stand seems to tremble and our footing is suddenly unsure,' says professor of linguisitics Deborah Tannen.[4] What many women don't appreciate is that men are often *equally* frustrated by their inability to understand what women want. To overcome these differences, men need more cues from women. Blake, 42, agrees: 'Men approach things from a different view. Women have to explain to a man what they expect and want at times.' The difficulty comes when a woman doesn't know what she wants. 'Men become confused when women communicate about an issue, because sometimes women want it resolved, and sometimes they do not,' says psychologist Bill O'Hehir. 'And sometimes a woman doesn't know whether she wants it resolved, until after she has talked about it.'[5]

'A woman's fundamental complexity is hardest to understand. For the most part men have simple relationships with one another. The world is easier to navigate that way.' *Trevor, 30*

'I find women mercurial. Men are usually the same each time you meet. This makes women both interesting and frustrating, as you find yourself continually making adjustments to your approach and behaviour to fit in.' *Craig, 58*

WILL SOMEONE PLEASE TELL ME WHAT YOU WANT?

When I asked men about their relationships, many admitted they had no clear idea what was expected of them. They talked of trying hard to please their partner, and of their disappointment when they failed to do so. 'My hypothesis is that if men knew how to meet women's needs, they would only be too happy to do so,' says psychologist Toby Green.[6] But as Tim, 25, pointed out, the problem is that most men remain in the dark where women are concerned. 'Most men find it difficult to work out what women want,' he said, 'as women have a tendency not to say directly what is wrong. So when a man tries to address what he sees as the problem, he is normally way off the mark.' Joel, 20, has a different take on this: 'Often women are way more interested in what their wannabe friends think. They sort of check you out – they're kind of playing with you – and I'm having to behave like something I'm not.'

HOW MEN SHOW THEY CARE

Many men work hard to make meaningful gestures towards the women in their lives, but women don't always see these gestures for what they really are, because they are interpreting them through a female lens. 'For a man romantic love is worship,' suggests Irma Kurtz. 'He doesn't want to do great things with a woman, he wants to do them *for* her . . . he wants the female to keep her mystery and apartness.'[7] Irma Kurtz has a point. When we take a closer look at what men do for women, we can begin to see the depth of meaning that often lies behind the seemingly simple, often practical gestures men make towards the women they love.

How do men like to show their affection? 'I bring a girlfriend flowers, cater to her requirements, show her how special she is. I might draw a picture of her, as I like to draw,' Joel, 20, told me. Blake's expressions of love are more down-to-earth: 'If your man brings home a pay cheque, takes care of the car and the home, provides and is protective, and brings you flowers every now and then, he loves you.' Harrison, 65, finds himself torn between making conventionally romantic gestures and being more creative: 'I am told that flowers have magical properties, and I have sometimes resorted to them, and I must admit they rarely fail on the occasions that I do. But being a man I feel that is too easy a solution and often strike out on my own, and am surprised to find myself sometimes misunderstood.' Ray expresses his love for Sue by taking care of her, by being considerate, by 'teasing, loving, defending and showing off to her. Listening to her, sometimes at least, and taking guidance from her.' For him caring is also about stepping outside his comfort zone and tolerating friends, relatives, activities and preferences he doesn't care for.

'Men don't like to be pressured into gestures. The important thing is to act caringly. You shouldn't have to make special gestures to show you care,' Jason, 22, told me. Craig also spoke of how women sometimes ruin the special gestures men plan, by trying to organise them. He stressed how important it is for men to be free to express how they feel in their own time and way, otherwise what they do can feel insincere. 'I might on occasions bring home flowers, but if my partner said, "Why don't you bring home flowers more often?", it would spoil my feelings about doing this.'

The love men feel for their partner can surface in unexpected ways. Many worry about the safety of their partner out late at night, or when travelling alone.

Often men do put a lot of effort into their relationships, but because their gestures aren't seen as romantic, women sweep these gestures aside, assuming men don't care. Men are frustrated to have their gestures ignored or taken for granted. It is very important to men that their home is protected and maintained, and just as important that their partner is safe. Women frequently overlook these practical acts of love, because they assume men should be doing these things anyway. When we step back a bit, we realise this dynamic isn't very different from the despair women feel about the amount of work they do around the home. Unblocking the toilet, fixing the blind or mending an appliance aren't particularly glamorous jobs, but to men they are significant gestures that demonstrate their commitment.

'We show we care by checking the woman's car is safe, that the tyre pressure is okay, and the radiator is topped up, so she won't get stranded.' *Lee, 48*

The love men feel for their partner can surface in unexpected ways. Many worry about the safety of their partner out late at night, or when travelling alone. This concern often amuses women; some find it suffocating or controlling, because they don't understand where these impulses come from. Some years back, I was about to start a new job and a retired friend called to wish me well. He then went on to discuss the best way for me to get to work. At the time I was mystified by his suggestions as to how I should get to and from work, as the route was relatively straightforward. Looking back, I can now appreciate how much he cared about *every* aspect of my new job going well. Gordon's gone now. I'm only sorry it's taken me well over a decade to understand the love he was showing by his suggestions.

ABOUT MEN'S EMOTIONS

While men fail to understand what women want in many situations, this does not mean they don't care or are incapable of emotional depth. Who is to say that the way a woman expresses love is more valid than the way a man demonstrates his love? Our responses are coloured by our expectations and comfort zones. When women see life from a purely female perspective, they don't feel comfortable stepping beyond it. Too often we allow our expressions of love to be shaped by films and advertising, and leave little room for genuine heartfelt gestures.

Daily we are bombarded with the extravagant gestures people are supposed to make to show that they care. But do we really want the impossibly intricate textures of our relationships to be dictated by the demands of consumerism, or do we want to discover a more meaningful space where men and women can meet? There are far more profound gestures to be had in relationships than those that come with flowers or expensive perfume. When I was growing up my father would often bring home a small, unexpected gift for my mother – a ripe pear, a book he had found in a second-hand book-shop – tiny gestures that were genuinely thoughtful and loving.

To fully explore these possibilities, women need to learn more about the nuances of men's lives. What tiny gestures would *they* appreciate? What do they do that is taken for granted? Once women can begin to explore this territory, a new world will open up for them. They will begin to understand and appreciate the subtleties of men's emotional make-up, and discover that men are *not* devoid of emotion.

Men also feel hurt and bewilderment, and they too long for tenderness. It's just that rarely do they express these needs. After a lifetime of suppressing all they hold in the hearts, it is hard for men to change overnight. The shutting down of boys makes them shy and vulnerable about feelings as adults. To be expressive is new and dangerous stuff for these men.

'Most men are taught by their fathers that emotions, especially senti-mental ones, are to be hidden away or, at the very least, undiscussed. That is why most men show affection in more subtle ways that don't require much emotional investment: a hug, a kiss on the cheek, or flowers.' *Trevor, 30*

MEN CAN ALSO BE SHY

Men's shyness around emotions is apparent in many ways. Some men are so uncomfortable when emotional issues arise that they will make a joke or change the subject. They are then labelled as unfeel-ing, when in fact it is just that they daren't risk exposing how they feel. Others are prepared to tread new ground, but they need to do so with great care. The essential shyness many men experience around emotions can often be seen in the way they give presents. Most gift-giving is done quietly, tentatively, as if it isn't a big deal. Men act in this way so they won't feel exposed or disappointed if a present fails to please. Yet when we look closer, we can see the depth of feeling they have invested in such gestures.

'It's not true men don't have feelings,' says American family therapist Michael Gurian, 'there's nowhere safe to express them.'[8] For men to feel free to express what they feel, we need far greater understanding of their needs than most men currently enjoy. The difficulty for men is that many of the assumptions society makes about their emotions and many other aspects of their lives are based on little more than anecdote and stereotype. Over time many men have become so isolated that they find it hard to let others in. But as clinical psychologist Alon Gratch points out, when men are given the opportunity to open up, they 'Invariably reveal a dramatic, bold, and amazingly vulnerable inner self.'[9] Time and again this was my experience during my interviews. I was constantly amazed by the emotional depth and honesty of the men of all ages I spoke with, most of whom were complete strangers to me.

'You can't pop in and have a cup of tea with men. You hang out, have a beer, watch the rugby. There has to be a plan, a purpose for getting together. That's why a lot of men spend a lot of time by themselves.' *Tony, 26*

'Most of my friends are women. Men are kind of loners in the way they are put together, so they spend a lot of time alone. Guys don't talk about triviality, except sport. We don't have the excuse for bonding, except over sport.' *Craig, 58*

Women may not realise it, but many men envy what they perceive as women's capacity for happiness, their fluid sense of freedom and self-assurance. With women, men get a taste of life beyond the gnawing competitiveness that colours the lives of most men. That is why so many men enjoy the company of women, and treasure the women friends in their lives. As one male friend explained to me,

'There's not all the competition bullshit when I'm with women.' It's much harder for men to be as relaxed as women, because competition is evident in almost everything men do together. They keep up the competition so they don't have to revisit the shame they were made to feel when they tried to be tender as boys.

'I feel it is very important for me to present myself as strong emotionally, and physically, even more so.' *Mitchell, 26*

This need to always prove they are strong forces men to play extremely limited roles in their relationships, cutting them off from the warmth and nurturing everyone needs in order to thrive. Psychologist Steve Biddulph goes further: 'Most men don't have a life. Instead, we have just learned to pretend.'[10] This is a very sobering statement, and one that was echoed recently by a male friend of mine when he admitted that it was only now that he is in his 40s that he feels he can be himself. How many men never get to experience this freedom, even in later life, we may never know.

'Women have very little understanding or sympathy for the hardships of men's lives.' *Lawrence, 33*

WHEN WOMEN ARE WAY OFF THE MARK

Men do need more help to understand women. But what was interesting to me during my interviews with men was the number of times they talked about women failing to understand them. Some went further, admitting they were so worn down by this that they allowed women to believe what they wanted, even when they were jumping to the wrong conclusion. Many men choose the line of least resistance, because they feel they are not as articulate as women in dealing with personal relationships. These men talk of feeling overwhelmed in discussions, and of how their partner always has to have the last word. 'On paper, some men are magnificently, hugely, poetically emotional,' says Irma Kurtz, 'but in spoken Malespeak they seem timid and even dumb, particularly to a woman who is busy pouring out her feelings as fast as they occur.'[11] Men often find women overpowering verbally and emotionally. Their reactions literally silence men. When talking of his emotionally needy girlfriend, one of clinical psychologist Alon Gratch's clients actually admitted, 'She takes away my ability to respond.'[12]

'I think that due to the way most men react to situations, especially those involving emotion, we give the impression of being a little one-dimensional and almost predictable. I find that it is often easier to react in the expected way than to have to explain myself.' *Tim, 25*

It is important that women realise that many men don't feel heard in relationships. This problem is partly one of *approach*. Not only are women generally more articulate than men, they are also usually more aware of *nuance*, and they love detail. Men, by contrast, tend to take things at face value. The way women converse is not only confusing to men, it can make them wary, because they feel that everything they say is picked apart.

'Having a conversation with women is in many ways like having a conversation with the boss. If you're having a conversation with a few guys, it's often quite benign and banal even. It doesn't have different levels that someone then throws back in your face later. It's like, "I had no idea that you felt that way about water, so that means we can't have a new house, because that means it will have an environmental impact," and I go, "Whoa, I didn't think there were that many layers to what I was saying."' *Alex, 35*

> *It is important that women realise that many men don't feel heard in relationships.*

GETTING MEN TO OPEN UP

The ways in which many women now choose to express themselves are often counter-productive when dealing with the men in their lives. This is not a plea for women to get back in their box, but to better understand the dynamics between men and women. Psychologist Toby Green describes the effect many women have on men as 'the whiplash of the male psyche'.[13] She is not encouraging women to agree with everything men say or do, so much as trying to help women see that men share the same insecurities.

Often women can't see the very real vulnerability beneath the tough-guy exterior, so they go into arguments with their guns blazing, determined to meet what they perceive as strength with strength. Seeing this, men start to back away. Their retreat often makes women even more determined to resolve the issue, so they press the point. It's their way of trying to get the men to open up, only to achieve the opposite, and so everyone ends up frustrated. Perhaps it's helpful here to return to an earlier comment a number of men made when speaking with me, when they said they appreciate women who are able to be more open and less combative. 'Women may believe that because men are so disconnected that they appear fine,' commented Rowan, 41, 'that they're tough – bullshit. That they don't feel – bullshit.'

The ways in which many women now choose to express themselves are often counter-productive when dealing with the men in their lives.

Being around men who are disconnected can be challenging, as so much remains locked beneath the surface. My conversations with boys and men showed me that they do not shut themselves down as a matter of personal choice. They do this to protect themselves from hurt. Psychotherapist Roger Horrocks describes this closing down of men as a form of castration. '[Castrated men] function from the neck up. Their bodies are deadened, and therefore their feelings are not available to them. It's hard for them to cry, to be warm, to melt, to love.'[14] The end result is that as the emotion inside these men builds, it gets to a point where they dare not let it out.

Tom Wingo, the central character in *The Prince of Tides*, is such a man. 'I thought I had succeeded in not becoming a violent man, but even that collapsed. My violence was subterranean, unbeheld. It was my silences, my long withdrawals, that I had turned into dangerous things. My viciousness manifested itself in the terrible winter of blue eyes. My wounded stare could bring an ice age into the sunniest, balmiest afternoon.'[15]

This glacial state is an extreme one, and when finally such emotions are released, it may well be in the form of a violent outburst. More often than not this kind of outburst will come out of left field, leaving friends and colleagues shocked and surprised at this seeming meltdown. Sometimes men are so shut down that they lose all sense of boundaries, which can cause them to endanger themselves and others. We see this when men become addicted to work, to risk-taking activities or to questionable business ventures. At its most extreme, the long-term suppression of these feelings can lead to a breakdown or suicide.

Everyone loses out when men shut down. Often women get so frustrated by what feels like an impenetrable wall around men, they try to coax or manipulate them out of their shell. Men are very aware of this and feel cheated, which is not surprising, because no-one likes to be manipulated. Clinical psychologist Alon Gratch offers a more positive way forward, suggesting women take careful note of what a man talks about and what he chooses to remain silent about. 'While a man may not talk about his emotional self, if you listen closely, you will find indirect evidence for its existence in everything he says – or doesn't say.'[16]

'Often there is enormous grief at all the wasted years of emotional deadness. And also great rage that this deadness was imposed on him, or demanded of him.' *Psychotherapist Roger Horrocks*[17]

Men and sex

WHAT ABOUT IT?

Often the only place men feel they can open up and express emotion is in bed. As a result, women tend to assume that men only want sex. Men derive great pleasure from sex – casual sex, as well as sex in committed relationships. 'There is a time and place for both, just never let one take the place of the other,' Ray, 50, told me. Evan, 27, took a different view: 'Just because you stay in a five-star hotel, doesn't mean a four-star hotel will never do.' Trevor, 30, agreed: 'There are occasions for less-sentimental interactions that can be equally satisfying, though in a purely physical way.'

Now sex is more freely available than in the past, men and women have more opportunities to have a variety of partners. The sexual freedom men and women enjoy can be liberating. Many men appreciate the greater level of honesty around sex, and the fact that women are more open about whether they want sex. But this doesn't mean men can't and don't make clear distinctions between casual sex and sex in committed relationships. Many men and women also appreciate the opportunity to ensure there is sexual compatibility before making a long-term commitment.

'Yes, men are under greater pressure. But so they should be! I understand that before it was all about "Wham, bam, thank you, ma'am",
and not at all about mutual pleasure and love. I think men of my
generation are better educated in this area and therefore it's what is
expected of us, and also what we expect of ourselves.' *Matthew, 27*

With this greater freedom, new pressures have also emerged.
When I asked men if they felt under greater pressure to perform
sexually, most agreed, but they could also see the benefits. 'It means
people are free of restrictions: to write their own life scripts, choose
their own experiences, and thereby have more poignant, personally
meaningful lives,' said Doug, 52. Craig, 48, said: 'Sexual liberation
has highlighted the importance of legitimate sexual pleasure, particularly for women. I think more women enjoy their own bodies these
days.' Rowan, 41, also felt that these changes were positive: 'Now we
can get on with the business of loving each other!'

'I think that sexual liberation may get people too focused on sex too
soon in a relationship. So that when they come up for air, they finally
take a good look at the other person and find that they don't have
all that much in common, but the relationship limps along anyway,
going nowhere.' *Greg, a counsellor*

ON THE NEED FOR INTIMACY

Even though some sexual experiences are little more than casual
encounters, many men do desire real intimacy. This is not always
easy for men to achieve, however, because popular culture is focused
on sexual performance. This constant emphasis on the mechanics of
sex can also be confusing to men. The instant familiarity that sexual

liberation offers can lead them to mistake this for true intimacy, and lead to shallow or dysfunctional relationships. Most women want to be loved and respected, and worry about whether 'he'll care' in the morning. What is rarely taken into account is that many men are also concerned about these things.

'I don't have a girlfriend at present. You either have a girlfriend and have physical contact, or you don't have a girlfriend, so there's no physical contact. I was so craving contact. It's terrible. Some of my friends go off to hookers, but I couldn't do that. I went and had fortnightly massages instead. It helped, but it's still terrible.' *Tony, 26*

'I found it very difficult to come to terms with relationships after the breakdown of my marriage. A lot of women only seem to want to approach relationships on a physical and material level. It was like there was no interest in the inner person.' *Craig, 58*

What one wants in a relationship and what one gets can be quite different. 'Respect for each other seems to be a modern casualty of relationships,' observed Nigel, 72. When *feeling* is taken out of the equation, women can become little more than objects of a man's desire – something to have alongside the new car, the new job. It is interesting to note that when I spoke with some high achievers about relationships, one or two talked of their large homes and incomes, and their attractive partner, all in the same breath.

'I was in a management position and things were going quite well. My second wife was nine years younger than me. It was kind of cool to have a cute wife. I felt I'd lucked out some.' *Ryan, 50*

What women don't always realise is that men are frequently intimidated by them in relationships, because men perceive women as holding the sexual power. So, as much as they yearn to get close to women, there is a nervousness that can be inhibiting. Often this process starts early. 'By addicting boys more to girls' bodies than vice versa, we make boys feel less than equal to girls. This reinforces boys performing for girls, pursuing girls, and paying for girls to compensate for their inequality,' says author Warren Farrell. 'The greater her beauty, the more he will have to pay — and therefore earn.'[1] Women are now depicted as powerful, sexual individuals in charge of their own destinies, which can place even more pressures on men to perform. 'Because some women no longer need men financially, paradoxically that has heightened men's awareness of their financial reputation,' said David, 36.

PERFORMANCE ANXIETY

How are men and boys to respond to the popular representations of women? Women have fought hard to be taken seriously, and in many areas they have succeeded. Yet when women are glamourised and objectified in magazines and on billboards daily, it doesn't make sense to turn around and place the blame solely on men for women being viewed so one-dimensionally. As Susan Faludi points out, 'Glamour is perceived as a female principle, but really it is an expression not of inherent femininity, but of femininity's merchandised facade.'[2] While most men can separate fantasy from reality, many of the images they now come across are so carefully crafted by marketers that some do mistake one for the other.

'I feel greatly offended sometimes by the sort of billboards that continue to thrust sexuality in my face. I feel very manipulated by that, because at the same time it's not really on offer, and it's for money.' *Justin, 43*

Men find the often edgy representation of women exciting and intimidating. What is often not recognised is that the more graphic representations of women not only de-humanise women, they disempower men. 'Pornography overpowers males, not females, by inhibiting them and making them feel less than adequate in terms of their penis size and general performance,' psychologist Bill O'Hehir explains.[3] This not only leads men to fear that women are unattainable, but heightens their concerns about their bodies, and about how to express their sexuality appropriately.

> 'What passes for the essence of masculinity is being extracted and bottled – and sold back to men. Literally, in the case of Viagra.' *Susan Faludi*[4]

Magazines don't help with their endless editorials on sexual performance. A recent cover of *Men's Health* contained the slogan 'Master the Art of Sex'. Inside were several pages offering 'red-hot romantic advice' to enable the reader to become the 'ultimate lover'. This section covered everything from sex on a beanbag to how to boost penis power, and a warning not to take Viagra with a big meal. The many sexual positions covered include The Cowgirl, whose instructions confuse more than they excite: 'Lean back with your shoulders against the foot of the bed and feet on the floor, supporting most of your weight. She then straddles your midsection and uses her legs to thrust. Even if she's never been the jockey type, she'll have a hard time resisting this invitation to ride.'[5]

IS GOOD SEX ENOUGH?

Like women, men need good information on sex, but they also need to be encouraged to use their imaginations to express their feelings and have fun with sex, and create greater intimacy. Without intimacy even good sex can fall short of expectations. Psychotherapist Roger Horrocks has worked with many male and female clients over the years who, while experiencing great sex, sought therapy, 'Because of a deep sense of incompleteness or deprivation inside of them. They are not suffering from a lack of pleasure in their lives, but are still suffering from a very early lack of holding, containment, nourishing, which impairs their capacity for intimacy and fulfilment as adults.'[6] Don Edgar agrees. In *Men, Mateship and Marriage* he indicates that in studies of divorced couples, well over half report a high level of satisfaction with their sex life.

> 'I think sex is a big issue. It promises you things that it doesn't deliver. You want intimacy – it's the ultimate intimacy. It's the holy grail. You're trying to get to this holy place, but when you get there it doesn't deliver.' *Tony, 26*

Genuine intimacy takes a relationship beyond a purely sexual level. It also respects the fact that there are parts of every person they need to keep for themselves, so everyone can genuinely be their own person. Without this level of intimacy and respect, sex can so easily become a desperate and disappointing experience. In the middle of a passionate affair, Mark in *The Naked Husband* suddenly realises, 'We have the trappings of intimacy without its substance . . . I cannot hold her any closer, but I cannot get close at all.'[7]

> 'Making love is very close and intimate. It can be scary as you have nowhere to hide. Your partner sees you for who you are.' *Lee, 48*

TAKING RELATIONSHIPS DEEPER

Without a language for intimacy, and the freedom to allow it to develop, many men will remain locked in conquest and performance. Men yearn for intimacy but they need women to help them understand that intimacy is not just about pleasure, but about subtler feelings and expressions. In intimate moments we see our partners at their most vulnerable, their most real, and we love them for it. When women realise how much of a risk it is for men to feel vulnerable, they can better appreciate all that intimate moments offer. Partners who can respect what it takes men to allow themselves to be vulnerable will be able to take themselves and the men they love to even deeper levels of intimacy than they thought possible.

> 'There is a real fragility inside that men work hard to protect, because it goes against everything they were brought up to, to show their feelings to women.' *Craig, 58*

Most women are more comfortable with intimacy because they learnt it first when they were little girls. They were encouraged to explore and enjoy intimate moments, and to develop their own repertoire of gestures and experiences that were meaningful to them. Just as a woman's expression of intimacy is more diverse, often so is her experience of her body, because of the many nuances of self-expression she may have explored while growing up.

> 'There was an assumption that engaging in a lot of sexual activity meant that you were more of a man, although looking back it is pretty clear that was not the case. But I guess it takes a meaningful relationship to show you that.' *Tim, 25*

True intimacy requires a great deal of trust. It challenges men, after a lifetime of having to prove they are strong, to allow themselves to be more open, more real. 'It amazes me that men are willing to die for patriotism, or look face-on to twelve huge men charging at them in order to do them bodily harm,' says Toby Green, 'yet they are terrified to put their hearts on the line. They'd rather be dead or bashed up.'[8] Men need first to establish a high level of trust, before they can enjoy the profound sense of relief and satisfaction that a genuinely loving relationship offers. When this does occur, men come to understand the essential difference between sex and making love.

> *The next step is for women to get to know men better, so they can create intimate moments that speak to men's emotional needs.*

CREATING INTIMACY

While many men yearn for more texture to their relationships, few know how to ask for them. In a recent *Reader's Digest* poll, 31 per cent of the men said they wished their partners were more affectionate.[9] One man said he longed for his wife to give him a hug now and then, but even though they had been together for some time, he had never told her of this. What is heartening is that younger men are far more comfortable seeking and expressing intimacy. They find it easier to relate to women, and to be more articulate about their own needs.

> 'Don't get me wrong. We need you. We need your love and acceptance ... Men do want women's bodies. But most want more than that; they want love.' *Stan Dale*[10]

The next step is for women to get to know the men in their lives better by taking time to listen more and by recognising that men and women share the same basic needs and anxieties. When they can achieve this, they are more able to create intimate moments that speak to men's emotional needs, which will in turn inspire men to find ways to fulfil their needs. While this cannot transform a relationship overnight, it can help start the process.

Perhaps one of the keys for men and women is to be more patient with each other, rather than trying to force the issue, or losing patience and moving on the moment things don't seem to be working out. Intimacy is not just about togetherness. Nor is it about being able to read every part of each other. Genuine intimacy is about allowing the true depth of meaning experienced in a relationship to fill us, and to then fuel the rest of our lives, so that we're more able to give ourselves passionately to whatever we're doing.

'I've got a hunch. It's a hunch about the need at the heart of all of us. It has to do with being held. Deeply – tenderly – like a baby. Held with laughter. Held with tasty food. Held with song. Held with long walks on this good, good earth. Held with gratitude. My hunch is that we all need more holding than we currently get.' *Kent Hoffman*[11]

The best relationships are a dance of possibilities that inspire men and women to move beyond their concerns, misunderstandings and limited perceptions, so they can taste real intimacy. That does not mean that at times relationships aren't still complex and bewildering. It is heartening to remember that in spite of our many differences, the chemistry between the sexes remains. This often mysterious chemistry continues to surprise us and to nudge us in new directions. 'For good or ill, Eros is always two steps ahead of us,' writer Helen Garner reminds us, 'exploding the constraints of dogma, turning back on us our carefully worked out positions and lines, showing us that the world is richer and scarier and more fluid and many-fold than we dare to think.'[12]

When things fall apart

WHAT HAPPENS WHEN RELATIONSHIPS BREAK DOWN

When relationships start to disintegrate, men often feel they are falling apart. Although most will not show it, men are extremely vulnerable at this time. During a break-up most men are unlikely to talk to anyone – even though the situation at home may be grim and they need desperately to talk. They prefer to keep their pain and confusion to themselves, because even in extreme moments they believe they should appear strong. 'The worst of it is, no-one will ever know what happened tonight,' admits Mark in *The Naked Husband*, as his marriage falls apart. 'I won't mention this fight to even my closest friends. This is my focus now, keeping the truth from others.'[1] When men keep quiet about their relationship break-ups, often they only make matters worse. Tragically, it is their unwillingness to share vital parts of themselves that frequently prevents their relationships from being healed.

'We don't like to risk exposing our inner self. It's a self-defence mechanism. So when we do, and the relationship then goes sour, it cuts deep.' *Craig, 58*

There are many good reasons why men keep their thoughts to themselves. Many are too devastated, too hurt, too shy, too shocked to share their relationship woes with friends. For most of their adult lives, and often long before adulthood, silence has become their way of surviving in the world. Yet while keeping their thoughts and needs to themselves might help at work, behaving this way at home can be disastrous, because most women don't want the strong silent types; they expect far more from relationships.

The increase in the breakdown of relationships has come at a time when men are genuinely confused about what is required of them. It is not that men want to turn back the clock, so much as discover what they can do to create meaningful lives that will give them the love and respect they long for. 'The well-worn path that men have walked down as the dominant sex for centuries is now littered with road blocks that they don't understand, and for which they don't seem to have a map,' reflected Morris, 61, who has spent years as a professional counsellor.

PAST THE USE-BY DATE

Today, relationships are as disposable as anything else. So when things start to go wrong, it's almost a given that partners should move on, even though the statistics on those who do are less than encouraging. Now the vast majority of divorces are initiated by women, and are not due to abuse or adultery, but to women feeling they no longer have as much in common with their partner as they once did. This flies in the face of the view that assumed a woman left because terrible things must have happened.

When things are not going well, men are more inclined to stay in a relationship. 'Men press on regardless, because they have been raised to do so. Never mind if you feel depressed or sad or lonely, or bored or angry or uninterested,' says psychotherapist Roger Horrocks, 'keep the flag flying.'[2] We cannot blame men for wanting to soldier on without saying a word. The simple fact is that society doesn't want to have to deal with men in distress, because it's much more comfortable for everyone if men keep on pretending things are all right. The bottom line is, however, that whether men admit it or not, they, like women, are devastated by the loss of love. As Steve Biddulph reminds us, 'The loneliness of men is something women rarely understand.'[3]

THIS CAN'T BE HAPPENING

When a woman says she wants out, more often than not her partner is stunned because he failed to read the signs. This is not because men are stupid, but because often they have been left out of the loop about how their partner is feeling. Unlike men, most women don't hold back about their lives. When things go wrong, most women seek support from those around them. As they talk through their problems with family and friends, it gives them the chance to come to terms with their feelings and to determine their position. They will no doubt talk to their partner, but often not in such detail, so he will be largely unaware of the full spectrum of their concerns.

'Her every feeling has been analysed and reinterpreted by her friends, her mother, her sister . . . She has spent hours brooding, thinking things through about their relationship,' academic Don Edgar explains.[4] As most men don't have access to this level of debate about the ways in which their relationship is failing, and because it is harder for them to pick up on emotional nuances, more often than not they are genuinely surprised and traumatised when everything turns sour. The more emotionally shut down a man is, the more of a shock this is likely to be.

When the final breakdown occurs, a man faces the loss of his home, and the nurturing and security of his relationship. As his partner is generally the one who has put the effort into friends and family, men can lose touch with their shared friends and acquaintances. If he is unable to express the many emotions that overwhelm him, often he will feel as if he were disintegrating. As family court counsellor Peter Jordan points out, with separation men not only face the loss of the person they were closest to, but the person who is best equipped to help them handle this situation.[5]

Suddenly these men lose someone to live for, to work for; someone with whom they can be safe and intimate, and share things; someone who understands the different textures of their lives, their likes and dislikes, their friends, their family. According to psychologist Toby Green, men draw their identity from their relationships with 'the important people' in their lives. 'Their sense of well-being is always attached to someone as a lifeline.'[6] It is no surprise then that when I talked with these men about their separation they also used such words as 'devastated', 'cheated', 'betrayed' and 'extremely hurt'.

MEN ON THEIR OWN

For most men the trauma of separation and divorce persists, not just for weeks and months, but for years. In 1985, when Peter Jordan examined the effects of separation and divorce on men, he found that men appear far more intimidated than women by the vulnerability, isolation and helplessness of a relationship breakdown. 'Men are just as dependent as women,' he explains, 'but their dependency is conventionally concealed.'[7] Because separated men tend to keep their desperation to themselves, friends and family assume they are well able to take care of themselves. However, this is frequently not the case.

Often by the time a couple separates, the woman has dealt with most of her anger, denial and grief at the disintegration of the relationship. So separation can be a liberating experience because she is now ready to get on with her life. Yet all too often it is not until his partner is gone that a man starts to deal with the ramifications of being on his own. He then has to deal with his anger, denial and grief, before he can begin to see his way clear.

> *Men appear far more intimidated than women by the vulnerability, isolation and helplessness of a relationship breakdown.*

Unfortunately it is not until their relationship is finished that many men are fully able to value what they have lost.[8] That is not to say women don't have second thoughts. Studies show that in the year following divorce, many men and women wish they had put more effort into resolving their difficulties. Significant numbers also experience a second crisis twelve to eighteen months after divorce, when they weigh up their losses and the challenges ahead.[9]

In Peter Jordan's study, nearly all the men interviewed admitted to being 'openly distressed' about their situation. Between one and two years after separation 55 per cent continued to think about their ex partner 'a lot'; 49 per cent of the men felt they should have tried harder to make their relationship work; 36 per cent believed their separation or divorce was 'a horrible mistake'; and a further 39 per cent felt they would never get over the experience.[10]

> 'A man who has seen his marriage become alimony payments, his home become his wife's home, and his children become child-support payments for those who have been turned against him, psychologically feels he is spending his life working for people who hate him.'
> *Warren Farrell* [11]

During separation and divorce most men feel the system is weighted against them. The men I spoke with often talked about being 'done over' by their wives and the courts. 'Once the profit motive is taken out of divorce, both for women and lawyers, then families will stay together,' Blake, who is now divorced, told me. This view is echoed by Dan Jarvis, research and policy director for the Michigan Family Forum. 'It is the very system, which also destroys many salvageable marriages. A person filing for divorce is often pleading for help, but not knowing where to turn, they seek a lawyer and find themselves locked in battle.'[12] Still society finds itself unable to consider what divorce does to men, leaving them not only vulnerable, but desperate, as many struggle unsuccessfully to pick up the pieces.

> Men are reluctant to share intimate details or talk in depth about their concerns, not just because they prefer to be private, but because loyalty is central to them.

THE IMPACT OF SEPARATION AND DIVORCE ON MEN'S HEALTH

The terrible angst many men suffer on separation can have a big impact on their health and wellbeing. In Peter Jordan's study, 81 per cent of the men reported suffering from sleeplessness after their relationship ended; 70 per cent said they cried; 63 per cent felt their energy levels had reduced. These symptoms are not only associated with distress, they are the kinds of symptoms people experience when facing death and significant loss. Even the men who felt more positive *before* separation experienced greater problems with being positive and maintaining good health *after* separation. Of the men who sought help, most tended to do so only from family and friends, not professionals.[13]

The majority of men are reluctant to share intimate details or talk in depth about their concerns, not just because they prefer to be private, but because loyalty is central to them. 'Getting a man to open up about what he considers to be his partner's faults is difficult,' says psychologist Toby Green. 'Men feel this is treacherous. They seem to be participating in an act of disloyalty. They often couch their language with, "This is only my opinion"; "I'm not saying she's a bad person"; "I don't want to say anything bad about her".'[14]

> 'When my marriage failed I too went into grief like I'd never felt before . . . I cannot stop remembering that we had something good for a while, and losing that has left an emptiness that just goes on hurting. My life improved from being married, but when it ended I became unable to hold onto a positive outlook on life anymore.' *Bradley*[15]

Once the separation is formalised, many men feel very alone, regardless of how good or otherwise a father or husband they have been. They are reluctant to seek formal help because they have no wish to reveal just how vulnerable they feel, and because they tend to regard support services as ineffectual or for women.[16]

HOW THE HURT LINGERS

In his 1996 follow-up report, Peter Jordan found there was an increase in *all* the physical complaints he had canvassed with the men. These divorced men admitted to experiencing more sleeplessness, headaches, poor memory, reduced energy, excessive tiredness and tight muscles ten years down the track, even though 72 per cent had re-partnered over that time.[17] It was the overwhelming grief men felt at having been cast loose that prompted relationships psychologist Toby Green to set up the Men's Room, a group for men to talk about the pain caused by their failed relationships.

The men I interviewed shared this pain. 'Even though I was the party that initiated the split, and even though I had a partner to go to and I knew I had to do what I was doing for my health, it still cost an enormous effort on my part,' explained Michael, 50, who remained in an unhappy marriage for two decades for the sake of his sons. 'I lost about ten kilograms. I can't tell you the number of sleepless nights I had worrying about how it was all going to pan out. It lasted about six months, and then it started to improve.'

Many men wish they could turn back the clock after separation and divorce.

It is no surprise then to discover how much more vulnerable separated and divorced men are to suicide. As *Good Weekend* columnist Alan Close points out, 'When men feel isolated they drive cars into trees. Women buy a bar of chocolate and sit in front of a funny film on TV.'[18] While this is a generalisation, divorced men in Australia are three times more vulnerable to suicide than any other group.[19] We need to recognise the terrible grief many men face during divorce and separation, and find more positive ways to help them deal with this. If we don't tackle this issue they will continue to be at risk.

Men and their health

WHY MEN'S HEALTH IS OF CONCERN

Even though we continue to regard men as strong, they are vulnerable in many ways. Their health and wellbeing remains a major challenge for them. Women fare better in terms of overall health because they are more in tune with their bodies and are more likely to get help when feeling unwell, while men's lack of focus on their health has very real consequences.

Frequently men ignore vital symptoms because they are shy about talking about their bodies, and because they hope these symptoms will go away. This can be very frustrating and worrying for those around them, but as clinical psychologist Ronald Levant points out, 'After a lifetime of numbing feelings, men are often not aware of the physical symptoms of illness. While men will exercise to build muscles, exercise to build health is not nearly so appealing.'[1]

A recent study of twenty countries highlighted how much more at risk of premature death men are than women, regardless of their age. 'Being male is now the single largest demographic factor for early death,' says researcher Randolph Nesse of the University of

Michigan. 'If you could make male mortality rates the same as female rates, you would do more good than curing cancer.'[2]

Men need to be encouraged to value their health and to feel comfortable admitting they are sick. When men fail to do so, they put themselves at risk. As psychologist Bill O'Hehir points out, men's health is not just a medical problem, it's a *social* problem. 'It's an issue of lifestyles, attitudes and values, gender roles, and restructuring of these, so that they are not emotionally and physically destructive.'[3] When talking with men about their health, I found they would become vague and evasive, as if their health were irrelevant.

> *Men's lack of focus on their health has very real consequences.*

Overall men tend to live on the edge and take more risks than women, which makes them more prone to injury. And while their adventurous streak is due in part to their nature, it's also a product of the way they are brought up. Few of us are surprised to learn that men are five times more likely to be victims of accidental drownings, and three times more likely to die in car accidents than are women.[4] We've all heard of men going for a swim, taking their boat out or rock-fishing when the conditions are less than ideal and ending up dead. Not only are men dying at a greater rate in all age groups than women, they have higher levels of death for many common illnesses. Yet in spite of this, still they are less likely to seek help – to go to hospital, to see general practitioners, counsellors, or complementary health practitioners.[5]

> *While the life expectancy for men in developed countries is a lot better than it was fifty or 100 years ago, over this time the gap in mortality rates between men and women has widened.*

I was concerned to note that while the life expectancy for men in developed countries is a lot better than it was fifty or 100 years ago, over this time the gap in mortality rates between men and women has widened. In 1995 the average life expectancy in developed countries was just under seventy-eight years for women, compared with seventy years for men.[6] In spite of this there has been little modification in the way men and boys choose to live.

We now know that boys are more at risk of injury or death, yet still we encourage them to be adventurous, while going to great lengths to ensure little girls are kept safe from harm. Generally more boys than girls have mental health problems, including disruptive and anti-social behaviour, but again this does not influence the way we raise them. Instead we allow the mythology of boyhood to obscure the reality, and so boys remain at greater risk of injury at school, in sport and at play.

WHEN BOYS BECOME MEN

The health challenges boys face continue into adulthood. When we examine the many conditions men are susceptible to, we can begin to see how and where they are most at risk. Heart disease – including heart attacks and aneurisms – is by far the biggest health concern for men, and one of the areas in which men's failure to maintain good health is clearly detrimental. For a 40-year-old Australian man, the risk of having coronary heart disease during the remainder of his life is one in two.[7] The next-highest killer is lung cancer, followed by chronic obstructive pulmonary diseases such as emphysema and chronic bronchitis, prostate cancer, then bowel cancer.[8] And while testicular cancer claims a relatively small number of men each year, it tends to strike men under 33, most of whom are not aware that they may be at risk.[9]

Osteoporosis is another area that affects a significant number of men. Yet, while most women are aware of the effects of osteoporosis in later life, most men are not. This is largely due to the fact that osteoporosis has only recently been recognised as a significant health problem facing older men. It is now believed that one in three men over 60 will have a fracture due to osteoporosis each year. Up to half those men who survive a hip fracture may then be physically disadvantaged and require ongoing nursing care, while one in five men who suffer a hip fracture will die within six months.[10] Again this is something too few men are aware of. These men are not just statistics, they are fathers, husbands, grandfathers.

> *Having spent their lives trying to be independent, most men fear any form of dependency, so they postpone seeing the doctor until they are really sick.*

WHY MEN DON'T THINK ABOUT THEIR HEALTH

A recent study showed that men and women don't differ greatly in their level of physical exercise or their diet[11] – so why are men's health problems increasing? Where men differ from women is in their reluctance to seek medical help. For many men their health isn't even on their radar. In one study of rural Australian men, most of those interviewed didn't see their health as an important factor in their lives. Almost half the men surveyed said they 'never, or hardly ever' thought about their health, while one in ten only considered their health when they were sick. Many of these men equated their health purely with their ability to work.[12]

There are many reasons why men pay little attention to their health, including a lack of literature on men's conditions and how to deal with them. In a recent study, a *Medline* search for the years between 1980 and 2002 sourced just under 8000 articles using the keywords 'women's health', compared to 179 articles using the keywords 'men's health'. A closer examination of these entries revealed that 28 per cent of those on men's health were devoted to HIV infection.[13] We need more editorials on men's health issues to help men become more aware of their bodies and more comfortable seeking help when things go wrong.

WHY MEN DON'T SEEK MEDICAL HELP

Men tend to regard seeing a doctor as a sign of weakness. Having spent their lives trying to be independent, most men fear any form of dependency. They postpone seeing the doctor until they are really sick, so many conditions aren't picked up until later on. These men don't want to be seen letting their illness get the better of them, yet tragically that is what they end up doing. To some extent this reluctance to see a doctor is understandable with older men, because they grew up in an era when there wasn't much money for medical assistance. Even if they are in a different financial position now, still many men fail to see a doctor when they are unwell.

Time spent in waiting rooms is another major reason why men don't visit doctors;[14] not because men are impatient, but because they worry about time away from their work. In one study, tradesmen were seen as a particularly hard group to attract, because of their long hours, and the difficulty in leaving their work, even for a short time.[15] Many men also commute long distances to work, which is another disincentive to seeking medical help. And in certain 'macho' professions, such as the armed forces, image plays a key role. Men don't want to compromise their standing by seeing a doctor unless it's absolutely necessary, and so again often their visits come too late.

Aware of male attitudes to health, Cancer Research UK has designated June as Men's Cancer Month. It set up a message board on its website to encourage men to share their stories. Sports presenter Russell Fuller, 29, was the first to post his battle with testicular cancer on the website, to encourage other men to open up. 'Men generally don't like talking about their feelings as much, and losing a testicle like I did can be embarrassing, and almost like a loss of face,' he admitted, 'but I'm a very open person and talking about it was an invaluable help. My friends and family were very supportive, made a few jokes and did wonders for my state of mind.'[16]

Men's reluctance to visit doctors is also due to the fact that they don't have much experience in seeking medical help.

More recently health professionals have realised that many men fail to use health facilities because they are frequented by women and kids, and staffed by female nurses. While steps are now being taken to employ more male nurses, health centres remain staffed predominantly by women.[17] Men's reluctance to visit doctors is also due to the fact that they don't have much experience in seeking medical help, unlike women who are more used to going to doctors with their own health issues, while pregnant and with their children. And unlike women, who have made pap smears and breast screening part of their routine, men rarely make use of regular health screening procedures.

The increased workloads of doctors doesn't help the situation. Overall doctors have less time to spend with individual patients, so often there isn't enough time during a consultation for male patients to get sufficiently comfortable to voice their concerns.[18] Women are also generally much better at asking doctors for additional information during their consultation.

FAMILIES COME FIRST

The pressure of being the breadwinner is another significant reason for men failing to seek medical help. Phillip, 54, a semi-retired
carpenter, told me he had been bleeding from the bowel for twelve
months before he went to see a doctor. He admitted to being 'nervous and frightened', but the pressures of owning his own business,
getting his kids 'set up' and supporting his wife's return to university
over-rode these medical concerns. Phillip was fortunate: his polyp
proved benign. His doctor did, however, point out that, had he left it
any longer, he would have been in trouble. Phillip's is not an isolated
case. Since researching the book I have learned of a number of men
who have hidden tumours, severe pain and other extreme symptoms
for years before they sought medical help because they feared what
the outcome might be.

> *Men need to know they are not letting others down by being sick.*

Men in relationships often fare better than single men, because
their partners tend to persist where health issues are concerned.
Women will not only insist their husband see a doctor, but will
spend the time and effort required to find the right treatment until
the problem is fixed. When Cancer Research UK analysed the calls
they received, they noted that over twice as many phone calls were
made by women than by men; 45 per cent of all calls seeking information on prostate cancer were by women, as were 40 per cent of
the calls inquiring about testicular cancer.[19] Once we understand the
deep need men have to be useful to those they love, we can begin to
see why they regard health problems as inconvenient. Men need
to know they are not letting others down by being sick.

This tendency to underplay or ignore their health permeates

men's whole lives. Even when men receive a fatal diagnosis, it's not uncommon for them to keep quiet about it, partly out of fear and partly to save their family from pain.

Men battle on alone with health issues because they think they are doing the best by those they care most about. What they don't realise is how devastating their silence and/or their failure to seek timely help can be for family and friends. Perhaps if men understood this, they could give themselves permission to do things differently.

> *Until it's acceptable for men to adopt more positive ways to de-stress, without being seen as weak or a loser, they will continue to bottle things up and drive themselves too hard.*

MEN UNDER PRESSURE

Psychologist Bill O'Hehir believes that stress is perhaps the single most important issue in men's health.[20] Many men don't even realise they are stressed, and few do anything about it. Generally when women are under stress they will ring a girlfriend, see a movie, go shopping, have a massage, light candles and take a long bath, or put on a face pack and watch television. When men are stressed they tend to work harder, or resort to alcohol and other stimulants, adding to the already considerable pressure they are under.

Frequently the only time men stop is when they get home; then they collapse on the sofa and fall asleep. While this crash-and-burn way of living has become commonplace for many men, it is hardly conducive to good health or happy relationships. Yet until it's acceptable for men to adopt more positive ways to de-stress, without being seen as weak or a loser, they will continue to bottle things up and drive themselves too hard.

Ultimately the ability to care for one's health is about valuing *oneself* sufficiently to make the time and effort to be healthy. Before we can encourage men to do this, we need to examine more closely the many messages men receive from early childhood that encourage their compulsion to perform and provide. Making the decision to chill out is no easy task in a society that values people for what they have and what they produce, rather than who they are.

When men are not able to be true to who they are as *individuals*, they are unable to lead genuinely fulfilling lives. Men who are locked into this way of living frequently experience what Bill O'Hehir calls 'significant inner stress'. Men need a bigger vision of what being masculine can hold. They need to know that by taking their health seriously they are taking care not only of themselves, but of those they love.

Men's take on work

HOW MEN FEEL ABOUT WORK

Work is a big part of most men's lives, but almost all the discussion about men at work focuses on the men at the top, and the power they possess. Yet while these men dominate the headlines, they are only a fraction of the men who do work. Some men are captains of industry, barristers and politicians. They have prestige and influence, and are well rewarded for their efforts. These men are decision-makers, and are possibly more in control of their destinies than the rest of us.

Yet for each of these men, there are thousands who have little influence, few choices and modest resources at best. These are the men who work on assembly lines, drive our buses and trains, keep our streets safe, and maintain our roads, waterways, parks and public buildings. Work for these men is an absolute necessity. Their prime focus is on doing a good job and staying employed. They do not have the luxury or stimulation of formal career paths. Many of these men will do the same job their whole lives. These men are not power hungry. They have little or no power. Yet their work and commitment are as essential to our communities as the contributions made by professional men.

One of the reasons men have received bad press in the workplace is their need to compete. Some men do bring a competitive spirit into the workplace, but not all men behave this way, or at least not destructively so. Competition in the workplace isn't limited to men, and competition is not necessarily a bad thing. Without a competitive spirit, few enterprises would thrive. When properly harnessed, competition can bring new life and direction to the workplace, inspiring and focusing all who work there. A positive spirit of competition helps motivate individuals to get out of bed in the morning. This is certainly Matthew's experience. 'My job has its highs and lows, like anything, but when it's high it's out of the stratosphere!' he told me. 'I love being challenged every day. My job has the winning and losing nature of sport that really appeals.'

UNDERSTANDING THE NEED TO SUCCEED

Work can be a positive outlet for men's desire to make things happen. The problem comes when men don't know how to switch off. Today many men are overly focused on work, and lack other elements in their lives. Yet just because these men are giving their all to their jobs does not mean they *enjoy* working this way. For the majority of men, to do anything other than work hard isn't a choice. Now that women are also experiencing the many pressures of work, they are more able to understand the love/hate relationship many men have with their jobs.

The difference for women is that over the course of their working lives, many will have the opportunity to dip in and out of paid work, and to change direction. Most men do not have this choice. In spite of the greater fluidity in roles, the vast majority of men still need to provide for those they love, because their families need their income, and because society still expects men to assume this responsibility.

'If a man said, "I don't want to go to work any more, I want to stay at home," or some such thing, that would make him a wastrel. It's natural for men to do something. It may be something they hate, like hard physical labour. It might be something they really enjoy, but they're not going to sit there and be idle, they will do something.' *Alex, 35*

PUTTING THEIR FAMILIES FIRST

While not all men are driven simply by the need to care for their families, many are. For some this might mean ensuring there is food on the table and a decent place to live; for men on higher incomes it might mean paying for private school fees and holidays, private health insurance for the family, and a nice home in a desirable suburb. Regardless of their assets or income, all these men are providing for loved ones. They are doing what is regarded as 'the right thing'.

> *For the majority of men, to do anything other than work hard isn't a choice.*

This desire to provide is not a thing of the past. When two people with equally promising careers get together, it is still assumed the man will be *prepared* to take on the major financial commitment for their life together. There is rarely an assumption a woman *should* be the principal provider, even if this proves to be the case. 'There is still a feeling in today's society that the man is the main bread-winner, although whether this is in fact true is up for debate. Hence there are pressures on men to have a good job, a good income, to provide,' explained Tim, a 25-year-old marketing professional. To this end, Tim is studying for his MBA while working full-time. Tony, 26, agreed: 'Even in my generation, I feel as though there is still the pressure to provide for my future family financially. And even though just as many women are in the workforce, they still want a man to provide for them.'

> 'I went out with an identical twin. It was all very confusing, because the other twin was going out with a guy who was working. I was a full-time student at the time. Their mother was a lovely woman, but she'd always make a big deal about what kind of presents the girls got at birthdays and Christmas. I don't think she meant anything by it, but it was really hard – it put me under a lot of pressure.'
> Mitchell, 26

While this need for men to provide might seem outdated, in practice it is alive and well. Men are acutely aware that their ability to provide a certain lifestyle has a huge influence on who ends up with whom. It's not just in fairytales that the hero wins the heart of the most desirable woman. And even though a young woman may be confident, capable and well-educated, the first question her parents and extended family are likely to ask when a relationship becomes serious is what kind of work her prospective partner does. Rather than risking looking like a failure by choosing a job they love, most men apply for the highest-paying job they are capable of, and/or one that offers the most prospects.

It's not just women and their parents and families who cause men to think this way; men place this pressure on themselves and each other. When men meet, one of the first topics for discussion is what they *do*. For many men, they *are* their work. This is one of the main ways men establish their sense of self, and earn the respect of those who count.

'Society judges men a great deal. That whole hierarchy thing that begins at primary school keeps going. The money, muscle and power positions in career is where the whole thing is perpetuated.' *Blake, 42*

'Perhaps the biggest challenge for men is to develop a sense of identity outside of what you do for a living. Without my work, who am I? What am I? Men are expected to work full on, full-time, and they have an image of themselves as the breadwinners. I know of a very few "house husbands", and don't know how they deal with their "status" in society.' *Nick, 53*

Gore Vidal sees the pressures men are subjected to as social conditioning. 'The thing that makes an economic system like ours work is to maintain control over people and make them do jobs they hate . . . Once a man has a wife and two young children, he will do what you tell him to. He will obey you.'[1] While not everyone holds such a radical view, the pressures on men with families cannot be denied.

> *Being well paid helps make jobs that would otherwise be unbearable, bearable.*

WHAT IS WORTHWHILE WORK?

The pressure on men to provide is very focusing, and helps explain why they often tend to view work more objectively than women. This ability to stand back helps men survive their many years at work. For most men work is a transaction: the investment of a certain amount of effort, in return for an agreed level of remuneration. The amount of money men can earn is central to this equation, because relatively

few working men have the luxury of simply seeking personal fulfilment at work.

'Even though I really do love my work, I would give it all up for more
time with family and friends.' *Kris, 35*

Being well paid helps make jobs that would otherwise be unbearable, bearable. Recently a friend of mine who helps organisations
manage change was touring the plant of a leading brick manufacturer
and met one of the men whose job it was to unload the bricks from
the oven. It was clearly repetitive and gruelling work, and the heat
in the area around the furnace was so intense it was almost unbearable. She found herself asking this man how he coped. His response
was immediate: 'It means I get to take my family on holiday for three
weeks every year.' This is the reality of work for many men.

'Work's pure misery for most blue-collar men. Why would you do it
unless it's for your family?' *Ryan, 50*

Wealthy men can also find themselves trapped at work, because
they have no options or sense of their choices. One of the most
tragic cases of this was a man I met during a formal dinner. He was a
high-flyer who worked for a leading multinational. After a series of
successful business ventures, which netted him several millions, this
man had taken on his current role, in which he was responsible for
the company's performance in more than a dozen countries. During
dinner, he admitted to a secret passion for photography and confessed that more than anything he would love to run a photographic
agency. The only time this man, who was well into his 60s, was animated was when he was talking about photography. It was unclear

to me whether the pressure to remain in the corporate world came from this man's family and peers or from within. What was obvious was that he felt compelled to remain in corporate life to feel worthwhile. There are thousands of men with similar stories, and as long as men are encouraged only to seek their value outside of themselves, it will continue to be hard for them to place any value on who they are *intrinsically*.

> 'I'm working with a woman in her late fifties. She divorced and is now interested in another man, but it's kind of depressing to hear what she says about him. She's clearly not that much in love. She says he's nice, but she's also brought up that he's wealthy, and that's clearly an attraction. That made me feel very uncomfortable – it's like we have to perform our whole lives.' *Tony, 26*

MEN WHO HATE THEIR JOBS

Because men don't talk about their difficulties at work, often families and friends have no idea of the weariness and quiet desperation men feel at having to continue to get out of bed in the morning and go to work. Like women, many men feel suffocated by the roles they must play – maintaining the house, paying the mortgage, remaining strong and committed to their job, even though they too yearn for time out.

Along with the quiet desperation they experience, many men feel guilty for wanting their working lives to be different, especially when they're perceived to be in a good career position and earning good money. Yet unless these men can *better* their prospects by bringing in more money and/or enjoying greater influence, most will endure jobs they hate, not just for a couple of years, but for decades. They do this because they are worried that if they step away from

193

what they have committed to, they will lose the love and respect of those who matter.

> 'People want so much today. A couple of generations ago people lived in small houses with big families and were happy. I'd love to be working part-time, or to have that option.' *Blake, 42*

The despair men experience around work is more prevalent than is often imagined. And providing for those they love and respect has become more onerous for men over time. Not only have their own material aspirations escalated, so too have those of their partner and kids. In many cases this has led to an even greater sense of despair. 'Everything's become so materialistic,' complained Blake, who feels pressured to maintain the lifestyle his wife and kids have come to enjoy. On more than one occasion Blake has attempted to talk to his wife about scaling back a bit, but to no avail, so he feels locked into a profession he has come to hate.

HOW BOYS SEE WORK

Men get the message about what's expected of them often while they are still relatively young. In his article 'Men and Dangerous Work', columnist James Novak related a conversation he had with his teenage son about work and the many expectations ahead of him. 'Sometimes I get scared that I won't get a job that will allow me to take care of myself and my children when I grow up,' his son admitted. It's hard to believe a teenage boy would feel these pressures so keenly, but as James Novak points out, 'My son is coming to grips with the central question that men face, and have faced for ages, as regards their sexuality, "How can I be perceived as a man if I cannot take care of myself and my family?"' [2]

Men find work isolating – not only because they may well end up doing something they don't care for, but because they are forced to spend so much time away from their families. The split a man faces between family and work is relatively recent. Until the Industrial Revolution, when there was a mass migration to the city, men worked from or close to home, and were able to enjoy the warmth of their family around them as they worked. For most men today this just isn't an option. Undoubtedly some men do use work as an escape from family life, but many do not.

> 'I really only work for the money. If someone would pay me the same, and I could just stuff around enjoying my life and my family, I probably wouldn't do this at all.' *Steve, 44*

Cameron, 32, told me it wasn't until he was a father that his own father admitted his grief at being absent from home as much as he was. Cameron's father was a professional man in a senior position with a high-profile financial company. Although he had never said anything to anyone while he was at work, Cameron's father sorely missed his time with his family. 'He's told me how much he wanted to be home when we were little, but because of his job he felt the pressure to stay late at work,' said Cameron. 'The sad thing is we all felt the same way. I remember time and again sitting at the dinner table waiting for him to come home, only to have the phone ring to say he would be delayed, so yet again his dinner was put in the oven.'

THE COMPANY MAN

Many men do get satisfaction from their work. As long as men can see something *tangible* for their efforts, they can at least take comfort in the results. But for many men who have routine jobs, often it's hard to feel productive. Many become anxious and worry about whether they are being sufficiently productive to keep their job, because they know their loved ones rely on them for their wellbeing. The anxiety men experience around work has become more acute as the downsizing and restructuring of organisations has become commonplace.

Now there are a whole range of issues men have to deal with at work, because many of the old rules no longer apply. Dependability, hard work and long service used to be the cornerstones of success, but now there are only the quick and the dead. In the current smoke-and-mirrors environment at work, it's much harder for men to know whether their face still fits, because those running organisations keep changing their minds about what is required.

'Men are expected to be tough, to bear any workload, to confront problems and so on, and sometimes these expectations are not in the self-interest of the individual man.' *Kieran, 58*

Physical appearance and personal presentation are also more important than ever at work, placing even more pressure on corporate men in particular to continue to fit the mould. This preoccupation with youth has created a much narrower window of opportunity for men to excel, because it leaves the mature men in the workplace with very little room to move. Add to this the challenge of keeping up with technology, and one can begin to sense the growing desperation many men face at work, especially fathers. Excellent product knowledge and finely honed experience are no longer enough. If a man doesn't continue to refine his skills, especially his technical skills, he will be left behind. Against this shifting backdrop, family men in particular are all too aware that, regardless of what's happening at work, their mortgage and other financial commitments still need to be met — which frequently can't be achieved without them, even when their wife is also working.

'It worries me that young men are getting such high-grade jobs so early, because the job's a lot harder than what it should be. Then, by forty they're past it, and [the] workplace misses out on terrific experience and ability.' *George, 60*

As men grow more concerned about their jobs, they work harder to ensure they remain with the pack. This often means they will see less and less of their families. Then, when finally they do make it home, frequently their families are resentful of the time they have not shared, or hardly even notice they are there. Because men are raised to keep their concerns to themselves, rarely do loved ones know just how tenuous their work lives have become, so once more these men feel out on a limb.

'I feel that I am growing more tired more easily as I age, which is not an earth-shattering insight, but it is something that males have to deal with in the workplace, and that can be confronting.' *Kieran, 58*

With the rise in the power of the corporation has come an increasing sense of powerlessness felt by those working in these organisations. For men supporting families, trying to prove they are 'with the program' can be very demanding professionally and personally. Those who do 'get with the program' are often overly exacting of themselves and others, making the road even harder. It can be extremely frustrating and disheartening to work closely with 'company men' as they continue to push staff and colleagues beyond what is reasonable.

I had a boss who was extremely exacting. One day I found him bent over his desk; he had had surgery the day before and was in a great deal of pain, but he had insisted on coming to work. Individuals who go to such extremes place everyone under huge pressure. 'Corporate Man, in particular, lives and dies for, and by, his performance evaluation,' explains clinical psychologist Alon Gratch. 'Performance and performance anxiety are intrinsic to men's masculine insecurity.'[3]

MEN AND OVERWORK

When men become addicted to work, they are more easily manipulated by the system and driven to manipulate others. While these men may see themselves as helping create a brave new world, often they become victims of the very cultures they give their lives to. The story of Apple in the early 1990s illustrates this point. The company was pulling out all the stops to release their hand-held computer, the Newton, for summer 1993. As the project was running almost a year late, the designers in particular were expected to 'deliver'. The pressure these men were under was too much for some designers. A number of engineers admitted to breaking down and crying after working eighteen-hour days. One suffered a mental breakdown and was jailed. Another committed suicide.[4]

The Japanese have coined the term *karoshi* to describe those who literally work themselves to death. While most working men may not reach such extremes, many do push themselves to the limit. The more worn down they become, the fewer options they can see for themselves, until they end up as simply yet another grey-faced man in a suit. I spoke with Matthew, who works in computing. At 27, Matthew is already well aware of the pressures at work. 'I would love to work less hours . . . than I do. But if I'm working on a large tender, or whatever, sometimes I can work a couple of twenty-four hour days in a week,' he admitted. 'I don't think you have a choice to do any less in the world in which I work, if you want to be successful.' While this energy and commitment may benefit Matthew's company, few individuals can sustain this pressure for any length of time. Long term, it's a recipe for burnout.

THE MEN'S CLUB

One of the many things men enjoy at work is the opportunity to be with other men. During interviews I was surprised to learn of the tangible sense of comfort a number of men experienced in working with other men. After returning from the Vietnam War, Dan, now 58, enjoyed working in the steel mills driving powered forklifts and operating the rolling machine. He has no doubt that being around men helped him get his life back together. 'I enjoyed it being ninety-five per cent men working there, because when men get together, they "let it rip",' he explained. Stanley, 70, a retired police officer with two grown daughters, also enjoyed working with men. He felt that the introduction of women into the police force towards the end of his career shattered the bond the men had shared. 'It was a worry,' Stanley explained, 'because not all men behave well around women.' He was concerned about these women and felt he had to keep an eye out for them.

> *Even when men choose to step out of work for a while, many find themselves itching to get back, because they long for the routine, the camaraderie, the sense of achievement.*

DO MEN AT WORK *REALLY* HAVE IT ALL?

The current dissatisfaction with work is partly due to our expectations. Something happened to our attitude to work in the 1960s, when almost every aspect of the status quo was under fire. Suddenly work was not only expected to provide a decent standard of living, it became an opportunity for self-fulfilment and self-expression. The women's movement helped consolidate this with its emphasis on work, and the belief that work would give women the power and satisfaction they longed for.

While there have been many gains, this heightened focus on work led men and women to believe that work could be all-fulfilling. It also took consumption to a new level. Now we consume many times more than we did twenty or thirty years ago. Our children have become locked into this same cycle, causing far too many households to become slaves to their credit cards. As we have already noted, for the many men who are the main providers in their family, these increased expectations can be almost unbearable.

> 'For both men and women the contemporary sales pitch is: you can do whatever you like. But I actually think that as you get older and mature more, while this may be possible, it's not necessarily desirable. We've created a much more competitive environment, where anyone can do anything, and this can end up being very daunting for both sexes.' *Alex, 35*

FINDING FULFILMENT

In spite of the many pressures they face, a lot of men do get a great deal out of work. It is here that often they feel most at home, because at work they have the chance to make their mark, to test themselves against those around them and to enjoy a sense of community. That is why when work is taken from men, they often experience a tangible sense of grief and loss. Even when men choose to step out of work for a while, many find themselves itching to get back, because they long for the routine, the challenge, the camaraderie, the sense of achievement.

While men tend to make more hard-nosed choices about the kind of work they will do, and how they choose to operate at work, there was nothing in my interviews with them to suggest they have any less need than women to feel fulfilled at work. What is different is they are more able to be resigned about a lack of personal fulfilment in their work, because it's looking after their children, partner and home that fulfils them.

'I have some friends in companies who have hated their work for a year, or in some cases for twenty years.' *Ivan, 48*

In spite of the angst and confusion many men feel around work, as one respondent noted, it is one of the ways men can prove to themselves they're alive. Work enables men to feel validated. It can inspire them to build something that will remain long after they are gone. When men can have a wider range of choices about how and where they work, when a greater number of men can share the burden of providing for their families more equitably, or at least gain more recognition for the critical role many play, and when more men are able to have time out – then men will get even more out of their work.

Risky business

DANGEROUS WORK

Aside from the handful of men at work on the fast track, there are many men who undertake back-breaking, often demeaning or dangerous work every day of the week. More often than not these jobs are essential to the community, but because we don't hear much about the risky, soul-destroying work these men do, rarely do we give them any thought. 'Work is a dangerous place for men,' states James Novak, when talking of the numbers of men who get injured at work.[1]

> *Injured men are not just statistics; they have homes, personal aspirations, partners, siblings, parents, children.*

In 1999–2000 in Australia, compensation was granted for 346 work-related deaths – and most of these concerned the deaths of men. Eighty-four of these fatalities took place on the journey to and from work, and the remaining 262 deaths took place as a result of work activities.[2] These figures don't include the fatalities that were not awarded compensation, or the hundreds of men injured but not killed at work each year. Nor do they take into account the men exposed to harmful chemicals at work, which they bring home on their skin, hair, clothes and tools, or in their car. These chemicals can not only kill or affect a man's health, they can also alter a man's sperm, affect a man's sex drive and ability to have an erection, or may even affect the health and normality of his unborn child.[3]

> 'You had to take the tap handles and dip them in acid. It would bring them up nice and clean, then we would dip them in another solution to clean the acid off. We had no masks or nothing, except for glasses. That was the job. I never did like it much. After a while I was running to the toilet once or twice an hour with diarrhoea. I was no use to them, so I had to move on.' *Dan, 58*

The literature on workplace accidents tends to focus on lost productivity – accidents on the job are often referred to as 'lost-time' accidents. There is plenty of material on the kinds of accidents taking place at work, but information on the *human* cost is much more difficult to obtain. Yet these injured men are not just statistics; they have homes, personal aspirations, partners, siblings, parents, children.

By failing to take into account the *human* dimension of the dangerous work men do, society encourages men to take this same attitude towards their jobs. When I interviewed men whose jobs have an element of risk, rarely did they acknowledge this risk. Peppi, 78, told me without a hint of concern that in a former job he had had to drink 2 pints of milk a day to offset the effects on his stomach of the chemicals he ingested while working with spray-paint. When these men talk about their work, often they talk about their *usefulness* to the company, rather than the poor health and safety standards they were subjected to.

By failing to take into account the human dimension of the dangerous work men do, society encourages men to take this same attitude towards their jobs.

POOR MEN, HIGH RISKS

There is no doubt that of all the men at work, poorer men are at greatest risk. Australian research shows they experience the highest health risks, and suffer higher mortality rates and disability levels.[4] These men are not only largely invisible to society, they are often most vulnerable to the push for profits. In a recent PBS *Frontline* interview, a number of such cases were highlighted, including that of Ira Cofer, a mechanic whose sleeve became entangled in a conveyer belt. Because of layoffs, Ira was working alone at the time of his accident. He was crying out for assistance for more than two-and-a-half hours, but with no-one to come to his aid, he was forced to watch and feel the belt rub his left arm to the bone.[5] This is all the more shocking because it is not an isolated incident.

'The average man in our culture takes the work that is available for him. If that work is dangerous, dirty or has little status, he will still do that work, so as to be grounded in our culture. Any work which pays at least an average wage will give him an identity as a man.'
James Novak[6]

Even where safety standards are high, the work culture can often undermine men's health and safety.

An employer doesn't have to be negligent for employees to be at risk. Warren Farrell tells of a garbage man who, over the course of his job, had several packs of human blood burst and spatter him; picked up what turned out to be low-level radioactive waste; had battery acid splashed on his clothes, and hot ashes – which had been dumped in the rubbish – ignite the back of his truck.[7]

Even where safety standards are high, the work culture can often undermine men's health and safety. Mining has long been regarded as one of the least healthy workplaces for this reason. While the pay is high, so too are the risks, especially for those working in remote communities. Not only does mining have a big element of danger, often the long hours and isolation can lead to substance abuse. The combination of stress, long shifts and working around the clock means miners are often out of sync with their body clock, making them more vulnerable to accidents and such ailments as heart problems, poor sleep, stomach disorders and mental health issues. Add to this the strong macho culture in mining, and it's not hard to see why these men are at risk.[8]

According to Men at Risk, a non-profit organisation devoted to educating men, the jobs with the highest and most frequent fatality rates are those involved in outdoor occupations – truck drivers, farmers, construction workers and airplane pilots, because these men are vulnerable to extreme weather patterns. Those who work at night and work alone; and those who handle money in fast-food outlets, convenience stores and petrol stations are also ten times more likely to be killed at work than the average worker.[9] It is important we fully acknowledge and respect the very real risks many men take to do these jobs, and continue to improve workplace safety to further minimise the risks.

DISASTER RESPONSE

Search and rescue is another high-risk area for employees. Too often we take it for granted that these men and women will save people from burning homes, cut the injured out of car wrecks, dredge rivers for missing persons, or plunge into the surf to rescue distressed swimmers. Often it's not until we face such monumental tragedies as 9/11 that we begin to appreciate what these men do day in, day out. In such moments these men become human again. Three hundred and forty-three firefighters lost their lives trying to save those trapped and injured after the collapse of the World Trade Center, but the danger didn't stop there. Now additional firefighters, police and other workers at Ground Zero are facing disabling, if not terminal illnesses because much of the dust resulting from the disaster is proving highly toxic.

Over 300 firefighters have had to leave work due to illnesses that developed after working at Ground Zero, and as many firefighters again are set to retire for the same reason. Firefighter Steve Strahl, whose bravery received front-page coverage, now has throat cancer.[10] Detective Walcott, 39, who worked on investigations at the site, now has leukemia.[11] Detective Williamson, 43, who also worked at the site, is fighting pancreatic cancer.[12]

THE NIGHTMARES THAT REFUSE TO GO AWAY

Working in these high-risk areas can also make men psychologically vulnerable. For Damian, who spent fourteen years in active police service, the worst part of policing was dealing with injured children, and telling families their loved ones were gone. 'I'd rather attend a crime scene any time,' he admitted. Every day thousands of police officers face suicides, fatal accidents, rapes, murders, robberies and drug incidents, risking their lives and their sanity to do their job. At times Damian found it hard to go home and listen to everyone else's worries – not because he didn't care, but because none of these things seemed so bad by comparison. Yet like most men in this situation, he tended to keep quiet about what had happened to him at work.

Dave, a policeman of many years' service, said that even though he has been retired for over a decade, he can still remember every case he worked on. 'It leaves a lasting memory,' he reflected. For him one of the hardest parts of the job was participating in post-mortems. 'It never gets any better,' he admitted. At the same time Dave is quick to point out the job was about helping victims of crime. 'Often they were really suffering, but if I could do something, then at least I could help ease their pain.'

While things are changing, for generations men have done jobs that are dirty and dangerous with inadequate training or protection. When Dave was recruited, his police training consisted of a three-week course in law and firearms. 'Then we were given a uniform, a pistol, a set of handcuffs and a baton, and let loose on the streets.' After a difficult day on the job, the only chance Dave had to debrief was over a beer with his mates after work. While conditions have clearly improved, with counselling and other services now available to officers, there is still fallout. A recent *Sydney Morning Herald* article on police trauma reported that 60 per cent of the 300 to 400 officers discharged each year from the force are suffering from post trau-matic stress disorder. Organisational psychologist Dr Peter Cotton felt that the stress came from the very real trauma police officers face on the job, and from the perceived lack of support they receive for doing their job.[13]

Damian began suffering nightmares after attending the scene of a fatal road accident, where a young man had lost control of his car. The car had rolled over a bank and ended up upside down, some distance below the road. When Damian arrived at the scene it was night. With the absence of street lights, he found it hard to see the extent of the damage the car and its passengers had sustained. He and his partner tried to calm the young driver while they searched for his five-year-old brother, who had been sitting next to him in the car. The little boy was nowhere to be seen. But then as Damian scoured the darkness, he saw two small feet sticking out from under the car. Although he and his partner realised the little boy was probably dead, they tried everything they could to extract him from under the car before back-up arrived. Twenty years later, Damian still has nightmares about this incident, as night after night he continues to try to rescue that little boy.

WHAT IT TAKES TO CAPTURE WORLD EVENTS

We are now learning more about the trauma suffered by journalists and photojournalists in major disaster and war-torn areas. Few journalists who report in extreme situations admit to the chronic distress they feel, let alone the very real dangers they face in this line of work. In 2001 alone, 100 journalists lost their lives, and many more were traumatised by what they had experienced. Studies on post-traumatic stress disorder in journalists show that when they continue to be exposed to disturbing events, the more acute their symptoms are likely to be.

Photojournalist Don McCullin explained his feelings on reporting in war-torn parts of the world. 'Going to war is not an easy thing for me to get rid of . . . I can still smell a mattress that was burning in a house in Cyprus when I went to my first civil war. There were three dead bodies lying in that house, and the sweet smell of the warm blood in the early Mediterranean morning. People don't realise that smells, as well as vision, can be a very powerful memory. I don't care how strong a man thinks he is, eventually he will need an emotional arm around him.'[14]

Until we fully recognise that psychological distress is a likely outcome of these jobs, men will not feel encouraged to talk about the impact their job has on them, let alone to seek help. Things are starting to change. One positive step forward is the establishment of the Dart Center for Journalism and Trauma, a global resource for journalists who cover trauma and violence, which has an Australasian branch.[15]

Much of the danger men have faced at work has remained hidden, partly because men didn't fully realise the risks they were exposed to, and partly because they haven't always spoken up about the health and safety issues at work that they *were* aware of. As we learn to handle these issues more effectively, we will not only transform the experience of many men at work, but the lives of their families and communities as well.

Becoming a dad

MEN'S TAKE ON FATHERHOOD

In spite of what people may think, most men are not just focused on what happens at work, especially once they become a dad. The process of becoming a father is an exhilarating, often complex experience for men, because while there are many ways men can now fulfil their role as dads, most are still locked into the role of breadwinner. Being a good provider remains an important way in which a man can demonstrate his love for his family. Many men continue to take pride in ensuring their families are well cared for, but they also yearn for other ways to express their love for their children.

> *Without a father's physical and emotional support, it's much harder for a family to be secure and to thrive.*

Men currently lack the recognition of just how important their role of providing for a family is. Society tends to forget that without a father's physical and emotional support, it's much harder for a family to be secure and to thrive. In recent times it has also become a whole lot harder for men to sustain the role of provider, as material aspirations escalate.

> 'It's nice to try to hold on to that ideal of being the breadwinner, and making sure that your wife and child are looked after.' *Adrian, 35*

Work is also a major issue for fathers, because many struggle to remain fully employed throughout their working lives, while others are swallowed up by their work. 'All the evidence suggests that they love their children and would die for them if necessary,' says academic Don Edgar. 'The problem is that they are dying for them (often through overwork and lack of balance in their lives), but the kids don't always notice and many fathers feel unappreciated.'[1]

> 'Fathers that I have spoken to tell me that they are caught between conflicting expectations of what a great father is; the reality of balancing life, work and family; and expectations from society that they be a fully engaged father, provider, protector and a loving partner.' *Colin George, The Fatherhood Project*[2]

REDEFINING FATHERHOOD

Things are starting to change for fathers. Just as women wanted to be liberated from the kitchen sink, many men now aspire to more time and/or involvement with their families. '[Men] want a better balance in their lives between endless work and more family time; they do want to spend more time raising their children in partnership with their women,' says Don Edgar. 'Unless we take a more positive view of male potential we will do an injustice to our sons and daughters by failing to draw on the unique qualities of manhood in their development of whole human beings.'[3] When dads get more involved with their children, new possibilities emerge for everyone.

Part of the struggle for fathers is the way they are represented. In films and media the focus is on either abusive fathers or the bland, one-dimensional figures promoted in the lead-up to Father's Day, rather than real men with real lives. Fathers can be much more than this. They need more recognition for everything they have to offer. 'When our daughter was born seven years ago, I suddenly became aware of the secret world of fatherhood,' says Duncan Fisher, director of Fathers Direct. 'I found myself, like many men, transformed by this new experience, this new life, entrusted to the two of us. Yet I was stunned to hear so few public voices echoing my feelings about becoming a dad. While I was brimming with excitement, thrilled with the potential of it all, I found myself surrounded by a public silence on fatherhood.'[4]

In spite of this silence, men are now redefining the whole concept of fatherhood, as they show more willingness and confidence in feeding, cuddling, toileting and playing with their children. It is interesting to read that Russell Crowe would rather be home with his son than at the Oscars, and that for Johnny Depp fatherhood is not just the best thing that's happened to him, but 'the only thing' that's happened to him.[5] Lachlan Murdoch walked away from his central role in the Murdoch empire so he could have more of a life with his wife and son. While we don't want or need high-profile figures to define our attitudes towards fatherhood, it is significant that they are now talking openly about being fathers when, just a few decades ago, even partners didn't get much of a mention.

'When we have kids I look forward to watching them achieve, encouraging them to experience everything they can. I look forward to the excitement and good times, to backyard cricket, and to the moments when you are brimming with pride in what they have done, no matter how small.' Matthew, 27

DO MEN REALLY WANT KIDS?

Not all men talk about having kids. This is not necessarily because they don't want them; often the subject is too personal. Many men long to be dads. When Neil, 34, thinks about being a dad, he looks forward to 'watching our child grow from a baby into a small adult, where they begin to develop their own personality, ideas and beliefs, and of course I look forward to playing with them.' Evan, 27, talks of 'providing everything that my little baby needs or wants. Increasing the close loving relationship that my partner and I have, to our children.'

While some men really want to be a dad, others slip into the role, coming to terms more slowly with what's required. A number of men I spoke with talked of giving fatherhood little thought until it happened. This doesn't necessarily make these men any less committed as fathers. Some men need the *tangible* experience of having their own child before they can understand what fatherhood means to them. What is clear is that fathers need far more support than they are currently getting to do the best job possible.

'Women have worked hard to win respect in the workplace, and now men are trying hard to win respect on the home front.' *Justin, 43*

THE EXPECTANT FATHER

When a man finds out he is to be a father, often this is an exhilarating and daunting moment. I was surprised to learn how anxious many expectant fathers are; men who worry they won't be up to the job. One study even suggests that men are more anxious than their partner,[6] and my research bears this out. When Lee discovered his partner was pregnant, he felt great, because they were going to be a family instead of a couple. 'We were very happy and looking forward to the changes and the challenges, with a little doubt and fear thrown in,' he admitted. Adrian, 35, soon to be a dad, talked of feeling petrified: 'You automatically kick into overdrive, because this is a big responsibility. You are now in charge of shaping that child in terms of how they're going to think, or feel, or what morals they're going to have. The responsibility side of things is frightening.'

'We are scared. We don't want to screw up. There is this perception in pop culture of the "maternal instinct" that guides women to make the correct and perfect choices for their children. Without that instinct, men feel lost. We remember when we were learning about cars and making some tweak to a 1987 Datsun B-210 that caused black smoke to fill the garage. We don't want to make a similar mistake with our kids. That fear, I believe, is part of the fear some guys have with having kids. They don't know what to do, and they freak out.'[7] *Jared Fiel, author of* Fumbling Through Fatherhood

Once these men come to terms with the enormity of becoming a dad, many start to look forward to the adjustments and bonuses fatherhood will bring. Unlike their partners, however, few of these men will receive encouragement, and even fewer will be advised on how to prepare for becoming a dad, because the vast majority of books on pregnancy, childbirth and parenting still focus on the role of mothers, or on parents as a whole.

As Michael Lamb, one of the world's leading experts on father-hood, points out, fathers don't just need to be motivated, they need skills and confidence. The way a father interacts with his child impacts his self-image and the health of his relationships — the more support-ive his relationship with his partner, the better able he is to be a good and supportive father to his child.[8]

LETTING DADS IN

It is odd that we have to find reasons why fathers are important to their children, when most kids are well aware that their dad adds a great deal to their lives. This lack of interest rubs off, meaning too few first-time fathers have enough confidence in their new role. They do not know the very real and positive impact their presence and approach can have on their children. Perhaps this is due in part to the narrow view some mothers still have of fathers as principally bread-winners rather than *active* parents.

Michael Lamb agrees. He found that while most men want to be involved fathers, the majority of women do not want their partners to be more involved than they currently are.[9] Things are changing, but even when fathers do get more involved with their kids, without meaning to mothers often discourage them by constantly correcting them or by taking over when they attempt to help.

When this happens, no-one feels satisfied. Men end up worry-ing that they're letting down those they love most, while mothers become exhausted and resentful because they have to do all the work. Apart from the expectations of what fathers and mothers are 'supposed to do', I suspect this issue is also due in part to a lack of confidence in new parents. Fathers want to help but don't know what to do, while often mothers feel they are ultimately responsible for the day-to-day care, health and wellbeing of their baby, and so they take charge. Both parents need encouragement to see that they each have a great deal to offer their child.

> *Too few first-time fathers have enough confidence in their new role. They do not know the very real and positive impact their presence and approach can have on their children.*

Although a man can never know what it's like to have a child growing inside him, this need not prevent him from playing an active role in his partner's pregnancy, in the birth of his child, and beyond – but he needs tangible support to do so. Often men do help out during pregnancy, by making meals, getting the baby's room ready, and by attending ultrasound sessions and antenatal classes. While this behind-the-scenes support can be very helpful to pregnant mums, often prospective dads yearn for even more involvement. They want access to good information and support, and the opportunity for feedback. 'Men get very little attention,' Cameron, 32, told me. 'They are hungry for information.' Increasingly health care professionals are realising how important it is to assist expectant fathers as well as mothers. Greater participation in parenting and antenatal sessions gives men the opportunity to discuss *their* experiences and ideas with other expectant fathers, and to talk about issues that are important to *them*.

HOW MEN FEEL DURING THEIR PARTNER'S PREGNANCY

Allowing men to express *their* thoughts and concerns helps draw them more fully into their role as expectant fathers. Men need to be invited to do so, because as Irma Kurtz observes, often they are made shy by the depth of their emotion.[10] This is particularly true of new fathers. While many are less expressive about becoming parents than their partners, this doesn't mean they don't experience a whole range of emotions as they struggle to play a more meaningful part in their partner's pregnancy. What a difference it would make if men helped women understand the depth of feeling they are experiencing at this time.

I was surprised to learn how anxious many expectant fathers are, men who worry they won't be up to the job.

When men are *actively* encouraged to be part of their partner's pregnancy, it helps them deal with their many thoughts and feelings during these critical months. Ray, a 50-year-old father of two teenagers, recalled 'a feeling of inadequacy for this new person getting ready to join us, fear that something would go or be wrong, and impatience that it was taking so long'. Having the opportunity to assist their partner in tangible ways helps nudge prospective fathers beyond their feelings of anxiety and helplessness. Lee, 48, whose son is now six months, remembers feeling happy and a bit more fulfilled during his partner Sara's pregnancy because of the back-up he was able to provide during her morning sickness. 'I prepared breakfast and brought it to her in bed. I felt supportive and "part" of her pregnancy,' he explained. 'Sara has since said that during the pregnancy and after that I was very supportive of her.'

The two central experiences for Adrian, 35, during his wife's pregnancy were being present at the ultrasound and feeling his baby move. 'If Kayt was asleep and I put my hand on her stomach, I could feel him moving around. It was amazing and creepy to have something wriggling around like that. It's a miracle.' It is interesting that Adrian enjoyed *private* moments with his baby while Kayt was asleep, pointing again to the shyness of men in intimate situations.

Encouraging expectant fathers to explore and articulate *their* feelings and experiences during their partner's pregnancy draws them into the process and helps them deal with their anxieties and excitement about this massive change in their lives.

The moment of fatherhood

WHEN THE BABY ARRIVES

After months of waiting comes the moment when the baby is finally on its way. This is another huge step for fathers, as well as mothers. These days fathers are able to be present at the birth of their child to experience this miracle first-hand. It's easy to forget that this is a relatively recent occurrence. When men were first allowed to attend the birth of their children, many were sceptical about the benefits, yet the countless fathers who had been left out found this exclusion difficult.

'During the delivery period at hospital, the closest I got to my children was looking at them through the glass viewing window of the nursery,' Nigel, 72, recalled. 'I found this exclusion frustrating, but it was the way things were done at the time. So I was pleased to have a go at nursing them for the first time, but it took some time to get in touch with them in a cuddly way.'

'No man is ever ready to become a father. But then something magic happens. The moment when that purply pink wrinkled thing stops

being an idea for you and becomes an independent organism, your
heart bursts with love.' *Jay Turley*[1]

Being part of the birth process allows men in on the mystery of
birth. Many of the men I interviewed spoke openly of their sense of
wonder. They talked of their child's birth as being 'magical', 'unbelievable', 'a miracle'. Boxer Kostya Tszyu believes the births of his
children to be the happiest moments of his life. 'You see your wife
and your kid and this feeling is very, very special. When you're holding your baby for the first time and he's screaming for you, it's a
feeling you cannot describe in words.'[2]

ADJUSTING TO THE BABY

As friends and family gather around the mother and baby, they are often
unaware of how overwhelmed the father may be feeling, and how crucial his back-up will be, so they can end up ignoring him. It is easy to
forget that girls have had more exposure to parenting – through play,
through observing the women around them, through magazine articles, television and film – whereas for most new dads this is brand new
territory. *Both* parents need assistance at this time. They need good
support from family, friends, and from each other.

> 'There seems to be a lot of support for mothers, possibly as there is
> a greater need, possibly as mothers may seek assistance, and fathers
> not doing so as they are supposed to be strong.' *Lee, 48*

There are many demands on fathers and mothers around the
birth of a baby. Unless fathers and mothers are aware of each other's
challenges, they can end up failing to appreciate what it is like for
one another at this time. Looking back to the birth of his children,

all now in their 30s, Nigel admitted, 'I didn't fully empathise with or understand the personal cost for Larissa — such things as tiredness, loss of independence, the crushing routines, or the demands of having three children in three years. It was to have a delayed, negative impact on my relationship with my wife.'

THE FATHER BOND

Men need time and space to develop a bond with their child, and need to trust their instincts, which while latent are very much present. Giving fathers this opportunity is essential for everyone involved. Every time we fail to assist and encourage them, we deny fathers the ability to express their tenderness and care.

> 'We all fumble. There's no right way to do it. But the paternal instinct is also very strong.' *Jared Fiel* [3]

> 'We were told after the birth there was a new mothers' class. I asked if fathers were welcome, and was told they were. I checked again before the first meeting that it was okay for me to go, and that they had the facilities for me to warm up expressed breast milk for Jasper. The whole thing was a disaster, because they changed the venue at the last minute, so there were no facilities. The woman leading the group had a name tag for everyone but me. She said I didn't need a name tag, because everyone knew who I was. It made me feel different. I just wanted a name tag like everyone else. So there I was with this very hungry baby, feeling very uncomfortable.' *Cameron, 32*

Recognising this need, Relationships Australia has now set up community programs for first-time fathers and their babies, and for primary-school children and their fathers, to get together and share information. The fathers who attend enjoy talking with each other and discovering new solutions to common problems. The program is going well, and the dads who have participated are now developing their own relationships with other fathers outside the program. As dads engage with their kids, they engage with their community and can enjoy this wider support, which in turn helps boost their confidence as fathers.[4]

Because previous generations of fathers were only expected to be breadwinners – and because this was all they were thought capable of – we can end up assuming that's all dads have to offer. Increasingly younger fathers are determined to prove that fathers and mothers can be equally nurturing and able to care for their children. Studies show that when an infant cries, a father's blood pressure rises to the same level as the mother's, and that when they are left to respond *directly* to their baby, fathers are equally able to understand what their baby wants, and are able to deal with it.[5]

FATHERS *DO* CARE

Part of the reluctance to involve fathers more fully in parenting comes from people not realising the depth of feeling most fathers have for their babies. It's interesting to learn that when their baby is born, men's testosterone levels drop. It is thought this also enhances their ability to nurture.[6] When asked, one man I spoke with described his feelings for his new baby as 'a violent kind of love, I feel so protective'. When men are allowed to express their feelings for their children, an extraordinary connection between father and child can develop from very early on.

'It used to be just me that I had to think about, now Evie is always at the front of my mind. I used to go surfing for half the day or a day

222

without thinking and now, after a couple of hours, I'm itching to get back and see what she's up to.' *Joel Parkinson, professional surfer*[7]

'My son is a joy to watch as he develops. Even when he is upset, he is just soooo cute. Even when he is crying, and I am rocking him in his cot for an hour, he is still cute. My feeling is that I'm his dad, and I will ensure he is looked after and comfortable. The song "He ain't heavy, he's my brother" comes to mind.' *Lee, 48*

> *When men are allowed to express their feelings for their children, an extraordinary connection between father and child can develop from very early on.*

In *Birth of a Father*, Martin Greenberg describes taking his tiny son out for walks. 'I talked to him about things we saw – about the sky, the ocean, the trees, the birds. And I told him what I was feeling, when I was happy and when I was sad. When Jonathan smiled and cooed in return, I felt that he somehow understood and accepted me in spite of my faults; and I felt elated by this unique sharing. At times like these I knew that he was very much aware of my presence . . . It was as if Jonathan was the door, the entryway, to my experiencing a new and different aspect of myself.'[8] An important part of letting fathers in to parenting is allowing them time on their own with their children, so they too can develop a level of intimacy.

'You will learn many things as you experience the journey that is fatherhood. It is a long journey of self discovery that can only be precipitated by the demand of having another human being's welfare totally dependent on you.' *Jay Turley*[9]

FATHERHOOD AND WORK

After the baby arrives, working life reasserts itself. Many women complain about how hard it is to combine motherhood and work, and to have to pretend they're not mothers while they are at work. Fathers often face the same dilemmas. To his dismay, Duncan Fisher suddenly realised he was expected to go back to work 'almost as if nothing had happened'.[10] The good news is that men are now fighting back, and making more informed choices about work, which are enabling them to be the kind of fathers they want to be.

Rarely does society acknowledge all the precious moments fathers miss out on to ensure their children receive the nurturing and support their income helps provide. 'By being a working parent you basically agree to miss your child's first steps, and virtually guarantee them a stronger bond with the stay-at-home parent,' Trevor, 30, pointed out. By working Trevor knows he helps ensure his kids are able to grow up in the most affectionate and supportive environment possible, and that they are well cared for.

> *Men are now fighting back, and making more informed choices about work, which are enabling them to be the kind of fathers they want to be.*

While it is assumed that spending long amounts of time away from one's family is part of what being the breadwinner is all about, increasingly Generation X fathers are choosing to draw the line. 'The commitment of the work/life/family balance is integrated into the work styles of Gen Xers,' points out demographics expert Julie Coates. 'While they are no less motivated to succeed, Gen Xers define success as including success at home and in life, as well as at work. The demands for flexi-time, family leave for fathers as well as mothers when a child is born or adopted, and time to attend children's school performances and teacher conferences are increasingly being met by employers.'[11] Even where organisations are less than supportive of parental roles, new fathers are choosing to draw their own line in the sand.

Jared Fiel was a newspaper editor when his first baby came along. 'I wanted to adjust my day so I wouldn't need to work awful hours every day, 2 p.m. to 2 a.m., but my boss wouldn't allow it, so I had to head to the dark side – public relations!'[12] Making this choice was tough for Jared, but he wasn't going to allow his experience of fatherhood to be jeopardised by working impossible hours.

Work isn't the escape many assume it to be for fathers. They too now want far more in their life. In a recent American workforce survey 82 per cent of men aged 20 to 39 put family at the top of their list; 71 per cent aged 20 to 39 said they would give up some of their pay for more time with their family. 'What we're now seeing is a transformation between generations and gender,' observes Paula Rayman, director of the Radcliffe Public Policy Center, and principal investigator of this study. 'Young men are beginning to replicate women's sensibilities, instead of women in the workforce trying to be more like the men.'[13]

In this same survey 96 per cent of the men and women felt that parents should share equally in the care of their children. There is still some way to go for fathers to be given more respect at work, however, partly because parenting in general is still largely a taboo subject for men to discuss there. 'When we interview men about work–family issues the whole thing blows,' says Professor Don Edgar. 'They spill forth a litany of family conflict, marital unhappiness, seething resentment against unfair expectations, and dislike of the male games so many of their colleagues play.'[14]

One of the difficulties for fathers and mothers at work are the role models the working world chooses to promote, which allow little focus on life outside work, let alone how people combine work and their family. In a recent article, journalist and working mother Deirdre Macken shared her experience around children and work, commenting, 'If you're at work, children are only tolerated in picture frames on the desk.'[15]

The way we represent work in the media doesn't help. 'Business magazines were (and still are) full of hero worship stories about "hard-nosed" executives who had to take the "hard line",' points out Daniel Petre, a father and former managing director of Microsoft Australia. 'We rarely gain an understanding of what sort of manager such people are or what sort of parent, spouse or friend they are . . . Often these heroes had discarded their responsibilities to their children and spouses; they had brought to many companies a culture of fear and intimidation and work obsession.'[16]

STAY-AT-HOME DADS

Some men are taking their parental role further by opting to be full-time dads. While these men are still a minority, they are gaining ground. When I spoke with stay-at-home fathers I was impressed by how dedicated they can be. Hogan is the proud father of three boys, two of whom are now in their teens. Like most parents, when he started out Hogan had to grapple with the basics. 'I had to learn how to hold, feed, dress, calm and nurture my first child during his early childhood years. As time passed, caring for the next two children became second nature.'[17]

Cameron, 32, is a stay-at-home dad to three-year-old Jasper. 'At first the hardest thing was Jasper's intensity. Now I'm really confident with Jasper. I can hold onto myself in the face of challenges. I'm the "go-to" parent, and I love that. Belinda now looks to me as to how to do stuff.' Making this choice is huge for men, not only in terms of their career and in how they are viewed, but because what they are doing is seen as being way out of the square. 'Initially Belinda and I mixed and matched being at home, with part- and full-time paid work. Now I'm full-time at home,' Cameron explained.

Dealing with the reactions of family and friends proved to be one of the biggest challenges at first. 'I had a very intense reaction from my mother when I announced I was leaving paid work,' Cameron admitted. 'She said I could end up really struggling. She asked what was going to happen to my career, or what would happen if our relationship broke up. But Dad said, "If you're happy, then that's the way to go." Since then he's confessed to me how much he wanted to be home when we were little.'

'I am able to serve as a positive role model for boys whose fathers work long hours and travel a lot, due to the nature of their job. And for the children who come from divorced households and don't have fathers in their lives, I am able to serve as a surrogate father.' *Hogan Hilling, founder of Proud Dads Inc*[18]

As with most full-time carers, these dads have had to find their way beyond the inevitable isolation an at-home parent faces. Some find full-time parenting easier than others. Not all at-home mothers are keen to let these fathers in. Michael, a 50-year-old father of two, talks of 'the occasional snub from mums in the playground, who think they recognise us from the sex offender registry, or wonder why we're not making a buck like their own husbands'.

Hogan has found his way beyond these complications by taking an active part in get-togethers with mothers. 'Many stay-at-home mums, who I meet for coffee or pot-luck luncheons at their homes, enjoy having me around. One mother said, "You bring a perspective on fatherhood that I never realised before. Thanks to you I now understand my husband a lot better."[19]

What dads have to offer

BEHIND THE ROUGH-AND-TUMBLE

For many men, fatherhood is their most significant achievement. Yet in spite of this, society remains nervous about letting fathers into the parenting process. Perhaps this is due in part to the way fathers behave with children. Certainly fathers are not as focused on ironed clothes and clean faces, and their play is more chaotic and rough-and-tumble, but as we will see, this may not be such a bad thing. Fathers have a lot to offer, but they need positive support to be the kind of parents they long to be. 'It's hard for fathers,' says Adrienne Burgess in *Fatherhood Reclaimed*, 'because they don't know what's expected of them in a concrete way.'[1]

> 'Many fathers are feeling alone and confused. The vast majority of fathers want to be at the birth of their children, they have dreams for their children, they want to be the best fathers they can be. They are under enormous pressure to be the engaged loving father and partner, a provider, protector and all-round super hero.' *Colin George, The Fatherhood Project*[2]

Clinical psychologist Ronald Levant agrees, pointing out that often men don't get involved around the house because they are constantly criticised or supervised by their partners.[3] This makes life particularly difficult for new fathers, who are already apprehensive about what is expected of them, and want desperately to do the right thing by their partner and new baby. When men are left to supervise kids, often they initially don't have the patience and experience mothers possess. Yet once they learn to *relax* into the role, they can begin to enjoy it and to feel they too are contributing to the lives of their little ones.

'It seems like it's more okay for dads to be involved later on. Like, mums can handle the kids while they're young, but once they're teenagers, then it's up to Dad. This sets men up. They're meant to troubleshoot, but many don't have the strength of relationship to do this, because the father hasn't a hard-wired bond with his kids from early on.' *Cameron, 32*

HOW KIDS BENEFIT FROM PLAY WITH DAD

The way fathers interact with their children provides the children with significant opportunities for development that they might not otherwise get. It's almost as if children sense this. Often kids prefer to play with Dad, because it's a freer experience. Dads do tend to be more spontaneous, and will often play with their child very differently every time they interact. 'It's also more arousing, so that you get an awful lot of stimulation, and it's often accompanied by a great deal of laughter and enjoyment,' explains Michael Lamb. 'There's quite a number of studies that have pointed to the fact that fathers engage in more playful "companion" types of interaction with their children, whereas mothers' interaction is less playful and a little bit more focused, a little bit more containing, less likely to rouse children.'[4] Initially mothers may not see any value in unstructured play, but once they become aware there are real benefits in it, they can begin to relax and appreciate what play with Dad has to offer.

'A baby's brain processes daddy differences as if it were building a complex jigsaw puzzle. The more successful a baby feels about each piece of information, the more the baby wants to keep adding on the new pieces. In other words, novel experiences with Dad build a baby's ability to anticipate certain events.' *Kyle Pruett* [5]

Kyle Pruett believes that fathers have a major role to play not only in helping build a baby's brainpower, but in assisting children with social interactions. 'In my own research I've found that when fathers are as prominent in their children's lives as their mothers are, children learn to negotiate two important, separate and different relationships. Having a distinct relationship with both a father and a mother from an early age equips children to deal with the broader, more diverse range of people they'll meet in the future.'[6]

THE IMPACT OF WORK

Many fathers don't have the luxury of spending a great deal of time with their kids, but they long to do so. Most fathers not only need to work, they have to expend serious time and energy on their job to ensure they remain employed so their family is secure. This creates for fathers very real pressures that are often taken for granted, as are the demands work places on them. 'Recent research in the US indicates that the increased time spent at work by American male executives means that, on average, even though they will retire at the same age as their fathers, they will in fact have worked up to ten years longer. This is due to the ever-lengthening working week,' says father and former managing director of Microsoft Australia, Daniel Petre.[7]

> 'Most dads would like to spend as much time with their children as women do. However, there is always the assumption that in the early stages the father will work full-time, and the mother will look after the children. I think most women encourage this stereotype, even though they do not like to admit it.' *Evan, 27*

It is time fathers were acknowledged for the nurturing they bring to their families as a result of the long hours they often work. Juggling home and work is not easy for anyone, and men can come to feel like strangers in their families when we fail to understand what they are attempting to achieve. This in turn can contribute to a father's lack of confidence as a parent, and to his reluctance to get involved with his kids once he does get home. 'In our world, a father feels unclear about his role as a man and father, forced to be gone at work, then exhausted and feeling guilty when he's home,' says family therapist Michael Gurian. 'He takes on less of a role at home, because he must take on an overwhelming role away from home.'[8]

The way fathers are often portrayed in ads and films and on television doesn't help. The stereotype of the lovable, incompetent father further undermines the important role fathers play. Dads don't have to be around all the time to leave their mark. What is important is that when they are present, their interactions with their children are meaningful. Mothers can help support fathers by letting go the reins a little. When mothers do this, they get a break, and fathers have the chance to get closer to their children in their own way.

When dads are 'let in', they can provide their children with a tangible sense of strength and safety, quite distinct from all the wonderful things mothers provide their children.

Fathers can take the need to provide too far, assuming that by loading their kids up with material possessions, they are giving their kids what they most need. Marketers work hard to give fathers the impression that this is what being a good father is all about, but the facts don't support this. A national competition was launched in Britain in the lead-up to Father's Day 2004, where primary school children were encouraged to talk about what they most enjoyed doing with their dad. This competition showed that it wasn't expensive holidays, computers or bikes that kids wanted, so much as time playing football, chatting at bedtime, being helped with homework, messing about, being cooked for, attending the mosque together, or going shopping.[9]

'A lot of us worry that being a good dad means paying for the latest new computer game or toy. It puts pressure on us to work harder, when in fact our children most want us involved in activities that cost nothing more than time.' *Duncan Fisher, Fathers Direct* [10]

A FATHER'S TOUCH LINGERS

When dads are 'let in', they can provide their children with a tangible sense of strength and safety, quite distinct from all the wonderful things mothers provide their children. One of my best childhood memories is of lying against my father's chest and feeling his deep Scottish voice reverberating through me as he talked or read me a story. It felt to me like the safest place in the world.

When talking with men of all ages I was fascinated to learn of their most significant recollections of their dads. McKenzie, now 49, didn't see his father much in his formative years, but his dad still managed to leave a lasting impression. He described his father as one of the last great adventurers. 'We would see him in between great adventures. So generally we didn't see all that much of him, even if we were travelling with him during these times. He always returned with big magical, worldly stories that seemed quite exciting to me at the time.' Now 61, Morris remembers when he was little his dad would always take him to the bathroom in the middle of the night: 'He would walk me out on his bare feet, so my feet wouldn't touch the cold linoleum.'

> *Dads don't need constant supervision,*
> *but they do need support and space.*

Today fathers are getting more involved, so even richer inter-actions are taking place. Although Owen is a busy IT executive, he takes his boys Mike and James camping. They had their first trip when Mike was two-and-a-half and still in nappies, and James was four. Other fathers showed interest and now Owen takes groups of up to fourteen dads and their kids, aged between 3 and 14, camping. He still takes his two kids away by himself. 'My boys help with the tent, and blow up their mats. They now play act camping together at home.' Owen goes crab-hunting and kite-flying with his boys as well. They also enjoy bus rides and building things in the shed, as well as bike-riding, and assembling model cars and planes. 'Then there's family activities with Mum – picnics, boating, and bike rides,' he explained.

'I have witnessed great acts of compassion and generosity by fathers towards their children and the children of others. Fatherhood is an opportunity for men to offer their substantial gifts to our children and our communities as mentors and fathers. When fathers develop these support and mentoring networks, we shall see a cultural change occur like no other.' *Colin George, The Fatherhood Project*[11]

Dads don't need constant supervision, but they do need support and space. When they are encouraged to develop their own rituals with their children, they can come up with some highly creative and worthwhile activities that will enhance their relationship with their kids.

Boys and their dads

DOES A LACK OF EMOTION MEAN AN ABSENCE OF LOVE?

Dads interact with their kids quite differently from mums. While some dads mightn't be as skilled at articulating their love for their kids, it doesn't mean they don't care. What is important is that dads are encouraged to be active fathers rather than onlookers – when dads are encouraged to have a fuller relationship with their kids, and to fully express what they think and feel, everyone benefits. Dads also need to know how much they mean to their kids. Nick's father had always wanted him to be a doctor, and was far from happy when Nick decided to take a different path. Finally he accepted Nick's decision, and wrote Nick a card, telling him how proud he was of him. 'The following day, my birthday, he died,' Nick told me. 'I was always grateful we hadn't parted with a gap between us.'

A BOY'S FATHER HUNGER

When I was at a gathering recently, a writer, now in his 50s, informed everyone present that his father had finally told him he loved him. The experience was clearly life-changing. Although I was initially sceptical

236

of the 'father hunger' that men talk of, the many interviews I have had with men proved my scepticism was ill-founded. For Father Dave Smith, a lack of a father is one of the biggest issues for the disaffected boys he works with.

'My father died when I was seven years old. That "father hunger" has stayed with me until this day. Being a father is my most important job. It's a humbling, confronting and joyful adventure. There is no blueprint.' *Cormac, 43*

Tragically, far too many men have been physically and / or emotionally absent from their sons' lives, and significant moments have slipped past. Often we don't realise how complex and fragile the relationship between father and son is and how easily it can be fractured. When a boy's lack of relationship with his father is not dealt with during his early years, often he will have little or no meaningful interaction with his father as an adult. Psychologist Steve Biddulph estimates, 'Thirty per cent of men today don't speak to their father. Thirty per cent have a "prickly" or hostile and difficult relationship. Thirty per cent go through the motions of being a good son . . . less than ten per cent of men are friends with their father and see them as a source of emotional support.'[1]

'The issues of the boys I deal with come back to their father time and again. It's boys who don't know who their father is, boys whose father has died, or boys whose father is absent that struggle the most.' *Father Dave Smith, Fight Club*[2]

Often when the importance of dads spending time with their sons is brought up, it is assumed boys need to be with their father simply to learn what it means to be a man. Recent research reveals that while it is important fathers share *masculine* values with their sons, sharing warmth and intimacy is equally important,[3] and certainly my interviews with men backed this up. The warmth and love a father gives his son is significant, because it helps provide an important base from which a boy can learn how to be a positive, well-rounded man.

> 'My dad is the old school, sort of tough and uncompromising. He doesn't talk about his feelings, it's all very superficial. We communicate through sport. We might sit down and watch a game together, but it's all small talk. We may only speak a couple of sentences.' Robert, 30

There is no better person than a boy's dad to teach him how to express himself, how to test his own strength, how to be confident, how to win and to lose. By being around their dads, boys also learn about acceptable behaviour, and what will happen if they don't behave appropriately. It is much easier for boys when they can learn these essential life skills in a safe and supportive environment, rather than by trial and error.

> *While it is important fathers share masculine values with their sons, sharing warmth and intimacy is equally important.*

It's not just loving, supportive words boys need from their dads, but shared experiences. When fathers are physically and/or emotionally absent, boys feel abandoned, cast adrift. What concerns me is how widespread the absence of fathers from boys' lives is. When thinking about his father, Ray, 50, recalled he was always either at work or in hospital with bouts of ill health. Nigel, 72, was never close to his father: 'I didn't know him, and he didn't understand a son who hadn't shared similar experiences as himself.' Doug, 52, experienced pretty much the same. 'We were not close,' he said of his father. 'We shared no activities or meaningful conversations.'

'I know that my father had a very strong father, who was very domineering, who wasn't there a great deal of the time. That probably brought on the way he treated me.' *Adrian, 35*

When boys don't experience their dad as a nurturer, they have no real sense of men as nurturers. This pattern has been repeated over the generations, and it is time for it now to be broken. 'Many of us have a place inside that is empty, yet consists of deep, pent-up and bruised emotions that are due to hidden societal expectations,' states psychologist Frank Cardelle. 'These emotions are also composed of longing for the loving, close contact we desire from our fathers.'[4]

When fathers create time for boys, often they give their boys far more than they imagine. As Kyle Pruett points out, 'A boy whose father has bathed and fed him knows that nurturing is something dads do. And when it's his turn to be a dad, he'll think of nurturing as part of his masculine identity, and he'll honour it.'[5]

All boys long to be validated, and there are many ways this can happen. I read recently about John Reiss, a dad with an inoperable brain tumour, who just before he died wrote his four-year-old son Felix three letters – for Felix's thirteenth, eighteenth and nineteenth birthdays. In these letters John told Felix how much he cared about him, and what he hoped for his son in the years ahead. The impact of these letters on Felix will no doubt be profound.[6] A dad doesn't have to be dying to do something meaningful for his son.

In the novel *Windmill Hill*, Paul and his father are not close, but one night while Paul is performing in his 'knockabout rock band', he catches sight of his father in the wings of the theatre. 'All I know,' he says, 'is that when he nodded to me, it felt like an ovation.'[7]

FATHERS ACHE TO BE LOVED

It's not just boys who yearn for love – this need for warmth and respect works both ways. As Steve Biddulph points out, just as sons hunger to experience closeness with their fathers, so fathers yearn for intimacy with their sons.[8] This was certainly the case for the men I spoke with. 'For a long time I felt pretty disconnected from the boys because of the divorce, but that gulf in recent years seems to be considerably mended,' Morris, 61, explained. 'The hugs that I ached for for so long now happen whenever we meet.' Recently Darren, 58, took me aside to tell me that he had received the most wonderful card from his grown stepson, which he found 'pretty moving'. In this card his stepson thanked him for being the closest thing to a father possible. Such gestures strike a deep place in a man's heart, making all the effort fathers invest in their children worthwhile.

'It is important to understand that although dads are good for children, children are also very good for the health and well-being of our fathers. Fathers need their kids.' *Colin George, The Fatherhood Project*[9]

'Every father, however much he puts on a critical or indifferent exterior, will spend his life waiting at some deep level to know that his son loves and respects him. He will spend his life waiting.' *Psychologist Steve Biddulph*[10]

Too often the barriers that have grown up between fathers and sons have been built on competition and misunderstanding. Adolescence can be especially trying for fathers and sons, as boys start to discover their own potential, and gain the physical strength they have longed for. This often coincides with the time when their fathers may be facing a mid-life crisis. As their sons grow more energetic and virile, fathers become aware of their own fading vitality, as their prospects fade, and they see that they are unlikely to realise many of the ambitions they held for their lives.

Academic Don Edgar agrees. He suggests the conflict between adolescents and their parents, especially their fathers, is often less about teenage rebellion than it is about the attitudes of their fathers. During the 1970s, while Don Edgar was researching adolescents and their fathers, he made some interesting discoveries. When the teenagers in the study were asked to agree or disagree with the statement, 'I take a positive attitude towards myself', over half the boys agreed, as did 41 per cent of the girls; only 7 per cent of their fathers agreed with this statement. An overwhelming 85 per cent of fathers disagreed with the statement, 'On the whole, I think I am quite a happy person.'

'These men were now in their mid-life, often stuck in boring jobs that gave them little satisfaction, and/or in marriages that had lost their gloss,' Don Edgar explains.[11] This is tough stuff for fathers and sons. But instead of rebuffing their sons, it is up to fathers to bridge this discomfort by establishing simple rituals they can do together that help warm each other's personal space.

'What an affront to them must be the exuberance and self-confidence of their teenage children. For youth, the world was their oyster, everything was possible, life had not yet played them too many losing cards; for their fathers, life had already closed in around them, their hopes had not been fulfilled, and envy of the life chances their children faced so cheerfully perhaps lay behind their gruff inability to handle any challenges to their parental authority.' *Don Edgar* [12]

SEEING FATHERS IN A NEW LIGHT

Men and boys need to understand so much more about themselves and each other. Only then will they realise that things are not always as they seem. One afternoon writer Yevrah Ornstein was thinking about his dad and the distance that had grown between them when he realised the only images that came to mind were *negative* moments they had shared. Realising these selective memories only helped reinforce his belief that his dad didn't love him, Yevrah wrote to his father about this. His dad wrote back, saying he wished to put the past behind them. 'The greatest surprise came when he revealed that he knew I had always believed this about him, and he just did not know what to do about it,' Yevrah relates in *From the Hearts of Men*. 'For the first time in my life my father became real to me, real in his admission of not knowing what to do, a fellow human being capable of confusion, hurt and feeling lost.' [13]

> The more the different generations of men understand each other, the more they will come to realise things are not always as they seem.

When dads can be real with their sons, they open up the way for them both to support each other, to be who they most long to be. Whatever situation dads find themselves in with their sons, it is important they allow themselves to be more open, more human, so they can make room for a more meaningful relationship to develop. When dads open up, their sons gain a much more realistic and richer view of what it is like to be a man.

ENCOURAGING GREATER UNDERSTANDING BETWEEN FATHERS AND SONS

One of the reasons dads and sons come to grief is that frequently they have very different expectations of each other. Increasingly the aspirations sons hold for their fathers are influenced by images drawn from television, movies and magazines, rather than from real life, while fathers are coming from the expectations they faced when growing up. As these expectations diverge, the likelihood of disappointment increases. When fathers and sons can let go of an idealised version of what they want from each other, they are then free to enjoy a more authentic relationship.

> 'When I was fifteen I couldn't believe how stupid my father was. When I was twenty I couldn't believe how much he had learned in just five years.' *Adam, 44*

Fathers do make mistakes, as do their boys. Like their sons, fathers need to be caught doing things right. Unless sons can do this, they become lost in the past. 'I began my life by being taken prisoner in my father's house,' says Tom Wingo in *The Prince of Tides*. But as Tom grows, he realises he too is powerful. 'I would begin my manhood by walking over him on my way out the door.' However Tom's journey doesn't stop there. 'My life did not really begin until I summoned the power to forgive my father for making my childhood a long march of terror.'[14]

Understanding what it is like to stand in each other's shoes helps bring perspective for fathers and sons. After hearing Robert Bly's poem 'At My Father's Wedding', writer Yevrah Ornstein realised for the first time what his father's life had actually been like. 'That my father had experienced incredible loneliness, that he didn't get what he wanted either. I realised that my father was a son too.'[15] There is

so much that fathers and sons can share. They have the capacity to
stretch each other's view of themselves and the world far beyond
what they thought possible.

> 'To encourage your child to be better than you are is important, but a
> lot of the older generation of males don't see it that way. If their child
> is doing better than they are, they get aggressive. It upsets them more
> than makes them proud. I always looked up to my father and thought,
> wouldn't it be great one day to be like he is. But he would say, "No,
> no, you're going to be better than I am," which I always thought was
> very, very nice.' *Adrian, 35*

WHEN FATHER–SON RELATIONSHIPS BREAK DOWN

When fathers and sons aren't close, hurt and misunderstanding can
so easily contaminate their relationship, causing the distance between
them to grow. The gap between generations has widened in recent
years, with the growth in technology and the rise of peer pressure.
Instead of feeling defeated, fathers need to find new ways to remain
relevant to their sons. Unless fathers are willing to work at this, it's
easy for boys to assume there is little their fathers can teach them.
This in turn makes boys more vulnerable to outside influences.

Today's boys are far more technologically literate and have greater
freedoms than in the past, but that doesn't make them more *mature*
or more able to make good decisions. All boys still need good male
role models. 'It is an argument for responsibility. It is an argument for
involvement,' psychologist Bill O'Hehir insists. 'It is an argument
for recognising the important role of the father in the family, which has
been lost.'[16] Just as dads need to work at their relationships with their
sons, they also need friends and family to help underpin their role.

Instead of feeling defeated, fathers need to find new ways to remain relevant to their sons.

MAINTAINING RESPECT

Whatever aspirations a father holds for his son, he must also respect his son's individuality and capability. Too many boys are sent to prestigious schools, or forced to take part in sports and other activities for which they have no interest or aptitude, purely to satisfy their father's ambitions. A personal friendship of mine failed when a father began pushing his nine-year-old son far beyond what he was capable of. Every time the child tried to explain his position, he was reminded of how much money was being poured into his schooling. This father wasn't interested in advice from friends, and lost several friendships as a result. These kinds of fathers do their sons few favours.

I learned recently of another young boy who was exhibiting extreme stress at school. After a while the teacher realised this boy was stressed because of the number of extra-curricular activities he was involved in. When this was pointed out to the child's father, his response was that he worked long hours in a high-stress job, and that he was simply conditioning his son to the realities of life. This might not have been so bad had his son not been seven years old.

'Boys need to be allowed to dream. You can't fulfil someone else's dreams. My childhood left me with a lack of confidence and self-belief. It's almost like you don't expect to be fulfilled. It takes time to change this – it doesn't happen overnight.' *Robert, 30*

Fathers can have an immense impact on their sons, and not always for good. Frequently fathers are unaware of how totally crushing critical remarks can be to their sons. The messages not to cry, to be a man, leave their mark. 'Even if the father perceives he's hurt his son, he often hasn't the skill to apologise, back down, communicate,' explains psychologist Toby Green.[17] Again this relates back to how boys are raised. When men are not brought up to recognise and articulate their emotions, they have little sensitivity for the feelings of others. Often these men will respond to difficult situations by withdrawing or with sudden, seemingly unprovoked expressions of anger, which sting their sons and leave them nowhere to go. If fathers don't learn how to articulate their concerns with care, successive generations of boys will continue to be emasculated, and they will emasculate others.

> *It is tragic when men cannot find meaningful ways to tell their sons all they hold in their hearts.*

A father's anger may be justified, but without an explanation, the prevailing memory for the child will be hurt and resentment. In *From the Hearts of Men* Yevrah Ornstein tells how he decided to join the Peace Corps.[18] When he spoke to his father about this, he was expecting his father's blessing. Instead Yevrah's father lashed out, leaving Yevrah feeling shocked. Yet once the situation had calmed down, his father explained that the thought of his son being thousands of miles away in a Third World country was too much, because if something went wrong he would be powerless to help. What a difference this explanation made for father and son.

It is tragic when men cannot find meaningful ways to tell their sons all they hold in their hearts. The men I spoke with who had angry or violent fathers talked of them with a mix of resentment and a deep sense of loss. Doug, 52, recalled his father as 'an angry man to be avoided. He seemed ignorant of my life.' Ray, 50, remembered his father's 'volatile anger and leather belt'. These and other men I spoke with weren't looking for perfect fathers, but for men who, even though they made mistakes and got mad now and then, were able to forge open, loving relationships with their sons.

> 'My father has always been caught up in his job. His family is secondary to the people he works with. He rings them every day, yet he finds it so hard to pick up the phone and ring me. It's eight months since I've had a call from him. He's too busy.' *Robert, 30*

DADS DOING THINGS DIFFERENTLY

I find it heartening that many grown men whose fathers were distant are determined to have a very different relationship with *their* kids. 'I think that it will be very interesting to see what the next generation of children will be like, as fathers are more open to communication about their feelings,' Adrian, 35, reflected. Fathers can be a lot more open with their sons, and those who are clearly get a lot more out of it. 'I am much more connected with my kids,' said Craig, a 58-year-old father of four grown kids. 'I know much more about them – how they feel, what they think. They have come to me with the most major issues they have had to face – from sex to buying houses, and continue to do so.'

> 'In this day and age it's okay to show your emotions. If our father and father's father showed any sign of emotion, it was considered a sign of weakness, or that they weren't male if they cried and openly hugged their children. It's a lot different now – I hope it is.' *Adrian, 35*

Ray, 50, has very few positive memories of his father, but he is determined to have a different relationship with his teenagers. 'I say, "I love you" every day, and really try never to miss. I spend time with them individually, both day-to-day and at events that are important to them. I talk to them about issues affecting the family, even if it is grown-up business.' David, 36, also has a very different parenting style from his father. 'I feel much closer to my sons than I think my dad ever felt with me,' he reflected. 'Don't get me wrong. My dad was wonderful. He tried to attend every one of my sports functions, and enjoyed taking my sister and I on outings to new places. But it was a much more superficial relationship than I feel I have with my boys. I hug them and they want me to. Not a day goes by that we don't tell each other that we love each other.'

'My dad did not play with me a lot when I was young. By contrast I play with our son. We roll on the floor. I push him up to the ceiling and he laughs. Watching him and hearing him laugh is great – it almost brings tears to my eyes.' *Lee, 48*

Fathers and daughters

DADDY'S LITTLE PRINCESS

Often dads enjoy a very different relationship with their daughters than with their sons. This relationship frequently contains a mixture of awe and protectiveness, and if it works well, it can be a wonderful experience for a father. He gets to play the hero, by providing for his daughter and shielding her from harm. To have a dad who is there for his daughter is a precious thing. My dad was always there for me, and left me with a very positive outlook towards men.

'As fathers we have a responsibility to protect our children, but there is, just by the nature of the human species, more instinctive protection of the daughter, a ferocious guardianship that might make dads feel like they're the knight in shining armour.' *Robin, 28*

'There is a "freshness" about a daughter, an innocence in the way that she sees the world, that makes me want to single-handedly make it a better place for her.' *Trevor, 30*

While most fathers love their daughters intensely, it can be hard for them to give their daughter sufficient space to develop in her own way. If dads are too protective, their daughters will end up feeling suffocated and resentful. Often daughters find it difficult to understand why their fathers are so protective, perhaps until they leave home and have a daughter of their own.

'You feel the need to protect daughters from the world, and especially from boys, because you know what you were like when you were young, so you end up on the porch with the shotgun. Even my little sister doesn't want to introduce any of her boyfriends to me.'
Adrian, 35

The difficulty for fathers is that they know the world, and they know men, and want desperately to keep their daughters safe from both. Irma Kurtz agrees. In *Malespeak* she suggests that for a father, his daughter is 'a pure container of all the female magic'. And aware of her vulnerability and potential, he feels duty-bound to protect his daughter 'from the brutal knowledge which must come in due course through the agency of another male.'[1] This makes a lot of sense.

'My oldest daughter tears me apart at the moment. Fathers feel so protective, it's difficult. I found pot in her room. She was suspended at school. I take a zero tolerance on that, whereas her mother turned around and decided she can drink a bit, and that if she wants to have sex, she can use a condom. I feel as if I'm standing on the bank watching her drown, and there's nothing I can do. I don't want to watch, and know I can't do anything. She's fifteen now, she's been like this since she was thirteen. I'm so disempowered and destroyed by it.' *Justin, 43*

Fathers are also special to daughters. They are generally the first man their daughter loves. With her father, a girl gets to explore the world of men. She can experience first-hand how men do things, what they like, and how they behave, talk and dress. When they have a good relationship with their father, daughters are able to grow up with a healthy male role model, which in turn makes them less vulnerable to men who are not. When fathers have positive relationships with the women in their lives, they help their daughters see how best to celebrate and navigate the differences between the sexes. Good fathers can be a wonderful anchor for their daughters as they seek to find their own place in the world.

'(My father) was the most faithful man a woman could ever have. Fighting all the way, he never once abandoned me, not even when I caused him pain. In the long run, my father was the making of me.'
Irma Kurtz [2]

WHAT HAPPENS TO GIRLS WHEN FATHERS AREN'T AROUND

Girls can suffer when they lack positive male role models in their formative years. Two recent long-term studies examined why among industrialised nations the United States and New Zealand have the highest and second-highest teen pregnancy rates respectively. Kenneth A. Dodge, director of the Center of Child and Family Policy at Duke University, and his colleagues discovered that girls with the highest rate of teenage sexual activity were those whose fathers left the family home before the girls turned six. Next were girls whose fathers left later on, followed by girls whose fathers remained at home.

The study also revealed that the American girls whose dads left home while they were small were approximately five times more likely to become pregnant as teenagers, while New Zealand girls in the same situation were approximately three times more likely to become pregnant in adolescence, than girls who had their dads at home. Among the many reasons for this, researchers suggest that girls in father-absent homes see mothers in and out of other relationships, and this, along with the destabilising effect of losing their father, causes these girls to be attracted to early and 'unstable bonds with men'.[3]

WHAT DAUGHTERS BRING THEIR FATHERS

There is much that a daughter can bring to her father's life. Daughters have the capacity to bring out tenderness their fathers might not even know they have. 'I was more open to give *emotional* support to my daughter than to my sons, possibly because I didn't have as many preconceived notions/expectations as to her future, as I did for my sons,' Nigel, 72, recalled. 'My relationship was more relaxed, and I was more able to be a friend, being more likely to show concern for her wellbeing rather than feeling let down if she didn't measure up to those "dreams" I had for her.'

Daughters are quick to learn that fathers are often easier to get around than mothers. 'I think as a father I tend to be more lenient with Lara and only take a hard line if absolutely necessary,' admitted Brian, 58. 'Lara is more helpful in domestic chores and more willing in general to help around the house, which clouds my judgement and makes me more acquiescent when it comes to being considered for extra funding for fashion, etc.'

'My daughter can still touch me like when she was born. On my fiftieth birthday she presented me with, amongst other things, all the notes I had written and put in her lunch box – the "I love you"s and "Hope you have a good day"s all came back in a rush.' *Ray, 50*

Being a father doesn't end when the kids leave home. It doesn't end when the kids get married and have their own kids, or reach middle age. While they might not talk about it, many fathers still hold their children close, feeling proud of them, concerned for them, hopeful for them, because that's what fathers do.

> 'Some day I know I'll be able to eat a meal while it's hot, watch a movie in silence, or go swimming without six bags of pool toys, but for now I try to relax and enjoy it. All of it, because it will be gone as suddenly as it came.' Jay Turley

Many men are surprisingly articulate about what being a dad means to them. 'I've learned a lot since I became a father,' says Jay Turley. 'I have become more protective, more self-reliant, more caring, gentler, stronger, and wiser. I attempt to provide my children with the image of a man, as I believe a man should be. This image keeps me from fighting with my wife as much as I used to. It forces me to fix the bookcase, and repair the bike tyre. It makes me, surly and reticent in the past, communicate with people, because I believe my children should. Some day I know I'll be able to eat a meal while it's hot, watch a movie in silence, or go swimming without six bags of pool toys, but for now I try to relax and enjoy it. All of it, because it will be gone as suddenly as it came.'[4]

> 'Being a dad has made me more in tune with the world and has given me closer attention to detail. In turn, that has made me a better writer, a better human being, because I have another outlet in which to express my emotions.' Trevor, 30

> 'Fatherhood is by far the best thing I have ever done in my life. It's also the one I work hardest at and am most concerned I get it right.' Ray, 50

Out on a limb

DADS UNDER SUSPICION

At a time when many of today's dads want to take a more active role in their children's lives, new challenges have emerged. It is good to watch men becoming hands-on with their kids, and to see how much everyone benefits as a result. Yet by getting closer to their children, fathers do also make themselves vulnerable to accusations of sexual abuse. Growing concern in the community about male sexual predators poses some very real challenges for men in general, and for dads in particular.

Some fathers are so affected by this growing fear of being seen as a perpetrator of abuse that they are reluctant to play with their kids – to bathe them or read them bedtime stories – just in case these gestures are misconstrued. Few are brave enough to interact with other people's children, even if they are a much-loved uncle or close family friend.

Dads are right to be concerned, because they are under close scrutiny. Many department stores routinely allow mothers into their son's dressing room, but as far back as the mid 1980s, fathers of young children were often not permitted into dressing rooms. When challenged about their policy, American department store JC Penney stated: 'The public perception is that men are voyeurs and molesters.'[1] In his book *Altered Mates*, journalist Tom Morton revealed a 1995 Qantas flight directive stating that unattended children were not to be seated next to male passengers. The following year male flight attendants on Qantas were no longer to take care of unaccompanied child passengers.[2]

> 'It almost makes you feel bad to be male, or to show some affection to children, or to play with them, because you think, "Are other people thinking I'm a weirdo or a paedophile or something?" If you were at the park on a nice day and saw a mum and her child, you would immediately have a positive reaction. Whereas if you saw a toddler with a man doing somersaults down the hill, it's like, "Who's that man, and where's the supervising mother?"' *Alex, 35*

We have all been in social situations where an enthusiastic child throws themselves at one of the men in the hope of a hug or a squeeze, and have witnessed the sudden nervousness felt by all the adults. This growing watchfulness doesn't leave the average dad much room to move, let alone men in general. Our children do need the best protection we can provide, but as academic Danae Clark points out, fathers have 'Come to represent all that is powerful, all that is potentially dangerous . . . In our urgent desire to fight off the patriarchy or to kill off the patriarchal father, we have killed off all "fatherness" and left our own fathers behind.'[3] It is good we are more vigilant about protecting children, but we need to encourage the men we trust to take a more active part in our children's lives. The only way we can do this is by inviting them back in.

WHEN FATHERS ARE FALSELY ACCUSED

One of the many challenges for some separated and divorced men is an allegation of abuse levelled at them by an angry partner. 'If the mother makes an allegation that the father has displayed violence (physical, sexual or psychological), the court is likely to limit him to supervised access, even if there is no substantiation that he has ever been guilty of what he is accused,' points out Felicity Goodyear-Smith, clinician and educator specialising in sexual assault. 'In many cases these actions have been taken without any corroborative evidence that the father has ever maltreated his child, [and are] often based solely on the testimony of the child's mother.'[4]

Apart from the patent injustice many fathers now face due to false abuse allegations, their children are then denied access to them at a time when these kids are at their most vulnerable. Not all allegations of abuse are false, but this has become a growing trend that has serious implications for all involved. Child support agencies are even more overworked as a result of false claims, as each allegation sets in motion a detailed procedure to establish its truthfulness.

Genuine cases of endangered children are increasingly being held up because of the growth in false allegations. In his 1987 report to the Select Committee on Children, Youth and Families, Douglas Besharov, the first director of the United States National Center on Child Abuse and Neglect, claimed that 65 per cent of all reports were unfounded after investigation, compared with 35 per cent of allegations in 1975. The further tragedy is that even if these fathers are found innocent, the stain of these allegations often remains with them.[5]

WHEN CHILDREN ARE ABUSED

Adults do need to be vigilant around children, and sexual abuse is not to be ignored. However, when men are seen first and foremost as predators rather than nurturers, their lives, and the lives of their children, and other children they interact with, are greatly diminished. It is important to have the full picture. Felicity Goodyear-Smith points out that neglect, not sexual abuse, is by far the most common form of child abuse. 'In 1994 about one million cases of child mistreatment were substantiated in the United States. Nearly half of these were cases of neglect, over a quarter were physical abuse, about ten per cent were sexual abuse, and the remainder were cases of emotional or other unspecified abuse.'

She also cites a large Canadian study, which examined 46 683 cases of child abuse, of which 49 per cent of mothers and 31 per cent of fathers were found to have committed some kind of abuse. In this same study, mothers had perpetrated 79 per cent of proven emotional abuse cases, and 85 per cent of proven neglect of their kids.[6] The purpose for mentioning these figures is not to underplay sexual abuse, or to denigrate the role of mothers, but to understand that child abuse comes in many forms, and that *all* forms of abuse need to be taken into account.

SETTING THE RECORD STRAIGHT

Some fathers do sexually abuse their children. This is unacceptable, but what does this mean in real terms? Certainly not all sexual abusers are fathers. Current research indicates that where sexual abuse is present in the home, stepfathers are far more likely than biological fathers to be involved. One study found that stepfathers were five times more likely to commit this offence,[7] while another study suggests stepfather abuse could be as high as seven times that of natural fathers.[8]

These figures are significant, yet they still don't represent the full picture, because not all stepfathers are predators. Many wonderful men take on other people's kids and do their best to provide them with a positive, nurturing environment. Surely the way forward is providing *greater* education for children, while at the same time encouraging fathers and stepfathers to be fully involved, positive, integrated members of their families.

Dads and divorce

WHEN DAD LEAVES HOME

Fathers are facing new levels of isolation, as increasingly relationships fall apart. While around 65 per cent of separations are now initiated by women, regardless of why a relationship has broken down generally it's the father who moves on, because someone has to move out and because they don't want the children's lives disrupted. Once fathers are on their own, many feel they have nothing to offer their families, when in fact they still have an important role to play in protecting their kids and helping them develop. The overwhelming loss many fathers experience is often paralysing, causing them to go into a permanent state of retreat. Many of the men I spoke with were distraught about their situation. Some cried. Others were barely able to keep their anguish under control.

'A father's approach to separation is coloured by his sense of loss. He is acutely aware of his personal loss at no longer sharing the daily lives of his kids. He has a social sense of loss, because everyone around him keeps urging him to move on. And he also experiences a structural loss as the courts and child support mechanisms seem biased against men.' *Belinda Pascoe, counsellor*[1]

Society does little to help men move beyond this paralysis, because it still tends to view separated fathers as superfluous, apart from their ongoing financial contribution. Many fathers don't fight for custody because they believe they're unlikely to get it, and because they believe the children's mother has far more to offer their kids. Often it is the absence of their children from their daily lives that these dads find most agonising. But because few understand this, they get little assistance with their overwhelming sense of loss. 'My brother divorced years ago,' explained Mick, who is now also divorced. 'I was no support to him, because I didn't understand what it was like for him.'

> Even though most breakdowns are caused by couples drifting apart, still the common view is that a separated or divorced dad can't be any good.

The bad press separated and divorced dads receive makes it almost impossible for them to be heard. Not only is their situation largely ignored by society, their valuable role as a dad is rarely taken into account. 'It seems unbelievable that we're having to mount a case that *dads matter*,' states professor of psychology Sanford Braver. 'Sometimes even to speak in defense of fathers is taken by some as the equivalent of bashing mothers.'[2]

WHEN MEN LOSE THEIR CHILDREN

While most people agree that having fathers around for their kids is a good thing, this just isn't happening for many children. In 1997 it was estimated that around 1 million Australian children under 18 were living with one natural parent and had a parent living elsewhere; 88 per cent of these children lived with their mother. Almost one-third of these children rarely or never saw their other parent; of those who did see them, 34 per cent never stayed overnight.[3]

Depriving separated and divorced fathers of a meaningful, ongoing relationship with their children isn't a great incentive for these men to remain active fathers, let alone be good fathers. As Michael Lamb points out, when fathers aren't around, the economic, social and emotional back-up they provide for their families falls away, or is inappropriately filled by others.[4] While abusive fathers forfeit their right to close involvement with their children, the majority of men aren't in this category.

'Most males in this situation become so disenchanted by the unfairness of the situation that they simply walk out on their responsibility. They then have to suffer the humiliation of being labeled as non-caring parents.' *Bill O'Hehir, psychologist*[5]

A lack of access to their children means these men are shut out of the many significant events in their children's lives. Not only do they miss out on the day-to-day nuances, frequently they have little input into schooling and other major decisions. The loneliness and the loss of the family routine are often achingly painful for these fathers, as many are excluded from Christmas and birthday gatherings, and don't even experience the joy of a call or a card on Father's Day or their birthday.

Even though most breakdowns are caused by couples drifting apart, still the common view is that a separated or divorced dad can't be any good. This view is so prevalent that often fathers come to believe this.

Children who do have access to their father benefit on many levels, as long as they are kept free of any conflict their parents might be experiencing. Fruitful ways of handling joint custody can be found. When fathers help make this work, they do their kids a great favour.

'Most separated dads are never told they are important. What men need most at this time is to have their role as a father validated – to know they're of value to their kids, even though the family has changed.' *Ray Lenton, family group counsellor* [6]

Family doctor Felicity Goodyear-Smith agrees. 'Children are much less likely to come to harm if they can maintain ongoing relationships with both parents,' she says. 'Regular contact between fathers and children should be actively encouraged and supported by our social service and the courts.'[7]

'My parents separated when I was fourteen. My sister went with Mum and I stayed with Dad. I would ride my bike to see Mum every weekend. My sister visited Dad fairly often as well. Every couple of years my sister and I would swap the parent with whom we lived. We did this from fourteen to twenty-three years of age, when I moved out to share with friends. My parents didn't seem to mind the "swapping" my sister and I did.' *Lee, 48*

ARE FATHERS *ALWAYS* TO BLAME?

There is no doubt that when families break up, children are extremely vulnerable. Society tends to blame absent dads for the problems their children then face. But not all fathers are absent by choice. Some separated dads simply don't have the money to support their family.

Many dads end up living in boarding houses or caravans, or they become homeless. Research shows that the least involved separated fathers tend to be those on low incomes who enjoy little if any wider back-up, while dads on higher incomes with better education are far more able to sort out workable co-parenting arrangements.[8]

'There's not that many dads that walk away from contact with their kids unless they have to. What does get to these men is the financial burden, the constant harassment and the false allegations. When they see how this is tearing their kids apart, then some do walk away. I had a client the other day that was moving away. He admitted it was a terrible thing, but he just didn't see he had an option as the abuse towards him continued to escalate, and it was affecting his kids. He was heartbroken.' *Ray Lenton, family group counsellor*[9]

According to Sanford Braver, author of *Divorced Dads*, unemployment is the single most important reason why divorced dads fail to pay child support.[10] In Australia unemployment among separated fathers can be up to three times the national average. Just because a non-custodial father can't pay child support doesn't mean he no longer cares. Some dads do let everyone down, but many struggle to remain part of their kids' lives, even when they have few resources. It is hard to imagine how distressed caring dads must feel in this situation. But because most men keep their thoughts to themselves, few of us will ever know the depth of embarrassment or despair these men feel at such times.

FACING UP TO THE FALLOUT

Whenever we consider divorce settlements and alimony, we tend to think of the top end of town, but this is about as far from reality as you can get for most men. Yet regardless of his income, a father is still expected to support two households: his new one and that of his family.

'When I had the children over school holidays, I had to wash their clothes every night when they went to bed, so they had clean clothes in the morning, because I didn't have the money for more clothes.'
Ryan, 50

Women and children are also financially vulnerable after break-ups. Children may still need full-time care at home, and their mother may only be able to earn a fraction of what their father earned. That is why women may receive up to 65–70 per cent of joint assets.[11] However, what is rarely taken into account is that the cost of this support can be inordinately high for some men. In a recent study it was found that the most disadvantaged men were those living by themselves, or as solo dads, and that one-quarter of sole fathers had incomes below the poverty line.[12]

'What we have to remember is that around 80 per cent of men involved with the Child Support Agency earn less than $30000 a year. You can barely support a family on this when you're all together. It's impossible to support your family when you're apart, so you end up living in poverty.' *Ray Lenton, family group counsellor*[13]

Governments do need a formal structure for child support payments, but what doesn't help is that dads in Australia pay child support *after* tax, while mothers pay no tax on the child support money they receive. Non-custodial fathers feel as if they are in a no-win situation, because the child support assessment is based on their gross income, and they have little if any input into how their child support contributions are spent, even when they suspect their children are not benefiting from their payments.[14]

> Access remains a key to encouraging fathers to support their families, not just financially, but in many other practical and positive ways.

'I know one dad who ended up in tears talking to [the] Child Support Agency. He's been told he has to go out and get a second job and find another $45 000 to pay his child's maintenance. He had given the Child Support Agency evidence he can't work as an executive anymore because his health has broken down after the marriage finished. He works as a manual labourer now. They have the medical evidence, but they're saying that's not enough.' *Justin, 43*

THE REALITY OF BEING A DIVORCED MAN

Most divorced men aren't leading bold, exciting lives free of care and responsibility. Many struggle to pay the bills, making it hard for them to get out and create a new life, let alone form new relationships, because they simply don't have the money. 'The process of dispossession is usually more painful for men than is generally understood. For the man who leaves, his prospects, unless he is wealthy, are rather bleak. The average man will probably live in a bedsit or one-bedroom unit to begin with, with few friends and scant furnishings,' says family therapist Terry Colling. 'For some men, the prospect of picking over the family's possessions is too hurtful and distasteful, so they literally leave with their clothes and little else.'[15]

'We're a lot more bonded to our kids than people think we are.' *Ryan, 50*

According to Bruce Smyth, research fellow in the Family and Marriage Program at the Australian Institute of Family Studies, one of the reasons information on the lives of separated dads remains scant is because many are living as boarders or in share accommodation in boarding houses or hostels, or in caravan parks.[16] Others have no alternative but to return home to live with their parents. Some end up on the street.

> 'I remember standing in the small two-bedroom apartment, holding an eight-by-ten picture of my son and daughter. The apartment was relatively empty, with sparse furniture and blank walls. I think that it was at that moment when I began to fully realize the complexities of being a divorced parent. I missed my children terribly. There were so many questions and concerns.' *Liam*[17]

The desperation many men feel has very real consequences for everyone, including their kids, who can be used as ammunition in the battle for control. Where there's a 'winner takes all' mentality, rarely does anyone end up winning. No-one wants children to be harmed in any way, but more equitable ways forward are needed.

> 'Fathers get so lost in the grief of loss. The net loss in relationship breakdowns is the loss of time with the kids.' *Ray Lenton, family group counsellor*[18]

Access remains key to encouraging fathers to support their families, not just financially, but in many other practical and positive ways. Separated and divorced fathers throughout the developed world are being torn apart by a system that frequently regards them as little more than 'walking wallets'. Too many men are expected to simply pay up and stay away from their kids, and when these men do get access they often feel more like visitors than parents.

'We as fathers love our children just as much as mothers do. We miss them when they are away, we think about them, and we want to be with them. Just because we happen to have the tragedy of divorce strike in our lives does not mean we stop loving our children.'
Blake, 42

It is important to note that not all men leave their relationships when they are unhappy. Many hang on for years. Studies show that while women tend to stay in an unhappy marriage for financial considerations, men tend to do so because they don't want to lose access to their children.[19] Michael, 50, admitted to remaining in his marriage for almost twenty years for this reason. 'I enjoyed being with the boys, going on holidays with them, working with them and doing schoolwork, taking them to sport and all that other stuff . . . By the time I did actually leave the marriage, my older son was already nineteen and my younger son was fifteen.' When these fathers do move on, the hardest part is often leaving their children.

GETTING ACCESS TIME RIGHT

Even though many fathers do care, society's nervousness about a father's ability to cope with their kids and their many needs after divorce is frequently reflected in custody arrangements. Most men only get to see their children once a fortnight, as it's assumed a loving father would be happy with this level of access, which is just not the case. What makes it even harder for these men is that few resources are thrown their way to help them make the most of their time with their kids.

'You often hear the comment that fathers in intact relationships don't spend much time with the children, but what everyone forgets is that's because the fathers are out there working. Yet when there's a break-up, mothers are puzzled as to why the men want access. It's only because Dad goes to work that the kids can do everything they do. While a dad's job is to help the household survive, most dads would rather spend more time with their kids, but someone has to work. It's just crazy.' *Mick, 42*

While many fathers haven't had as much practice as mothers at looking after the kids, and may not have the same range of community contacts, this is no reason to shut them out of their kids' lives. Sometimes a woman believes that because her ex wasn't an ideal partner, that makes him a hopeless father, but this does not necessarily follow. These are all very human responses to the trauma around break-ups. However, a better way forward is needed for separated dads, so they can become the confident, involved fathers many aspire to be. These men need active encouragement and recognition, and good literature and other resources to help them move forward.

The extremely limited time non-custodial fathers have with their children can cause them to over-compensate when they do get together with their kids. Many become so concerned to do the right thing that they become over-anxious about their kids' health and wellbeing, and rush them off to see a doctor for minor complaints. Or they are so worried that their custody time goes well, they become over-controlling. Many men I spoke with in this situation confess to being fearful and stressed when the kids are around, and find even the slightest upset with their kids devastating.

Because non-custodial dads are often seen as less than competent, these men are not likely to admit they're struggling, so many never get to experience the fulfilment they long for during access time. 'Stripped of any real parental authority, many non-custodial parents begin to focus not on parenting, but on being their child's friend,' explains psychologist Wade Horn. 'Far from making parents more effective, divorce often leaves children with one, often overwhelmed custodial parent, and one Disneyland Dad or Mom.'[20] Sometimes the relationship breakdown is so painful for dads that they disappear out of their kids' lives for a while; research shows, however, that fathers wanting to establish a good relationship with their children are best to do so *early* on. The longer this is left, the harder it is for everyone to adjust to the separation, and remain part of each other's lives.[21]

WORTHWHILE TIME WITH THE KIDS

Fathers need support to make the best use of time with their kids. We have all seen dads trying to keep their kids entertained in parks or fast-food outlets. Fathers need to know that it is not in a child's best interest to eat what they want when they want, to spend hours in front of the computer or PlayStation, to let their homework slide, to behave as they choose.

A non-custodial dad has to work extra hard to remain relevant to his kids, especially if he lives away from the family home and the kids' circle of friends. It can be difficult for these dads to pick up on the many nuances of their kids' lives when they only get to see them once a fortnight. Much of the debate to date has been on the *proportion* of time fathers have with their kids, but new research suggests fathers and kids need more qualitative, flexible time together that allows for a whole range of activities, including just hanging out together. As researcher Bruce Smyth points out: 'Fluid meaningful time cannot be scheduled, especially with children. It needs to be cultivated.'[22]

As children grow, so too do their social commitments. Non-custodial dads don't always understand that it's natural for kids to prefer to spend time with their friends, so they take any requests to do so as a personal rejection. Even last-minute changes to the hand-over of the children can be traumatic for these dads, because they are so overwhelmed by the days and weeks they spend in isolation from those they love.

'I'm conscious how angry and upset I get about my own daughter, who is now with her mother full-time. I'm a reasonably balanced bloke and in not that bad a situation, but you get desperate. You can see what happens with men wanting to get back at the family court and with suicide. These men are troubled with such feelings of power-lessness.' *Justin, 43*

How parents navigate their way through the break-up has a profound effect on their kids, because their children take their cues from the way their parents react in situations. It is easy to underestimate just how sensitive children are to their environment. Children learn to deal positively with conflict when they see their parents doing so. When marital relations have reached an impasse, often fathers withdraw because they lose heart. Mothers then try to compensate for this absence, so everyone loses.[23] Estranged dads need to know the importance of hanging in there – for their own sake and that of their children.

It was his own experience as a separated dad that inspired Brad Mander to set up Camp Connect, where fathers can take their kids.[24] 'It's not just a fun weekend away, but a learning opportunity,' Brad explained. 'There are workshops for kids, but they're mainly father-focused. It's a chance to spend quality time with the kids, but also to bring something back from the weekend. A big part of the week-end is seeing other dads deal with similar issues. Being able to talk about it and set up support networks, build friendships, and hear others tell their stories is important. It's a legacy for my own children, because I'm limited to what I can do with them with contact time.' What is especially heartening for Brad is what his own children get out of the weekends away. 'My kids keep asking when the next camp is. They're already forming relationships with other kids. And my son says he likes his time at Camp Connect, because he doesn't get as much time with Dad as he'd like.'[25]

'I was terrified at first when I was left with the kids. But then I real-ised what a privilege it was to be with my kids, when I got it right.'
Ryan, 50

SOLE FATHERS

While the majority of children in sole-parent situations are with their mother, there are a significant number of men who are sole parents, not just because of divorce and separation, but because of the death of a partner, or due to abandonment. It's often a lot harder for fathers to be sole parents, because most haven't had the same level of input into the intricacies of family life that women have. However, in spite of the challenge of helping their children feel safe, dealing with domestic chores and with their own issues, research suggests that resident fathers are equally able as parents as resident mothers.[26]

When Barney's wife walked out and left him with four children under the age of four, he was shattered. 'I just got on with it because I had to,' he recalled. After years of struggling with exhaustion and a lack of resources, Barney, now 55, can take pleasure in seeing his teenage children develop their various talents. Yet in spite of this, major challenges remain. 'What never goes is the often over-whelming sense of isolation,' he admitted. Here Barney was not only referring to the loneliness of doing everything on his own, or missing the physical and emotional comfort that comes with having a part-ner, but the lack of interest and awareness society has of men in his situation – the awkward moments when professionals and others ask where the child's mother is, just because he is doing something nor-mally done by a woman.

> 'It's been hard in all sorts of ways. I've had to work really hard at establishing the fact that I'm okay with other parents. When my daughter asks to have friends round I've made sure their parents know I'm a sole father, and they've been really good about it. My daughter's even had sleepovers, and that's been okay.' *Barney, 55*

Coping isn't the same as being properly supported as a sole par-ent. Few solo dads are fully able to relax and enjoy parenting. In a recent survey on loneliness in Australia, Dr Michael Flood indicated that sole fathers are the loneliest group of all.[27] At present there are an estimated 55 100 sole fathers in Australia caring for children up to the age of 15. Some manage to hold everything together. Those with few resources have tenuous lives at best. Some become homeless. Recognising these needs, the Canberra Fathers and Children Service was established in 2002 to provide accommodation for these fathers and their kids, as well as an outreach service for sole-father families living in caravan parks or other temporary accommodation. It also provides a range of additional services, including tips on how to cook healthy food and bargain shop.

'Most people just don't want to hear what is going on in my head. I feel lonely every day of the week. That's just part of my life. I have to deal with it.' *John*[28]

Too often society ignores these dads, forcing them to deal with the many challenges they face alone. It need not be this way. With more assistance so much could change for these fathers and their kids.

Life after divorce

LOOKING IN FROM OUTSIDE

As estranged dads and their kids settle into a new routine, often new challenges emerge. These dads frequently have to deal with the fact their children now have a stepfather, who appears to have taken their place. It's not easy for any man to see his children living with a stranger, a man who enjoys time with his kids that he longs for.[1] In the best cases, non-custodial fathers can continue to be supportive and build a good relationship with the stepfather of their kids. While some men achieve this, many don't. On top of these challenges, some fathers have to deal with accusations from their kids of not caring, or have to stand back and watch their children being brainwashed against them.

'I did have a little bit of a problem when my ex-wife moved in with another guy . . . When I took my daughter back from access visits, her mother would always send out the guy to come and get my daughter, so I always had to hand my child over to him. I said to the guy one time, "Do you love my daughter?" And he fobbed the question off, and said, "Oh, I don't know," and it hurt even more that my daughter would be in this relationship with this guy who didn't give a shit about her. I wanted to know she wasn't living in a relationship with an adult that ignored her.' *Doug, 52*

All these scenarios are doubly painful for fathers who have been let in on the miracle of birth and the joy of helping rear their children. After developing a meaningful bond with your kids, to suddenly be treated as if you're irrelevant is a big shock. Many estranged fathers get desperate; otherwise-reasonable men end up doing unreasonable or inappropriate things. In September 2004 Jason Hatch made world news when he and David Pyke scaled the walls of Buckingham Palace dressed as Batman and Robin. These men gained international coverage, but their stunt did little to convince anyone that they, or their organisation Fathers 4 Justice, were responsible. Their angst at lack of access to their kids was lost in their bizarre choice of protest, which could very easily have got them killed.

'My wife left me for another man about seven months ago. At the start she gave me access to my little daughter who is four. But over the time she has denied me access by making all sorts of excuses as to why I couldn't see my little girl. Now she says she wants to move on with her life and doesn't want me in the picture. I love my little girl and only want to continue to see her and be her father. It now seems her mother has chosen a new father. Am I supposed to just walk away and forget my little girl? I can't, I love her.' *Murray*[2]

WHEN FATHERS ARE MISREPRESENTED

It is hard to describe the very real sense of helplessness and anguish estranged fathers feel in these situations. This was evident in almost every interview I had with non-custodial dads. Pain and disappointment is often also felt by their children. In his book *Divorced Dads*, Professor Sanford Braver tells the poignant story of a student whose parents divorced when she was nine. Initially she saw both her parents, until her dad got a girlfriend and then vanished. Then one day, while in her final year at high school, she bumped into her father's girlfriend, and was devastated to discover her mother had deliberately blocked every attempt her father had made to see her.[3]

When children lack access to their father, the effects are often long-term. Rowan, 41, is starting to rebuild a relationship with his estranged father, since his mother passed away. After having been brought up to believe his father never mattered or cared, he has discovered his father is a completely different kind of man than had been portrayed. 'Dad's not at all like Mum said,' Rowan told me with a lingering sense of sadness. 'He's a sensitive man. He knows a lot and he's done some amazing things.'

A girlfriend of mine, who was brought up by her maternal grandmother, didn't discover until she was 40 that her father had been present at her birth, that he'd wanted to keep her and that he had paid child support for the first nine years of her life. These are not isolated incidents, but very real situations that deprive fathers and their children of years of special moments.

HANDLING STEP-PARENTING

The pain of separation is so extreme for some men that they cut off from their family altogether. For the men who have lost touch with their own kids, or who simply miss day-to-day family life, it is tempting to seek out a ready-made family to fill their aching sense of emptiness. In the desperate desire to have a family, a man may even be tempted to pretend his stepkids are his biological children, or to go over the top to show he cares. Sensing this, kids can be quick to take advantage. What these men don't realise is that overcompensating with children or stepchildren can be just as damaging as being heavy-handed. Unless a man addresses his *own* issues around his identity as a father, he can find himself dealing with an even more complex situation as a stepfather, as he tries to handle his biological children, stepchildren and the children from his new relationship. Many men do not consider these issues before entering a new relationship, and end up in an even less satisfactory situation.

> 'When I remarried, my wife already had two kids. I'd always wanted kids. That was a bit of a magnet for me.' *Ryan, 50*

WHEN STEPFATHERS WORK WELL

Being a stepfather is far more difficult than being a father, because it requires even more patience and sensitivity. Although many men do choose another partner when their relationship falls apart, and enter this new relationship with great enthusiasm, there are no guarantees it will work. While a new family can help lift a man out of his terrible loneliness and give him a renewed sense of meaning, step-parenting can be a lonely and frustrating experience. Research suggests that men have a higher chance of success at step-parenting when the children are young. Dealing with the intricacies of a new relationship and adolescent step-children is a far more complex scenario – with these heightened challenges comes a heightened risk of failure.

Frequently men find it hardest dealing with adolescent daughters, because girls often resent the closeness these men share with their mother. Boys, by contrast, frequently benefit from a warm, positive stepfather, both as a role model and as a buffer if their relationship with their mother becomes strained.[4] Stepfathers fare better when children can see them helping take care of their mother.

No stepfather wants a troublesome relationship with his step-children, but often this is the reality. It can seem a totally thankless task to continue to provide for kids who are determined to make life as difficult as possible. The temptation stepfathers then face is to retreat. Continuing to support the children's mother in her parenting is by far the best way forward. In a recent survey, stepfathers and stepchildren were asked what they felt worked best in the bonding process. Over half said they wanted conversation. Next, at 16 per cent, was working together. Additional activities, such as sport or help with homework, came far below this.[5]

Many stepfathers find their lack of authority difficult to handle, especially when facing resistance from stepchildren. This often leaves them frustrated and feeling like a stranger in their own home. Those men I spoke with who have pushed through these barriers advise other stepfathers to encourage children to feel comfortable talking about their biological father and about their feelings in different situations. The very fact that stepchildren want to talk with their stepfather indicates that genuine one-on-one time with each child in the home can make a difference. When stepfathers can give these kids time and demonstrate they care, without invading their space, they can start to build significant bridges.

SHATTERED LIVES

The difficulty in finding a more effective way forward for divorced dads may lie in part in our assumption that most families are torn apart because the father must somehow be to blame. This belief makes people fearful and defensive towards fathers, and even more protective of mothers and their children. Mothers and their kids need to be taken care of, but not all break-ups are due to infidelity, abuse or neglect. 'I just think any sort of value judgement that is made about any kind of relationship without being intimately familiar with the details is bound to be a naïve, silly black-and-white judgement, and more often than not it is a naïve, silly black-and-white judgement in favour of the woman, and that's just not right,' said Michael, a divorced father of two grown sons. While most relationships fail because couples drift apart, loss of their home, partner and kids is still often the end result for men in this situation. It's a huge price for men to pay for no longer being close. There is no point in trying to make something work that is no longer workable, but it is time to find better ways forward.

'I am aching beyond what I thought possible . . . I feel so isolated and removed from who I've perceived myself to be. I look in the mirror and just don't recognise myself any more. I miss feeling alive . . . I try to make sense out of what is left . . . For now, it's all I can do just to get myself out of bed in the morning.' *Awashen*[6]

All the trauma men experience around little or no access to their kids comes at a time when they are trying desperately to reconstruct their lives. Suddenly they have to find somewhere to live, while maintaining their work, sorting out the new financial arrangements, and filling in the hours they are alone. This process often exacts a high toll – many experience extreme stress, sleeplessness, tiredness and depression after break-ups for years afterwards, and some never recover.[7] 'I must say the hardest part of leaving was the sense that my children would have felt I was betraying them in some way,' Michael, 50, told me. 'I now see my sons every weekend. We meet at my parents' place for lunch, and then on Sunday night just the three of us go out for a meal together – it's great.'

WHEN SUICIDE SEEMS THE ONLY WAY OUT

It is good for everyone concerned when divorced men can find positive ways forward after being separated from their homes and their kids. When they lack the support to express their grief, anger and real sense of loss, many become vulnerable to suicide. Divorced men are at least three times more likely to commit suicide than any other group in Australia.[8] 'The period immediately after separation is the most difficult time for such men [at high risk of suicide],' says Dr David Crawford, who has examined the health issues separated fathers face. 'But look in the directory for services for separated parents — virtually all the services are for women. The way in which our services deal with separated fathers should be seen within the broader context of how society sees them and values them or, as is generally the case, ignores them.'[9]

> 'I felt suicidal plenty of times. You don't know how to handle the pain. It just becomes unbearable. It's the hunger for your child, it's that strong. When I was representing myself at court for custody, I got to know eight or nine others. We became very close, and stayed in contact. One of the guys who was very helpful to me blew his head off before the final hearing.' *Ryan, 50*

Society still doesn't realise that many fathers really do love their children. In a recent paper, researcher Bruce Hawthorne pointed out that often fathers grieve for the loss of children more than they do the loss of marital identity.[10] So, when the children go, some men feel there is nothing to live for. In his study of 4000 suicides, Professor Pierre Baume, head of the Australian Institute for Suicide Research and Prevention, found that 70 per cent were connected to relationships that had gone sour, and that men were nine times more likely to suicide after a break-up than women.[11]

Allan Huggins, director of men's health at Curtin University, states that unless the psychological issues men deal with around separation and divorce are resolved, these extreme emotions can result in murder/suicides. 'Ultimately they (men) see their situation as being totally hopeless, and then the realm of fantasy begins, where they want to take their children with them to what they perceive as being a better place.'[12]

'I felt suicidal plenty of times. You don't know how to handle the pain. It just becomes unbearable. It's the hunger for your child.' *Justin, 43*

Too many estranged fathers end up killing themselves because they don't see any other way out. After having had no contact with his daughter for approximately four years, Andrew Renouf discovered that after child support payments had been taken out of his bank account he had just 43 cents left. 'Since my last pay was also directly deposited on Friday, I now have no way of supporting myself. I have no money for food or for gas for my car to enable me to work,' he said in his suicide letter. 'I have tried talking to the Family Support people . . . their answer was "we have a court order", repeated several times. I have tried talking to the welfare people in Markham. Since I earned over $520.00 last month I am not eligible for assistance . . . I have no family and no friends, very little food, no viable job and very poor future prospects. I have therefore decided that there is no further point in continuing my life. It is my intention to drive to a secluded area, near my home, feed the car exhaust into the car, take some sleeping pills and use the remaining gas in the car to end my life. I would have preferred to die with more dignity.'[13]

'Financial stress is still the biggest issue in separated families, because you're living in poverty. It should be no surprise that so many men are killing themselves. When men then suicide they leave their families without any financial or social back-up.' *Ray Lenton, family group counsellor* [14]

Even though some divorced men keep going for their children, many still face the temptation to kill themselves, as Bruce Hawthorne discovered when researching Australian fathers in this position. 'Being a driver I have come to an intersection and seen a brick wall in front of me and you think, "If I put my foot down, it will all be over," but what is the point, I would never see my daughter again?' confessed one man. Another also shared his pain: 'I am not sure I have recovered because my inner feelings are pretty raw, I think. I spent so much of my energy attempting to recover my equilibrium. I had been thrown a real loop. I kept my job, but nothing else, apart from my relationship with my son'. [15]

Picking up the pieces

GETTING BACK ON TRACK

The good news is that those who find their way through the pain of separation can come up with positive ways forward for themselves and their children. A recent *Newsweek* article reported on a significant shift in attitudes towards co-parenting, prompted in part by Gen Xers who, having experienced the acrimony of divorce first-hand as children or teens, want to do things differently when their own marriages fall apart. This article suggests there is now a greater emphasis on mediation around divorce, which encourages a more open approach to estranged parents' time with their kids. Estranged couples are now starting to co-host children's birthday parties, and share family celebrations, holidays and other significant times of the year. 'Today, it's unacceptable for a father not to be involved,' states Professor Constance Ahrons. 'As we've moved towards more egalitarian marriages, we've also moved towards more egalitarian divorces.'[1] Such stories offer a great deal of hope, even though most couples might not be there yet.

THE CHANCE TO BE HEARD

A father can only begin to move on when he can face up to what is happening to him and seek help. Men need to share their stories and experiences, and to hear from others whose situation is no longer so raw. The Internet is an ideal medium for men in this situation, who often find one-to-one conversations too intimate. There are now some excellent websites that give separated and divorced dads a say, as well as offering back-up resources.[2] Being able to read first-hand how other fathers are feeling and coping, and to take part in chat rooms can help.

'Divorce is very devastating, and it takes time to heal from all the hurts that come with it,' admits Ron Miller, a divorced father who also grew up in a divorced home. 'As divorced dads, we have a choice on how to respond . . . We can continue to fight, blame and be angry, or we can choose to take the high road . . . It may include listening to your children complain or tell you how things are different at Mom's house. It may also include hearing false innuendos from your children coming from your ex-wife about you. No matter how many stones are hurled, you can still choose to be the leader and example to your children.'

As part of this positive approach, Ron advises others to accept their divorced situation as it is. 'Don't be too proud to read articles or books on what it takes to be a good dad . . . Give your children your complete undivided attention while you are exercising visitation . . . Don't waste the time arguing with your children over issues that pertain to you and their mother. Solve those issues with her directly during non-visiting hours . . . Finally, if you are struggling with depression, anxiety, or anger, do yourself and your children a favour by going to get counselling.'[3]

HOW DADS CAN REASSURE KIDS

The way fathers handle divorce doesn't only affect the quality of their lives, it can have a huge impact on their kids. When these dads are aware of their own emotional issues, they are in a much better position to help their children with their anxieties and confusions. Children of divorced parents need additional nurturing, and to know they are not responsible for the divorce. When they are with their dad they must feel free to talk about their mother or not, and must never be placed in the position of go-between. Ron Miller agrees: 'It is our responsibility as fathers to make sure we comfort our children concerning the divorce . . . Do not put your children in uncomfortable situations.'[4]

> 'Divorce has not changed the core fathering instincts that I believe every father possesses. The feelings are packaged with that of unconditional love. The need to protect your children from danger and misdirection, and the desire to guide and support. What has changed are the meanings of quality, communication and memories.' *Chuck Houghton*[5]

One of the many ways Daryl stays in touch with his son, Jack, is by making their shared time more meaningful by taking him to festivals, and teaching him about hunting, fishing, karate, photography and telecom repair. He has also started to teach him to drive on dirt roads. Daryl also builds bridges with his son's school by dropping by and introducing himself to Jack's new teacher each year, and giving them a business card with his contact details. This year Daryl gave Jack's teacher some self-addressed envelopes to mail him a copy of Jack's report card.

All this takes time, effort and sensitivity. When psychotherapist Bill Klatte looks back on his time as a solo father, he realises it was all worth it. 'For all the years I was away from my daughters I worked hard to stay in touch with them in spite of our physical distance, but I often asked myself if my efforts mattered at all,' he admits. Now his daughters are in their 20s, he has a different view. 'As I look back at it now, my involvement mattered tremendously. I am very close to my daughters today. I know that I was a powerful and positive influence in their lives then — and remain one still. I have a better understanding now of what helped me get through those tough years . . . The most important thing was a slowly evolving realisation of my importance to my children. As a social worker and psychotherapist working with divorced dads and never-married dads, I came to see how much a father's involvement mattered. I learned how hurt and angry children were when their father was out of their life. I discovered that I was a role model to my children when I was respectful to women . . . honest in my dealings with others and committed to a job well done.'[6]

MOVING ON

There are no overnight solutions to help fathers get over the trauma of divorce. For some the way forward is relatively straightforward, while for others it can take years to get themselves together. 'Feeling like a family again is good,' admitted Morris. 'It was highlighted one night when I started going out with Jane. The two of us, and the boys, were having dinner together for the first time. In the middle of it a friend phoned and when I went to take the call, I looked back and saw the family complete.' Having his boys there was so overwhelming for Morris that he broke down on the phone.

Sometimes the painful things that continue to happen to these fathers can threaten to alienate them from their kids altogether, because it can seem a more painful option to fight with their partner to stay involved in their children's lives than to walk away. 'Parents need to understand parenting is an active word, and that they need to move beyond getting even to doing things with their kids that are worthwhile,' group work counsellor and father Raymond Lenton explains. 'The fathers that are able to make this leap are often better fathers after separation because they try harder. Separated fathers frequently recognise this. These fathers give so much more in the short time they have in precious ways. To do this fathers need to make new plans – to consider what's working and what's not working. To remember what it was like when things were working and set new goals that are realistic. The key for men is to start to think about what the *kids* would want to do, how *they* would want them to act. It's about learning to behave as a statesman in the face of difficulties.'[7]

When estranged fathers are given a voice and a role, both they and their children are enriched. 'I spend every other weekend with my children, and it truly is quality time,' explained Chuck. 'Whether we are camped out on the couch, or watching the latest family movie, it is quality time. Without any effort our weekends are filled with memories. The times we spend fishing, and Zachary finding the courage to hold a bass that he caught, or when Hannah realised that her small hands could fit inside Zachary's baseball glove. These are lasting memories, and they are precious. I have learned that divorce doesn't mean the end of good parenting, and with an open mind and the ability to invite change, our memories will continue to grow.'[8]

When men retire

LEAVING WORK

As the years pass and men come towards the end of their working lives, many look forward to a new chapter beyond work. If they understand the choices available to them and are motivated to embrace these options, there is much they can enjoy in retirement, from travelling and volunteering, to pursuing long-held passions or simply relaxing with friends and family. If men leave the workforce without planning for this new phase, retirement can be a massive challenge as these men struggle to continue to feel useful.

'Men love to have something to do and somewhere to go.' *Keith, 72*

Older men need to feel worthwhile. In the world they grew up in, the pressure on men to perform was very real and often intense, because the wellbeing of their family was almost entirely dependent on what men could bring in. If they failed, their families were seriously disadvantaged, and their failure was apparent to everyone.

Over the years many of these men have achieved a great deal for their families and, after a lifetime of working hard, they have good reason to feel proud of their accomplishments. They have helped their children grow up in a far more materially secure environment and to thrive in ways they could only dream of. Yet though older men are ready to ease up, they don't want to be 'put out to pasture'. They want to continue to contribute to their family and community.

WHY OLDER MEN NEED TO FEEL USEFUL

Some men manage the transition to retirement with ease. Their lives are so full, they wonder how they had time to go to work. For many men, however, retirement is far from easy. Finding enough to occupy each day can be a huge challenge for older men, especially as they become less active, less mobile. Those who plan to do nothing are often the most disappointed, as boredom quickly sets in. Milson, 76, told me of a friend who had worked for forty years for the same company, at a job he hated. What kept his friend going were his dreams of being able to put his feet up. 'The problem was when he left work he retired from life and, within a year, he was dead.'

> Though older men are ready to ease up, they don't want to be 'put out to pasture'. They want to continue to contribute to their family and community.

The perceptions society has of older men once they are no longer at work can be equally challenging. As these men become more isolated from those around them, it becomes harder for friends and family to reach out. Blake, a schoolteacher in his early 40s, admits to being haunted by the sight of his neighbour, who worked until he was 65 and now spends his days wandering the streets. 'Work is a huge part of men's lives. It's their network and everything. It gives them a purpose to get out of bed. It's awful, but I can see I'm going to be the same at his age,' he confessed, even though he has a wife and kids in his life. One of the problems for men such as Blake is that they don't have to be very old to be regarded as 'over the hill'. As the culture of youth now dominates, more and more men feel displaced.

> 'There's a certain amount of emasculation that comes with ageing and losing one's status in society – a status that no amount of wigs, follicle transplants, Botox injections or material purchases can enhance, although it isn't for the want of trying.' *John Larkin, 40, author*[1]

Without meaning to, often friends, family and neighbours say and do things that make older men feel superfluous – something they have fought against their whole lives. Writer Jack Zinn captures this well in *Older Men's Business*. 'As men grow old, a curious thing happens to us. Like Lewis Carroll's Cheshire Cat in *Alice in Wonderland*, we start to vanish, a little at a time, until all that is left is a rather insubstantial form which, while clearly male and elderly, makes little impression on the world around us.'[2] Some men are more philosophical about this process, but that doesn't necessarily make it easier.

> 'It's hard to be treated as an irrelevancy.' *Nigel, 72*

UNREALISTIC EXPECTATIONS OF RETIREMENT

For those still in the thick of things, it can be difficult to understand just how bewildering and disappointing retirement is for many older men. For these men retirement isn't just another phase of life, it's their *last* phase. The fear and desolation this realisation can bring is immense. Nigel, 72, admitted that he's heard a number of male friends say that having left work, it were as if they died.

After a lifetime of making their mark and providing for those they love, these men can experience a terrible emptiness. Part of their problem is in the *planning* for retirement, because while there is plenty of information on financial security, there's very little material on the social isolation and health challenges that retirement can bring. Often the families of older men sense the landscape ahead, but generally it's not until retirement kicks in that these men realise just how different life is.

'Men tend to come through their working lives with a "production philosophy". Then as they get older, they get tired. They start to develop daydream ideas of being at home, of taking off and travelling around the country, of sailing off into the sunset, only to find it's not like that. Most of their relationships are linked to work, but when they leave work, their wider support disappears.' *Bob Nelson, manager of the Mary MacKillop Outreach Centre* [3]

Many men go into retirement with completely unrealistic expectations. As family therapist Terry Colling points out, 'When we as a society have great difficulty in enjoying our leisure time creatively during our working lives, why should we think we can magically transform ourselves into consumers of creative leisure in retirement? . . . Many people grow old before their time, not because they have worked too hard but because they are bored, they feel a sense of loss of purpose, lack of relevance, they're observers rather than participants.'[4]

After an active life at work, suddenly retired men find themselves with whole days to fill. All at once their previously busy lives can seem like a vast, terrifyingly empty terrain, with precious few of the qualities they had hoped for. Frequently this emptiness is compounded by the fact that their children and grandchildren have moved away, and their wives have full lives of their own.

FACING EARLY RETIREMENT

As more and more men exit the workforce, the challenges around retirement are growing. For many men, even a handsome payout soon loses its appeal, because they don't know what to do with themselves. Those men who actively plan their retirement tend to fare much better than those who don't. Stanley, 70, a former police officer, decided to take early retirement when he was offered an attractive severance package. But once he retired, he was in for a surprise. 'I had this wonderful idea of retirement. My wife kept asking me what I was going to do. I thought I'd just play bowls.' It didn't take Stanley long to realise he needed more in his life than bowls, so he got a security job at the Powerhouse Museum. 'It was a beautiful job. Nine to five. Dealing with people.' Stanley enjoyed the people content of his job, including the 'tricky customers', because after years in the police force, he was able to handle people with ease. This job gave Stanley a new lease of life. Once more he was occupied and useful, and he was able to use some of his professional skills in his new job. He ended up working another 'nine happy years'. This additional time in the workforce gave Stanley the chance to plan for a very active and fulfilling retirement.

After thirty-one years working for the same company, Jim was made redundant in his late 50s. He was fortunate because he got a job with a local printing company, where he worked for the next five years into his 60s, when he had problems with his knees. 'I looked forward to work – getting out every day, and getting on with it. Sometimes I'd work a twelve-hour day, but that didn't matter.' In spite of his setback, Jim's printing company would have been happy to have him back, but his ongoing battle with his knees prohibits him from working.

For Jim, retirement is, 'The worst thing that has happened to me. It's just so boring.' One of the lifesavers for Jim, now 67, is his weekly wood-carving class. 'I was into cabinet-making years ago, then I had to let it go. Now I'm back into it. You can go to the class for the whole day and take your lunch. You get to make friends, and you feel good.' Jim is also involved in a number of other activities, but still his overall perception of retirement is one of disappointment and bewilderment.

WHEN RETIREMENT COMES OUT OF THE BLUE

Not everyone gets the chance to plan for retirement. When mature men are retrenched, often they cannot find another job, so they miss out on several fruitful working years. In extreme cases, the shock of retrenchment can cause men to continue to get dressed in the morning and pretend they are still going to work, or to resort to drinking or gambling. Sometimes personal circumstances overtake men, demanding they retire earlier than expected. When Geoff was diagnosed with a degenerative disease, he had to retire immediately. 'It was devastating,' he recollected. 'All of a sudden I was doing nothing five days a week.' Hans had looked forward to spending a long and happy retirement with his wife, only to be forced to leave work early to nurse her after she fell ill. In these kinds of situations retirement can be an extremely difficult adjustment, as the many dreams these men had disappear.

OLDER MEN AS LONG-TERM CARERS

Many more older men end up spending their retirement caring for loved ones than most people realise. Currently one in three carers in the home is male, and 42 per cent of these men are over 60.[5] Not only are these men often wrenched out of the workforce to provide necessary care for loved ones, rarely do they get the same level of support as women in this position. This is due to their 'invisibility', and their reluctance to seek help. When Hans retired early to care for his sick wife, suddenly he was responsible for looking after two adult schizophrenic sons as well. His remaining four adult children went their separate ways, so he was left to deal with this on his own. 'The illness blasted the family apart,' Hans reflected. 'It's a bloody tragedy.' Now Hans' wife has passed away, this older man is left to look after his two grown-up schizophrenic sons on his own.

'I'm not saying the family neglects you. My children were very supportive during my wife's decline, but only one really understood my predicament as a carer, when she had to move in and look after my wife when I was unexpectedly consigned to a hospital bed.' *Gerard, 75*

By casting women in the role of carers, too often the very real sacrifices male carers make go largely unnoticed. David, a former jockey and steeplechase rider, began making plans for retirement. 'I was going to retire early, so we could travel. I'd got a van and everything,' he explained. But then his wife, Elaine, had a stroke, so David had to retire immediately. They never got the chance to travel, or to do many of the other things they had looked forward to. 'After a massive stroke in 1996, she couldn't talk or walk,' David reflected, 'but she used her eyes to talk to me. She had to have a [gastric] tube, and I had to do everything for her.'

Although David is no longer a young man, he would carry Elaine to the bathroom and shower. 'Love is a very strong thing. I would do it again, but only for Elaine. It was difficult for us both, because we were both private people. I had to learn about a woman's body. That made it difficult for Elaine.' David was told that Elaine would have to be institutionalised. 'I got them to teach me what to do, and I joined all the groups pertaining to her sickness – the stroke club, a dementia group, and so on. They helped me more than anything.' There were days when it was impossibly hard for David, but he always found ways around this. 'It's always important to give people this sick respect. I learned to say, "Would you like this?" rather than "Here something is," to give Elaine that respect.' Since Elaine passed away, David, now 72, gives talks and tries to encourage others in caring situations. 'I have a lot to say, because of everything that's happened.'

> By casting women in the role of carers, too often the very real sacrifices male carers make go largely unnoticed.

Even with support, often men feel the weight of responsibility on them in this situation. Aside from the physical toll such caring takes, the pressure is still on these men to maintain the family income. After retiring from a senior executive role, Gerard found himself returning to work on a contract basis while caring for his wife, who was suffering from Alzheimer's disease. 'I like to work, but I also had the expense of looking after my wife,' he explained. What impressed me when talking to these older men was their quiet heroism, as they are left to tackle incredibly difficult situations.

When the literary world looks back at the life of Iris Murdoch, it mourns the loss of a great talent. Few spare a thought for how agonising those last years must have been for her husband, Oxford professor of English John Bayley, as the woman he loved slipped slowly away from him. In a recent interview with *The Observer* about their final years, John Bayley described himself simply as 'someone who had the good luck to be there when a really rare bird appeared.'[6]

WHY OLDER MEN DON'T SEEK HELP

Tragically, the majority of men who struggle to adjust to retirement rarely seek assistance. It can be impossibly hard for these men to talk about their needs, when they have spent a lifetime suppressing their feelings. These men are silent not because they are proud or stupid, but because they were raised to be self-sufficient. That was the only way they could survive in the uncertain world into which they were born. This makes it hard for friends and family to know what to do to help. Often these men are so good at masking how they feel, family members may not even realise their father or grandfather needs help, and so their situation continues to deteriorate.

Because older men grew up in a very different world to today, they have little or no understanding of their *psychological* needs, let alone the language to express them. This inability to articulate their feelings of loneliness, fear or despair denies many access to more support and therefore to a more fulfilling retirement. For others it can prove fatal.

> The majority of men who struggle to adjust to retirement rarely seek assistance.

UNDERSTANDING OLDER MEN'S NEED TO BE SELF-SUFFICIENT

Today's older men grew up in the shadow of the Great Depression, when unemployment was rife. Thousands of men took to the road, just so they were one less mouth to feed. Many current retirees spent their childhood watching their parents battle hunger and poverty. For many it was an experience that would haunt them for the rest of their lives. From the age of 7, Jim, now 67, would walk the railway tracks near his home, picking up stray pieces of coal to put on the home fire. He never had shoes, not even for school. Vern, now in his late 80s, got a job taking charge of the milkman's horse while the milkman made his deliveries. Vern got his job at the age of 7, because he petitioned the milkman in the school playground. He was persuasive because he needed work – his father was unemployed, and literally every penny counted.

> I'm sure that many mature men will pretend to be hardy about living alone, rather than admit to loneliness and the need for more family interaction. For those who still lead busy lives, like me, this isn't a problem, but the male macho thing doesn't stop as you get older!'
> Gerard, 75

As these men reached maturity, war loomed, and so they went off to fight. On their return most missed out on educational opportunities, and worked long hours at often back-breaking or routine jobs. For the most part they did this willingly and *silently* for those they loved because, like the rest of us, they wanted their lives to count for something.

WHEN OLDER MEN BECOME INVISIBLE

The world has changed remarkably since these men were young. Tragically, what to these men was a *huge* achievement is now seen as commonplace. Today, food on the table, access to education and health services, the opportunity to live in peace, is a given. We're more interested in what we still want to acquire, in what we're doing tomorrow or next week.

> 'In older worlds there were things we could do, were designed to do, that nobody or no machine could do.' *Robert Kincaid in* The Bridges of Madison County[7]

As I began to learn more about these men's lives, I found it hard not to be moved by them. Stanley, now 70, worked for a number of happy years as a traffic policeman and in the police pipe band. When his wife fell pregnant, he left the band and became a police sergeant, to bring in more money. The band was Stanley's great passion. He loved every moment, but he gave it away to provide for his two now-grown daughters, who don't know of his sacrifice and probably never will. As far as Stanley is concerned, it's no big deal; he simply did what he had to for his girls. Women of this generation also sacrificed a lot for their kids, but because they were around their children more, their families are well aware of what their mothers and grandmothers did for them. Yet for this same generation, their fathers and grandfathers were often distant figures at best.

TALKING ABOUT WHAT MATTERS

Unlike successive generations, these men not only keep silent about their needs, they rarely talk about their most significant experiences, so their children know little about them. Their silence seems strangely out of place in our world of celebrities and larger-than-life characters who compete daily for column inches in our newspapers and magazines. This flesh-and-blood heroism of older men doesn't sit well with our preoccupation with youth and beauty, yet it has an aching poignancy, because it was these qualities that helped build the prosperity we now enjoy. Once we give the lives of these men some attention, we realise how much they deserve to be honoured, because they have fought and toiled, and faced situations we hardly dare imagine. No-one wants to see their life dismissed as of little or no value, and these men are no different.

We don't set out to *consciously* emasculate older men, yet every day in a thousand ways we do it subconsciously. Nigel, 72, makes an interesting point about the language of old age: 'There are few words in common usage to describe the wisdom of old age — our gifts, our history, our uniqueness — qualities which are effectively hidden under the umbrella title "old".' Without the language to express what older men have to offer, it's much harder to appreciate them. The language and behaviour of exclusion has a huge impact on older men. Sadly, most have become largely invisible to those around them. So, instead of their final years being filled with joy and contentment, these men are largely ignored and isolated.

'I think that families like to think they understand, but I don't believe anybody really understands what it's like to be an older man, except another mature man in retirement. I don't think that I ever understood what it was like for my father, who lived by himself in a Victorian country town for seven years after my mother died. Only now do I get some glimmers of understanding of what it was like for him.' *Gerard, 75*

On their own

WHEN OLD MEN ARE ABANDONED

One of the most heartbreaking aspects of talking with older men is in discovering how many lack the support of family and community, especially if they live alone. Most men won't talk about this outright, because it's too painful. Often the isolation many older men face isn't deliberate on the part of family and friends; it's just how things have turned out. With the increased fragmentation of families, older men frequently live alone without any back-up, because their children and grandchildren now live in other cities or countries. Even when their families live close by, older men are all too aware of the pressures work, family and commuting place on their adult children, and are reluctant to add to them.

'We come from an era when talking about yourself and your problems was seen as a weakness.' *Phillip, 54*

This isolation creates even more heartbreak for older men, as the rifts between them and their family grow. 'It hurts a lot of people,' said Jim, 67. 'The frustration boils up inside them, then it comes out and hurts the family.' A man's isolation from his sons can be especially painful, as unresolved tensions create what can seem like an impenetrable wall between them. According to psychologist Steve Biddulph, a man's issues with his own father often emerge in his attitudes to older men – in the way he respects or makes fun of them, is superior to them, or ignores them.[1]

> 'When blokes get older, they become "too old" for their kids, so Dad gets pushed aside. When my parents got older, I used to take them out for a picnic or a drive. Today kids don't even want to take their parents to the shops.' *Jim, 67*

When Henry was widowed, his two grown sons rarely visited or rang. Even when the family home was sold because it was getting too much, Henry's sons didn't offer to help him move, although they live close by. Sadly this is not an isolated case. As Bob Nelson, manager of the Mary MacKillop Outreach Centre, pointed out when I spoke with him, 'In extreme situations, these are the elderly men who die unnoticed, and are found by the gas man three weeks later.'[2]

ARE *WE* PART OF THE PROBLEM?

What has happened to make older men so invisible? It's not as if most of us go out of our way to ignore older men. Is it because they seem to be coping, so we leave them be? Certainly not all older men are wise and amenable. They can be as stubborn, autocratic and demanding as anyone else, but is this reason enough to abandon them?

Perhaps there is a deeper problem in our relationships with the older men in our lives. If pressed, many of us would admit to feeling awkward around them. We don't want to ignore older men, but because we don't know what to talk to them about, often that's what we do. How do we break down the barriers, and keep their dignity intact?

If we want to move past the reticence of older men, we need to learn ways to meet them where *they* are. When I started interviewing these men, I was surprised at how willingly they told their stories — how much they shared of their anxieties and aspirations, even though I was a stranger. They liked the fact I was *interested* enough to make the time to talk to them, and that their stories might be *useful* to others. As we talked I began to realise that the majority of these men had, to a greater or lesser extent, retreated from the world since retirement. They had become shy. Bridging the gap takes patience and imagination, but the benefits can be immense.

> We don't want to ignore older men, but because we don't know what to talk to them about, often that's what we do.

LOSS OF A PARTNER

Older men who are married have a far greater chance than single men of enjoying retirement, at least while their wives are alive. When their wives die, often the loss is devastating, because for decades these men have relied on their wives to care for them, to handle social engagements and deal with family issues, while they concentrated on bringing home the bacon. Once their wives are gone, even the practicalities of making meals, operating a washing machine or oven, or taking their medication in correct dosages and on time can be impossibly hard for these men.

It is easy to be impatient with their helplessness, but we need to remember that this was the way these men were raised. Even capable men can find themselves at a loss. Unlike their wives, they find it hard to stay in touch with family and friends, because all too often they don't have the confidence or the skills. Significant times of the year such as Christmas and anniversaries can be extremely painful, because they hold too many memories of how life used to be.

When one's life partner goes, so too does the physical warmth that comes with being with someone you love. The comforting touch and the kind gesture are the qualities that keep people going. 'The loneliness, the lack of a companion to share experiences with, to talk to during the day, to share the comfort of a double bed, all compound to aggravate the person's view of life,' explained Gerard, now on his own. 'Many older people, men and women, find it difficult to travel by themselves, which robs them of another opportunity to exercise the mind beyond the business of just getting through the day.'

'I was locked away with Elaine for almost twenty years. When Elaine left me I didn't know what to wear out. I still had flares hanging in the wardrobe. I had to learn about that all over again.' *David, 72*

Sometimes the warmth a man had with his partner can be found in different forms, sometimes not at all. David enjoys getting out with a lady friend. He still loves watching others dance at social events, but he no longer dances. 'I can't dance with another woman, I just can't hold them in my arms,' he admitted. 'I've found a lady friend,' said Gerard. 'We don't live together. She's divorced with three children, and lives ten minutes drive away. We get together when we can. We travel together and go to the theatre together. It doesn't completely solve the loneliness, but it sure makes life eminently more bearable.'

'Because I now live alone, retirement presents some extra challenges. How to find companionship. How to have stimulating conversations with someone other than the dog. How to keep the house in some reasonable state of tidiness. How to find time for hobbies and the mind-bending stuff after cooking, washing, ironing, shopping, mowing the lawns and raking up the leaves. Some of this could be solved by living in an apartment, but there aren't too many apartments where there is space for a model railroad, and/or where you can play the piano at any time of the day, when the mood takes you.' *Gerard, 75*

WHEN OLDER MEN 'LOSE IT'

When older men are unable to rise above their grief and bewilderment of losing their partner or are simply no longer able to do things they once could, they often go into a decline, failing to feed and take care of themselves, as they retreat even further from a world they can no longer relate to. If left unchecked, these men often end up suffering malnutrition, taking to the bottle or living in squalor. This isolation is compounded by the disintegration of community. And because nobody knows what is happening to these older men, it can seem like no-one cares. 'All they have are four walls,' said Jim. 'They want to talk to people, but they can't, because people will think they're weird.'

> *Even when older men move in with their families, their loneliness doesn't necessarily go away. Still their grief needs to be worked through.*

Unless families understand what is really going on with the older men in their lives, they can become so appalled to see their father or grandfather 'losing it' that they end up beating a hasty retreat.

This downward spiral in older men is painful for all concerned. It frequently coincides with adult children grappling with their own issues – their mid-life crisis, recalcitrant teenagers, or trying to remain employed in a difficult job market. Communication is clearly one of the keys. Even when older men do move in with their family, their loneliness doesn't necessarily go away. Still their grief needs to be worked through. Finding activities that make these older men feel useful, that affirm who *they* are, is essential. If not, the cycle of despair continues.

> 'So many older men end up living in an empty house with their wife passed away, because they're heartbroken.' *Jim, 67*

Although they might not realise it, widowers are relatively fortunate, because they often inherit a well-developed social network from their wives. Those men who have lived alone most of their lives, or who are divorced, generally aren't as lucky. Frequently their lives are more isolated before retirement, and this isolation tends to increase during retirement. This, along with poor nutrition and heavier patterns of smoking and drinking that are apparent in many of these men, doesn't make for a healthy and satisfying retirement.

One elderly man I spoke with, who is widowed and now in his 80s, confessed to me that one of the reasons he enjoys ballroom dancing is the physical contact. 'Sometimes I get a little cuddle,' he admitted. A friend told me how she took over the role of cutting her father's hair after her mother passed away. Her father, a retired doctor, was a man of few words, but once my friend realised how much her father was enjoying the physical contact while having his hair cut, she made sure she spent almost an hour on his hair, even though she could easily have finished in ten or so minutes.

A number of older men talked of how much they yearn to get to know the children around them, but feel compelled to keep their distance, because they fear their gestures may be misinterpreted.

One of the difficulties in dealing with older men is in recognising they have specific needs. 'Over recent years there have been substantial advances in our understanding of the lives of older women, but older men have been largely neglected,' says Professor Sara Arber, from the Centre of Research on Ageing and Gender, Surrey University. She emphasises the importance of assessing how older men are faring from *their* point of view rather than through a female lens, because the way men and women express intimacy and friendship is different. Men are more likely to chat with neighbours, whereas older women tend to interact by giving and receiving gifts, and making kind gestures. And even though older men may get out and about, because they regard the activities for the elderly as geared towards older women, they stay away.[3]

Not only are older men often isolated from the community, they have less and less contact with men their own age, as their male friends continue to die. Even a widower in his 50s or 60s can feel surrounded by women, while it is estimated that a man in his 70s will be outnumbered by women of his age at least two to one. In *Malespeak*, Irma Kurtz recalls a conversation with her father, Bill, who was finding old age a struggle because he had so few male friends. Everywhere he went seemed to be full of older women, prompting him to remark, 'Only old men die.'[4]

WHY OLDER MEN FIND INTIMACY HARD

Another dilemma older men face is in finding acceptable ways to become more intimately involved with those around them, when increasingly men of all ages are portrayed as predators. A number of older men talked of how much they yearn to get to know the children around them, but feel compelled to keep their distance because they fear their gestures may be misinterpreted. A close friend talked to me about her elderly father who, after an active work life and a huge interest in sport and coaching, would drive down to the local park and watch the kids play football or cricket. But then as her father aged, attitudes changed. Even though he longed to do so, he stopped going to the park, because he didn't want to be seen as a predator.

> 'I would love to kick a ball around with kids in the local park. My wife and I moved eighteen months ago, so we no longer have a wide network of friends close by. I really wish I could just connect with kids in the street, but I don't do or say anything. I don't want them to think I'm a paedophile.' *Phillip, 54*

Because older men are frequently excluded from expressions of intimacy by friends and family – because they seem so self-reliant – it's assumed they don't need the hugs and kisses, and small acts of kindness that older women enjoy, and so their isolation grows. Yet while older men have less experience in reaching out, this doesn't mean they are incapable of such gestures.

Some time back, while I was staying with my parents, an older neighbour called in to give me some of his first potatoes of the season. He was very shy about his potatoes, but clearly thrilled to see that his present was appreciated. For him this wasn't just a gift of potatoes, it was a gift of *himself*. Whether they show it or not, older men do need nurturing, acknowledgement and respect to warm their days, and when we can find meaningful ways to honour them, we honour ourselves.

Ending it

WHEN OLDER MEN FEEL WORTHLESS

When older men no longer feel part of those around them, they start to feel worthless. Their ability to maintain strong connections with family, friends and community is now becoming harder, as increasingly they feel they have little, if anything, to give. In previous generations, older men were able to pass on a whole range of skills to successive generations – from father to son, and through apprenticeships. But as their children and grandchildren inhabit a world of DVDs and cyberspace, so much of what these men know and value can seem of little relevance. Realising this, older men often assume they have nothing to offer subsequent generations, so they simply fade from view.

The invisibility of youth pales in comparison to the plight of older men, especially once they are living on their own. For far too many older men, their grasp on life is tenuous at best. Once these men believe they are worthless, it is often only a short step to believing suicide is the only way out. When feelings of uselessness are combined with the loss of a partner, and/or ill health, frequently life becomes unbearable for older men, and explains in part why so many choose to kill themselves.

It is estimated that in America alone someone aged 65 or over suicides every ninety minutes,[1] and the vast majority of these suicides are men.[2] By the time an American man reaches 75 he is ten times more likely to commit suicide than a 75-year-old woman. Australian men 75 years and older are five times more likely to commit suicide than women the same age.[3] Yet in spite of this, most of us are not aware that the older men in our lives are at risk of suicide, so rarely do we keep an eye on them.

WHY OLDER MEN SUICIDE

Without the challenges and stimulation of work, and with their wives and children busy with their own interests and concerns (or if their wives have passed away), often the question of what these retired men are to do with themselves weighs heavily upon them. There's a telling urban myth about a wife at a loss as to what to do with her husband. 'I married you for better or worse, not for breakfast, lunch and dinner,' she complains. 'Can't you go out and do something?' The husband nods, goes out to the garage and hangs himself.

> Far too many older men see suicide as their only option.
> Those who are widowed, divorced or recently bereaved are
> at a heightened risk of suicide.

'Our society has a great deal of ambivalence about ageing,' notes suicide expert Professor Yeates Conwell. 'On one hand we value youth, vigour, strength and traditional concepts of beauty. Older people do not fit that idealised image, so their suicides are not considered as the tragedies they are. It is a form of ageism. Behind that phenomenon . . . are two other processes. First, we fear ageing and death, and so we want to believe we will maintain control – we are more comfortable seeing suicide among elders as a "natural" choice, rather than an expression of pain and unbearable suffering. To do otherwise is frightening, too close to home. Second is our need, as a society, to see our elders as we, on an individual basis, wish or need to see our parents – as capable, strong, autonomous people. We will always be our parents' children, so it presents a painful conflict for us when they become in need of our caring . . . When a suicide occurs, however, we want to see it, for this reason, also as an expression of strength and autonomous choice, a "natural" end.'[4] Sometimes it's easier for us to rationalise or ignore situations than deal with them, and certainly this seems to be the case with older men. But without help, little is likely to change for them.

RECOGNISING THE SYMPTOMS

Far too many older men see suicide as their *only* option. Those who are widowed, divorced or recently bereaved are at a heightened risk of suicide. While families and friends need to be aware of changes in eating and sleeping patterns, withdrawal, a preoccupation with death, giving away precious possessions, crying for no reason, unexplained fatigue, difficulty concentrating, and a failure to take prescribed medicines,[5] depression is the main reason for suicide in older men. It can be triggered by everything from financial difficulties, a loss of social status and isolation, a breakdown in health and loss of mobility, looking and feeling old, a fear of dying a protracted death, to family upsets and unbearable physical pain.

Dr Eric Caine, chair of the Department of Psychiatry, University of Rochester Medical Center, New York, says that much of the depression in older people occurs because of multiple small problems – medical and otherwise – that become exaggerated in the mind of an individual. In his view, it is the accumulation of these factors, more than terminal illness, that triggers an older man's desire to 'end it'. According to Dr Caine, the real tragedy is that while 75 per cent of elderly suicides involve depression, two-thirds of these cases are late-onset depression, which is 'very treatable'.[6]

It's not just isolated older men who are at risk of suiciding, or those who are terminally ill. In one recent survey, two-thirds of the older adults who suicided in their late 60s, 70s and 80s were in 'relatively good physical health'.[7] Professor Yeates Conwell believes the major problem is that depression goes largely undetected in the elderly, because they don't think in psychological terms, and because doctors are so busy often they fail to detect these symptoms.[8]

Older men need help to find ways to continue to be useful members of their family and community, and to move beyond the fear of appearing vulnerable or not fully able to cope. When they don't get the chance to share the richness of their life experience, then we all miss out.

Opening up

TALKING ABOUT THINGS THAT MATTER

There are many ways for older men to move beyond their isolation. One of the best ways is to spend time around men their own age. John, a former advertising executive aged 72, was asked to set up and run Just For Older Men by his local neighbourhood centre. Just For Older Men provides fortnightly talks on subjects ranging from dealing with troublesome neighbours to organ donation, and subjects the men might otherwise avoid. 'The group talks about death frequently and deliberately,' John explained. 'We got the local funeral director in, and we've never laughed so much. The guys have never stopped talking about it.' What began with a dozen men now has up to fifty attending on a regular basis.

John also organises excursions, some purely for pleasure, while others are more information-based, such as a trip to the emergency department at the local hospital. Although it was hard to get the men motivated at first, once they became involved they began to enjoy their time together and now talk of the relief and pleasure they experience being around other men who understand their concerns. 'The men talk to each other about things that are real personal, and it's good,' confided Jim, a regular. 'I could do with this meeting once a week.'

'There are a lot of blokes out there who need to be pushed to get out and about. If I was the worrying type, I'd worry about their future, but I'm not, so I don't.' *John, 72*

One of the many bonuses of Just For Older Men is the opportunity these men have to share their medical experiences. It's not uncommon for them to reassure each other in the lead-up to medical procedures. The chance for these men to talk to others with the same complaint is invaluable because, by their own admission, they would be too embarrassed to talk about these things if women were there. The men also talk about solutions to family problems, instead of bottling them up and worrying about them. Even those who find it hard to open up benefit, because they have access to shared information, ideas and emotional support.

MEETING THE CHALLENGES

Physically and/or mentally active men do tend to fare much better in retirement than men who stay home and do nothing. Even those who have to watch their health can come up with new possibilities for their lives, if they are sufficiently motivated. After a major heart attack John had to take his health seriously. 'Before the attack I was a real slob,' he admitted, 'too much wining and dining over the years.' John responded by setting up a weekly walking group, Just Walk It, in association with the Heart Foundation.

After the end of his formal career, Milson, 76, decided to volunteer his services to developing countries through AESOP –

a non-profit organisation that provides management assistance to business and other organisations in the South Pacific and South-East Asia. For several years Milson worked on a variety of projects in different countries, including a feasibility study and plans for junior secondary schools on the island nation of Kiribati. Since drawing up his plans, eighteen schools have been completed on the outer islands, and two more are in progress. 'It gave me an immense amount of satisfaction,' Milson recalled. 'The architectural challenge wasn't as wonderful as seeing the schools built.'

> 'The highest mountain in the world is your doorstep, but you've got to be active and adventurous. If you want to feel better, go out and help someone in need.' *Peppi, 78*

VOLUNTEERING CAN MAKE A DIFFERENCE

It can take a huge effort for older men to step out and do new things. 'Stop seeing retirement as God's waiting-room. Forget about TV and keep moving,' advised Peppi, a 78-year-old widower originally from Sicily. Dan, a former Vietnam veteran, agreed. He was forced into early retirement after a heart attack, but has few regrets. 'I enjoy it, because for the first time in my life I can do what I want.' Dan does a variety of volunteer work. He was a volunteer driver for the Slovakian team at the Sydney 2000 Olympics, because his parents were from Czechoslovakia. 'There was a meeting-place in town for the team. We'd have a meal and a drink with them, and I'd have the same kind of meals my mother used to cook for me. It was very nice.'

Blake, who volunteers at The Men's Shed, a social/woodwork program for retired men, sees a real difference in the older men who join them. 'It gives the men a purpose to get out of bed. When they first come they're so euphoric, they're almost jumping out of their skins.' Phillip, 54, described his work at The Men's Shed as, 'The best job I've ever had – being able to provide skills and pass them on. There's so much that goes on here, it's an eye-opener to see what others are going through. Some men have nowhere else to go.' Apart from making wheelchairs for children injured by landmines, the men produce building blocks for local childcare centres, furniture for nursing homes, planter boxes for local streetscapes, and seats for council parks and gardens.

The Men's Shed participants have had numerous articles and photos of their work in the local paper. 'The men may socialise out-side The Men's Shed, sometimes having a meal at the local club or catching up for a drink,' explained manager Bob Nelson. 'They may also visit other participants at home when they are sick, and check on the wellbeing of participants who have been absent for a period.' At the time I was writing the book, two of these men were driving across the desert together.

HOW MATURE PETS CAN HELP

Another way older men are moving beyond their isolation is by adopting a pet. In the United States the elderly are being encour-aged to adopt adult pets from local shelters, through the Pets For the Elderly Foundation. While this scheme isn't just for older men, it can be particularly effective in helping older men get out of the house. According to the Foundation, the adoption of mature pets is ideal, because these animals are 'more likely to be calm, already house-trained, and less susceptible to unpredictable behaviour.'[1]

The presence of an animal in an older man's life not only warms his space, it can provide a non-threatening way to interact with neigh-bours. On its website the Foundation tells the story of a recently widowed gentleman whose cat died within weeks of his wife's death. In spite of his double loss, this elderly man insisted on living alone, even though he had stopped taking proper care of himself. In desperation his son got him a mature cat from the local animal shelter. Encouraged by this new presence in his life, the man began to eat more, and by the end of the first week an elderly neighbour had befriended the cat, and through the cat had got to know this gentleman.[2]

TELLING *THEIR* STORIES

Older men have a lot to contribute. One way of doing so is by getting the chance to tell *their* stories. Some older men get a new lease of life by exploring their family history, while family photos can be another way to get them talking. With encouragement, these men may be inspired to write down their stories. Taking the opportunity to visit places that are significant to them can also be invaluable. A friend of mine found a trip to the War Memorial Museum with her ageing father deeply moving. 'I'm not into war, but I was so moved by the stories of the soldiers, and of Dad's own accounts of some of the things he'd been through. He was so animated when we were there, it was like being with a different person.' Stories might emerge from a handful of old postcards, or from passports, war medals or immigration papers. Another friend, Sara, told me, 'I couldn't believe how many of Dad's stories were contained in his stamp collection. It was really moving to share that time with him.' Perhaps it's time to get out the family photos, or to put together a scrapbook of old photos, letters, bills and other memorabilia.

MOMENTS OF INTIMACY

One of the reasons we don't work at getting older men to open up is because we assume they have nothing to say, or because we think they don't have the depth of feeling or insight women possess. Yet in my many discussions with older men, this proved not to be the case. Time and again when talking of those they love, these men became animated and tender. For Geoff, now suffering a degenerative disease, he spoke of how his children have transformed his life. 'If I didn't have kids, I probably wouldn't be alive,' he admitted. 'I used to be a bit of a wild boy. I didn't think I was, but when I look back, I guess I was. I enjoyed fatherhood – something of your own flesh and blood.'

These days Geoff is separated from his wife and lives in a hostel, and his children are clearly his lifeline. The day we met he had risen early to pick up his son and take him to sports practice. Those few shared moments with his son were clearly one of the most important moments in his week. His son may never know how much that early-morning ride meant to his dad, but the immense love this man felt for his son was apparent all the same.

Concerns about providing and caring for their children often remain strong, even for older men with grown children. Sebastian, now in his 90s, continues to play the stock market so he can leave his two sons and their families well provided for.

Rarely do older men know how important their presence and their input is to their children, because they have become so used to taking the back seat. So, when their grown children ring and they answer the phone, they tend to rush off to get their wife, rather than chat with their kids. It is very poignant to see how often these men seem almost incapable of interacting with their children and grand-children, or telling them how much they care. We have all seen how older men sit back at family gatherings, as if they were onlookers rather than participants. Yet when these men can feel useful and involved, it's a very different dynamic.

'I was around yesterday putting in a clothesline at my daughter's place while her husband is away. It'll make things much easier for my daughter when the baby comes. I go around and mow the lawns when her husband's away, just to help out. But I never interfere when he's home, because it's not my place.' *Stanley, 70*

While these men may not say much, they are every bit as concerned for their children as their wives are. Morris, 61, confessed how concerned he was about a string of poor business decisions one son had made. He also worries about how happy his other son is in his marriage, because his wife is so controlling. Nigel, 72, talked to me about the instability of one of his children's relationships, and 'the collateral damage' this rocky situation was likely to have on his grandchildren. Ian, 76, had similar issues: 'When the younger family members split up, this can cause large problems for the oldies.' Many of the men also spoke of their concern at how highly geared their children were, and how little time they had in their lives, apart from work.

GRANDFATHERS DO CARE

Many of these men also care deeply about their grandchildren. Now a significant number of older men are being drawn into more active parenting, as they help out looking after their grandchildren. In a recent news report it was estimated that over 30 000 Australian grandparents were caring for their grandchildren. Looking after small children doesn't always come easily to these men. In one study grandfathers who were looking after their grandchildren said they wanted to help more with the day-to-day aspects of caring for the grandkids, but didn't know how. Others worried about the bills, and whether they'd live long enough to see their grandchildren grow up.[3]

Australian social researcher Jan Backhouse has done an in-depth study of grandparents. She believes that helping raise their grandchildren offers older men new possibilities to feel useful. However, she also points out that some men are more comfortable with this than others. 'Younger grandfathers do take on a supportive role. Those who are older often don't connect. They lack confidence. Small children get on their nerves. They upset their routine.' With a lifetime spent at work, one of the difficulties for many older men is that often they haven't been around the happy chaos of families. As they are not sure how to handle this, they tend to withdraw. 'I think they think they're not capable of doing these things,' Jan Backhouse told me. 'Too often women step in and take over, making men feel helpless.'[4]

Those who can get over these feelings often start to enjoy being a grandparent. 'It's a lovely feeling of all care and no responsibility, coupled with a sense of being loved for who you are,' said Nigel. 'It's nice too, to be introduced to their current world ideas – to see the world anew, as a little child.'

'My grandfather was always around. I remember catching catfish with him, and going on ferry rides on the Tigris River. He had his own room in the house, while everyone else shared. We weren't meant to go in there. I remember how still and quiet it was in that room, compared to the chaos in the rest of the house. He was definitely not invisible. He was always there. It was lovely.' *Mark, 32*

MEN ALSO LONG FOR GRANDCHILDREN

Like older women, many mature men dream about having grandchildren. This longing was apparent in a number of men I spoke with. 'I'm really looking forward to them,' confessed Phillip, 54. 'I hope I have one of those grandchildren who can't wait to get out of the car and see you.' Stanley, 70, centres his hopes around living long enough to enjoy time with his grandchildren. 'I wonder how long I have, but then I think, how selfish. But I really do want to see my grandchildren.'

THE MELLOWING PROCESS

Something happens to men when they age – it's as if they're finally allowed to be more tender, more human. The need to be competitive, to win at all costs, seems to dissolve, and a gentler, wiser person emerges. This came across repeatedly in how older men behaved and talked in interviews. The way these men expressed concern and admiration for their men friends was as gentle and generous as any woman.

'Often older men are not looked after properly in nursing homes. And when they're sick and frightened, they need a kiss and a cuddle, just like anyone else.' *David, 72*

Like women, these men also worry about older friends whose health is deteriorating, or who are no longer managing on their own. Again and again they described each other as good men, beautiful men, decent men, brave men. It's as if they have begun to see themselves and each other as we need to see them. When we begin to look at them in this way, we can see that in among all the things men wrestle with and fail at, there are countless men who are good, decent, brave and beautiful, who love their partners and their kids, and who in a thousand tiny ways try their best to be someone's hero.

In the company of men

WHAT KEEPS MEN APART

Throughout their lives too many men feel isolated. Yet there are few men, regardless of their age, whose lives cannot be enriched by the friendship of other men. Society doesn't focus much on the relationships *between* men, because this is not seen as significant, and so men now focus less on these friendships. Those men who do have strong friendships often find these relationships harder to maintain as life gets busier. Now that men frequently commute, work longer hours, participate more in the household and family life, there aren't many hours left to catch up with male friends. Even at social events there's an expectation that men should stay with their partner. Some women expect their partner to be around all the time, forcing men to negotiate time spent with male friends.

> 'It's not as acceptable as our father or grandfather going down to the pub. It's not as tolerated now. It's like, "Well if you do that, then where's the recompense? You have to take me to dinner." There has to be some sort of payback.' *Alex, 35*

Often women don't encourage partners to keep up their male friendships, because they don't realise how important it is for them to spend time with other men, even though they get a lot out of the time they have with girlfriends.

When a man is in a committed relationship, it is important he puts time and effort into his relationship. However, when men spend all their time with the women in their lives, everyone's world starts to shrink. He not only alienates himself from wider forms of support, he denies himself the opportunity for stimulation outside his work and relationship. Often women don't encourage partners to keep up their male friendships because they don't realise how important it is for them to spend time with other men, even though they get a lot out of the time they have with girlfriends.

'We're denied the opportunity to really express how we feel about each other because of competition and homophobia. It's like every time you have feelings for a man, you get worried, because it might be interpreted as being gay. You know you're not gay, so the best way to deal with these feelings is to keep up your barriers and push those feelings away.' *Rowan, 41*

It's not just women who put the brakes on men spending time with each other – so do men. Men are sensitive about the way they feel about the men in their lives. Some fear that by getting too close to the men they genuinely care about, this closeness might be misconstrued as them being gay. This discomfort is reinforced by the wider community, who are quick to jump to conclusions whenever they see men who are close.

While there is nothing wrong with being gay, no-one likes being labelled something they're not. Two young friends of mine were travelling together through Europe recently, and were annoyed to hear a couple of older women describe them as two 'lovely gay boys', when they were just good friends enjoying travelling together. Every time presumptions or jokes are made about a man's sexuality, unhelpful stereotypes are reinforced.

ALLOWING MEN TO SHOW THEY CARE

In Italy, Spain and Greece, and in many countries around the world, it is normal for men to embrace, to laugh and cry together. These men are clearly doing something right, because they are far less prone to suicide. When we sexualise every affectionate gesture men make, we imprison them. One of the most moving experiences I have had was at the funeral of a friend's son. To see my husband and this boy's father embrace heart to heart, to hold each other in an intense and deeply meaningful embrace, was one of the most powerful experiences of masculinity I have witnessed in a long time.

> *When we sexualise every affectionate gesture men make,*
> *we imprison them.*

It is time to liberate men from the narrow forms of expression that are currently deemed appropriate, so they can enjoy the same freedoms women do, to articulate all they hold in their hearts. Often men cling to the women in their lives as a way of avoiding intimacy with other men, because they have never known what it's like to fully trust men. It need not be this way.

Women can do a great deal to encourage this process, but first they need to understand its value. Psychologist Toby Green talks of one man who met with considerable resistance from his wife, mother-in-law and family when he announced he planned to attend Toby's men's support group. 'It was a bit of a shock to them all that I could benefit from this group support,' he explains. 'I think the single most important thing I have learned through this whole process is the importance of intimacy in a relationship.'[1] Why are we surprised that men also need support?

WHEN COMPETITION GETS IN THE WAY

Currently the opportunities for male bonding are limited. Friendships tend to grow through a shared interest in sport, or through work. Yet when these relationships are put under the microscope, often the men continue to compete with each other, rather than share genuine aspects of themselves, so their sense of isolation remains. Recently a girlfriend of mine confided her concern for her husband, who had taken to extreme sports after the untimely death of their son. Whenever possible her husband goes off with male friends to take part in dangerous mountain climbs and other death-defying feats, pushing his boundaries as a way of suppressing the terrible pain he holds inside. His wife, by contrast, has allowed herself to be supported by friends and family, and has slowly been able to move on from her own overwhelming sense of grief.

'Most blokes have trouble understanding love for another man that isn't sexual, so we go out there and throw ourselves into work and war and sport. We put our bodies at risk to gain the approval of other men. Spending time with men who are more open enables us to practice being authentic and vulnerable in ways we never have.'
Rowan, 41

APPROVAL OF OTHER MEN

Gaining the acknowledgement of other men is crucial to a man's sense of himself. Within this need to be acknowledged by male peers are often deeper needs that were not fulfilled by these men's fathers while they were growing up – not necessarily because these men were neglectful, but because that was the way things were. 'At a deep, deep level many of us had absent fathers,' explained Rowan, 41. 'Some of us had dads who disappeared. Others lost their dads to work, or because they were always remote. At some level we're all hankering for that. Many men try to get this through a rugby club or becoming part of the old boys club at work, where there's little opportunity to be real. They feel there's safety in numbers in these gatherings, but still everything gets held in. I reckon 80 per cent of men in Australia have no true male friends.'

> Gaining the acknowledgement of other men is crucial to
> a man's sense of himself.

When I asked men whether they spent time with their male friends, many admitted they preferred spending their spare time with women. 'I love my women friends – they give me guidance. It's great having a non-sexual relationship with women – it takes the pressure off, and you learn a lot about women,' said Lance, 23. 'I have two really good male friends, but I rarely spend time with them,' explained Craig, 58. 'I have more female friends, and I find it more relaxing going out to dinner or going for a walk with them.'

Others felt differently. 'When you've got good mates there's a level of unconditional mateship. Even though we don't understand every-thing about each other, we understand what we're going through. It's less serious. You don't have to worry about the relationship – it's more casual,' Joe, 20, told me. What Tim, 25, enjoys about time with his male friends is, 'Not being nagged at for vulgar habits. The camaraderie of being subjected to the same pressures and oppressions. Delight in how men get into things and have whole other lives and interests, apart from their jobs and families.' Lawrence, 33, said, 'It's much more relaxing to be with male friends because you can say what you feel like. It's so nice to spend time in an all-male environment. You don't realise it till it happens.' For Lance, 23, there's 'happiness' being around male friends: 'friendship, good times, someone you can fall back on when things go wrong.'

'With the right male, relaxing together can be an opportunity to unburden oneself of the right stuff, that one cannot express to one's wife and others. It is good to have someone to confide in about male issues and struggles. Women do not really, in my opinion, want to hear that their man is struggling over certain issues.' *Kieran, 58*

Quality time between men comes in many different forms, and can be valuable for all concerned. Recently I was talking with a family friend who married an Iraqi girl. After initial worries about the possible clash of cultures, he was pleasantly surprised at how welcoming the community was. While he spends most of his spare time with his wife and baby son, he looks forward to community gatherings and to the chance to have time with the men. He finds the company of the older men in particular comforting and validating. He enjoys hearing their stories and telling his own stories, while his wife enjoys relaxing with her women friends and family.

'I first came across the men's movement in 1994 when I'd split up with Belinda. I go every year to an annual men's festival. It gives me a real sense of belonging, family, shelter and protection. It also exposes me to diverse models of masculinity. There's time for reflection and mentoring. It's informal and supportive. I also go to a fortnightly men's group, which gives me time for reflection and support. Then there's a quarterly gathering, which has been life-changing.' *Cameron, 32*

ENJOYING TIME WITH OTHER MEN

Men's groups do seem to work for many of the men who attend them. What is impressive about these men is their positive sense of self, and their ability to express themselves with such humour, humanity and ease. The men's groups Cameron attends have had a dramatic impact on him, because while he loves his wife and young son, time with men feeds another part of his life. When asked what he gets out of it, he admitted that it feels like coming home. 'Sometimes I feel a sadness when I get there, because I realise how much I've missed it. I feel enormously affirmed as a man. It's a wonderful thing to be.' This was also Rowan's experience, once he settled into his men's group. 'When I first went to a group I was very covert,' he explained. 'Now everyone is so relaxed and at ease with each other. I guess it's summed up in the saying, a friend is someone who knows all about you, and still likes you.'

'Men's groups give men the chance to get together in a supportive space, beyond judgement and unsolicited advice. Life is mostly about conformity, especially for men. Time together frees men from these expectations. This is important because our young men in particular are expected to conform even more, so they party hard and keep their distance. Often they don't realise how vulnerable they are, especially as they're now hitting the brick wall a whole lot younger.' *Soren, 56*

'Men need the company of men,' Rowan told me. 'I heard Ian Lillico, the founder of Boys Forward, talk recently about the young men in rural West Australia, who are committing suicide. He said that suicide is taking our most passionate, sensitive, creative young men because there are no role models for them. If they're not drinking themselves silly, screwing around, scoring, or driving at high speeds, they're quickly made to feel they don't fit in. They assume there's something wrong with them.'

When boys never get to taste what it really means to be a man, they grow up in the shadows, pretending to be something they can't quite grasp, but when a boy or a man understands what it means to be male, everything changes for them. They have a clear sense of themselves, and of the kind of man they would like to be.

> *Suicide is taking our most passionate, sensitive, creative young men because there are no role models for them.*

The media is full of the many evils men have committed. No-one denies men have done some terrible things, but they are not alone in this. There are also many courageous and inspiring aspects to masculinity that deserve our attention. When we encounter the more profound expressions of masculinity, they can be extremely powerful experiences for all involved.

In *From the Hearts of Men*, Yevrah Ornstein tells how he came across an older man who was fishing on a beach in Fiji, and was mesmerised by his presence. 'He had made his living by using his body, and he exuded an incredibly beautiful muted power that felt very masculine to me. In his presence and within this shared moment, I had one of the profoundest and most pleasant experiences of feeling my own deep masculinity that I have ever felt in my life,' he explains.

'This man engaged those parts of myself, gave them permission, voice, elevation and song. He was simply being himself, his natural and beautiful self, and he gave me the gift of meeting him on equal footing, and the gift of me being myself.'[2]

'To enjoy the comfort of other men and be held close, to allow stories that have never been told to be told is a huge thing for men. Men have lived with pain for too long. Being with other men in a genuine way takes a man beyond the need to constantly perform, to a place of potency, beyond their anger, sadness and despair, enabling them to genuinely love a woman, be a good father, enjoy everything good it means to be a man, and to allow all those around him to enjoy this also.' *Soren, 56*

'We're finally getting glimmers of other ways to be,' said Rowan, 41. 'More and more men are stepping out of the mould and are showing they can be comfortable being themselves, without compromising their masculinity. We're seeing men holding babies in their arms, taking their kids out in strollers, and doing all kinds of things they never used to do. We don't have to wait for every man to do this for things to change for men. We just need enough of us to start modifying our lives in little ways to enable the rest of men to make a shift. When we do, we'll be more empowered, because we'll be less dependent on women, which will make life easier for them. Our health will skyrocket, because we'll no longer have all the stress of having to keep everything inside, because we won't feel we have to stay with current stereotypes.'

The way ahead

There is much to be done to break down the barriers that exist between men and women, and between men and other men. The first step is to better understand men — to see them as they are, and not how we assume them to be. We can only do this by meeting them where they are at.

We also need to understand the essential loneliness that many men and boys experience, and to see the very real impact this has on them, and on their families and friendships. We as a society need to be more aware of how we contribute to this isolation in the way we raise boys, and through our ignorance of the impact the culture of violence has on boys.

The suicide of men and boys is also of concern. We publicly mourn the loss of men in war, yet during the 1990s more Australian men ended their lives than were killed in World War II. There were fewer than 600 Australian men killed in Vietnam, compared with over 17 000 men who took their lives between 1990 and 1999.[1] It is important we realise that it isn't just boys and young men who are at risk of suicide — so too are men in middle age, men facing separation and divorce, and older men.

330

There is so much men want from their lives. They ache to be loved, understood, accepted, but rarely can they find the words to express these needs. It is time now to encourage men and boys to talk about their feelings in ways that are appropriate to them, and to articulate the many issues that they have been silent about for far too long. At the same time, we need to venture into *their* world, embrace *their* perspective, because it is only through greater openness that new ways forward can be found.

When we take time to listen to men we learn so much. We discover that not all men are obsessed by their work. Many remain in jobs they hate, to support themselves and those they love. For many of these men, the time and effort they put into work is their way of demonstrating they care. We also learn that for most of the men who become fathers, being a parent is every bit as precious to them as it is to mothers.

We want so much from men, yet often we fail to help them attain these things. We expect men to be good fathers, but provide them with few resources to achieve this. The good news is that fathers are now embracing their role in new and wonderful ways. This is a significant step forward, because dads offer their kids a whole range of experiences that are central to their development. The more we encourage fathers to be an active part of their families, the more their children and partners will benefit.

One of the great disadvantages for men is that society has always seen them as strong and capable. It is time now for us to examine the areas where men are vulnerable, so we can minimise the situations in which men are currently at risk. The more we understand, the more the solutions become apparent to us. For example, when we know that men can be as vulnerable as women during a relationship breakdown, we are able to help them deal with their pain, so they don't become yet another suicide statistic.

While there are many differences between men and women, there are many more similarities between the sexes. Just as women have felt undervalued, so too do many men. They try hard in their own way to enrich the lives of those they care about, and are disappointed when their efforts fall short. They too have great aspirations for their relationships, even though they rarely talk about this.

So many possibilities await us, but first we must attend to the many needs of young men and old. Right now our boys are in need of greater nurturing. They also require more protection from the largely dysfunctional male role models that popular culture offers them. Grown men need to find richer and more productive ways to express themselves individually and collectively, and to be supported in achieving this.

Rarely when considering the lives of men and boys do we consider the plight of older men, especially those who live on their own. In recent years older men have become largely invisible to us, making them vulnerable to suicide. After surviving so much, and working hard to create the prosperity we now enjoy, these men deserve far more from life than they presently enjoy. We need to find ways to draw them back into our families and communities, for their sake and our own.

As we consider how men might move forward, we are reminded of the importance of friendship. One of the great lifelines for many women is their friendships with other women – our men also need this enrichment. Without this opportunity, men can easily lose essential parts of who they are.

Men need to move beyond the current narrow definition of masculinity, as today's men inhabit a very different world from their fathers and grandfathers. They cannot be equal to the many challenges before them unless they can hold a greater vision for themselves.

This is new ground, but one that offers huge possibilities for the future. It is time now for men to begin to express all they hold in their hearts, so they can liberate themselves and others. We as a society can assist them by openly celebrating the many wonderful qualities that men already bring to our relationships, our communities, our world.

Notes

WHAT *IS* IT ABOUT MEN?

1 Ross D. Parke and Armin A. Brott, *Throwaway Dads: The Myths And Barriers That Keep Men From Being The Fathers They Want To Be*, Houghton Mifflin, Boston, 1999.
2 Joe Tanenbaum, *Male and Female Realities: Understanding the Opposite Sex*, Candle Publishing Company, Sugar Land, Texas, 1989.
3 Robert B. Clyman et al, 'Social Referencing and Social Looking Among Twelve-Month-Old Infants', *Affective Development in Infancy*, edited by T. Berry Brazelton et al, Ablex Publishing, Norwood, New Jersey, 1986, pp 75–94.
4 Robert B. Clyman et al, 'Social Referencing and Social Looking Among Twelve-Month-Old Infants', *Affective Development in Infancy*, edited by T. Berry Brazelton et al, Ablex Publishing, Norwood, New Jersey, 1986, pp 75–94.
5 T. Berry Brazelton, 'The Transfer Affect Between Mothers and Infants', *Affective Development in Infancy*, edited by T. Berry Brazelton et al, Ablex Publishing, Norwood, New Jersey, 1986, pp 11–25.
6 Ross D. Parke and Armin A. Brott, *Throwaway Dads: The Myths And Barriers That Keep Men From Being The Fathers They Want To Be*, Houghton Mifflin, Boston, 1999.
7 Dan Kindlon, PhD. and Michael Thompson, PhD., with Teresa Barker, *Raising Cane: Protecting the Emotional Life of Boys*, Ballantine Books, New York, 1999, p 108.
8 Peter West, *What IS the Matter With Boys? Showing Boys The Way Towards Manhood*, Choice Books, Sydney, 2002.
9 Michael Thompson et al, transcript of the panel, 'Boys to Men: Questions of Violence', *Harvard Education Letter,* Research Online, Forum Feature, July/August 1999, www.edletter.org/past/issues/1999-ja/forum.shtml.
10 Renu Aldrich, '*20/20* Airs Buck's Research on How Boys Communicate', *Advance*, University of Connecticut, 22 June 1998, www.advance.uconn.edu/1998/980622/06229809.htm; R. Buck, 'Non-Verbal Communication

Of Affect In Preschool Children: Relationships With Personality And Skin Conductance', *Journal of Personality and Social Psychology*, vol. 35, no. 4, 1977, pp 225–36.

11 Olga Silverstein, 'Think "Male" Not "Masculine"', *Speaking Freely*, Tips For Parents For Raising Boys, www.kqed.org/w/baywindow/speakingfreely/tips/tips_boys. html#olga.

LEARNING TO MEASURE UP

1 Myriam Miedzian, *Boys Will Be Boys: Breaking the Link Between Masculinity and Violence,* Anchor, Bantam, Doubleday, Dell Publishing, New York, 1991, p 271.

2 Peter Sheehan, *Perceptions of Violence on Television*, www.aic.gov.au/publications/ aust-violence-1/Sheehan.pdf.

3 See www.actagainstviolence.org.

4 Lyric W. Winik, 'The Toll of Video Violence', *Parade*, 11 July 2004, http://archive.parade.com/2004/0711/0711_intelligence.html.

5 Myriam Miedzian, *Boys Will Be Boys: Breaking the Link Between Masculinity and Violence,* Anchor, Bantam, Doubleday, Dell Publishing, New York, 1991, p 300.

6 Jim Garbarino et al, transcript, 'Boys to Men: Questions of Violence', *Harvard Education Letter,* Research Online, Forum Feature, July/August 1999, www.edletter.org/past/issues/1999-ja/forum.shtml.

WHEN BOYS GET TO SCHOOL

1 Deborah Tannen, *You Just Don't Understand: Women and Men in Conversation*, William Morrow, New York, 1990.

2 Ben Fordham, 'Bullying', *A Current Affair*, transcript, 4 March 2004, www.aca. ninemsn.com.au/factsheets/1843.asp; Dean Francis, dean.francis@aftrs.edu.au.

3 Michael Thompson et al, transcript of panel, 'Boys to Men: Questions of Violence', *Harvard Education Letter,* Research Online, Forum Feature, July/August 1999, www.edletter.org/past/issues/1999-ja/forum.shtml.

4 Jim Garbarino et al, transcript of panel, 'Boys to Men: Questions of Violence', *Harvard Education Letter,* Research Online, Forum Feature, July/August 1999, www.edletter.org/past/issues/1999-ja/forum.shtml.

5 K. Rigby, 'What Children Tell Us About Bullying', *Children Australia*, vol. 22, no. 2, 1997, pp 28–34.

6 Greg Moran, 'Teen's Explanation Given In Interviews With Psychiatrist', *Union-Tribune*, 16 August 2002, www.signonsandiego.com/news/metro/ santana/20020816-9999_1n16psych.html.

7 A.A.P., 'Private School Sued Over Assault', *Sydney Morning Herald,* 14 June 2005, www.smh.com.au/news/National/Private-school-sued-over-assault/2005/06/ 14/1118645796114.html.

8 Kerry O'Brien and Tracy Bowden, 'Parent Rejects School's Response to Bullying

Finding', *7.30 Report*, transcript, 7 February 2001, www.abc.net.au/7.30/stories/s243511.htm.

9 Evelyn Field, 'Parent Rejects School's Response to Bullying Finding', *7.30 Report*, transcript, 7 February 2001, www.abc.net.au/7.30/stories/s243511.htm.

10 Ben Fordham, 'Bullying', *A Current Affair*, transcript, 4 March 2004, www.aca.ninemsn.com.au/factsheets/1843.asp.

11 Joe Tanenbaum, *Male and Female Realities: Understanding the Opposite Sex*, Candle Publishing Company, Sugar Land, Texas, 1989.

12 Peter West, *What IS the Matter With Boys? Showing Boys The Way Towards Manhood*, Choice Books, Sydney, 2002.

13 Deborah Tannen, *You Just Don't Understand: Women and Men in Conversation*, William Morrow, New York, 1990.

14 Don Edgar, *Men, Mateship, Marriage: Exploring Macho Myths And The Way Forward*, HarperCollins, Sydney, 1997.

15 Dan Kindlon, PhD. and Michael Thompson, PhD., with Teresa Barker, *Raising Cane: Protecting the Emotional Life of Boys*, Ballantine Books, New York, 1999, p 37.

16 Olga Silverstein and Beth Rashbaum, *The Courage To Raise Good Men*, Viking, New York, 1994, p 119.

BIRTH OF A HERO

1 Maria Burton Nelson, 'Bad Sports: Football, O.J.Simpson, and Wife-Beating', *New York Times*, 22 June 1994.

2 Colette Shulman, 'Raising Boys', *We/Myi, The Women's Dialogue*, vol. 20, no. 4, 1999, www.we-myi.org/issues/20/raising%20boys.html.

3 Anna Quindlen, 'Public and Private: The Good Guys', *New York Times*, 11 April 1993.

4 See www.ffasa.org.

5 Edgar J. Shields Jnr., 'Intimidation and Violence by Males in High School Athletics', *Adolescence*, Fall, 1999, www.parentsurf.com/p/articles/mi_m2248/is_135_34/ai_60302517/pg_2?pi=psf.

6 Josephson Institute of Ethics, Data Summary, Sportsmanship Survey 2004, 13 September 2004, www.charactercounts.org/sports/survey2004/beliefs.htm.

7 Josephson Institute of Ethics, Data Summary, Sportsmanship Survey 2004, 13 September 2004, www.charactercounts.org/sports/survey2004/beliefs.htm.

8 Child Protection In Sport Unit, www.thecpsu.org.uk.

9 Nathan Vass, 'When Sports-Mad Parents Go Too Far', *Woman's Day*, 20 December 2004.

10 Peter West, *What IS the Matter With Boys? Showing Boys The Way Towards Manhood*, Choice Books, Sydney, 2002.

ANGRY YOUNG MEN

1 Dr John R. Lee, 'Teenage Boys' Perceptions Of The Influence Of Teachers And School Experiences On Their Understanding Of Masculinity', *Australian*

Association for Research in Education Conference, University of Sydney, December 2000, www.aare.edu.au/00pap/lee00106.htm.

2 Dr John R. Lee, 'Teenage Boys' Perceptions Of The Influence Of Teachers And School Experiences On Their Understanding Of Masculinity', *Australian Association for Research in Education Conference*, University of Sydney, December 2000, www.aare.edu.au/00pap/lee00106.htm.

3 Roger Horrocks, *Masculinity In Crisis: Myths, Fantasies and Realities*, St Martin's Press, New York, 1994, p 97.

4 Dr John R. Lee, 'Teenage Boys' Perceptions Of The Influence Of Teachers And School Experiences On Their Understanding Of Masculinity', *Australian Association for Research in Education Conference*, University of Sydney, December 2000, www.aare.edu.au/00pap/lee00106.htm.

5 Dan Kindlon, PhD. and Michael Thompson, PhD., with Teresa Barker, *Raising Cane: Protecting the Emotional Life of Boys*, Ballantine Books, New York, 1999.

6 Interview with Father Dave Smith, 28 July 2005.

7 Peter West, *What IS the Matter With Boys? Showing Boys The Way Towards Manhood*, Choice Books, Sydney, 2002.

8 Interview with Ray Lenton, 30 July 2005.

WALKING ON THE WILD SIDE

1 Kay Donovan, *Tagged*; for further details email magneticpics@telstra.com.

2 Douglas A. Gentile et al, 'The Effects Of Violent Video Game Habits On Adolescent Hostility, Aggressive Behaviours, And School Performance', *Journal of Adolescence*, vol. 27, 2004, pp 5–22, www.mediafamily.org/research/Gentile_Lynch_Linder_Walsh_20041.pdf.

3 Douglas A. Gentile et al, 'The Effects Of Violent Video Game Habits On Adolescent Hostility, Aggressive Behaviours, And School Performance', *Journal of Adolescence*, vol. 27, 2004, pp 5–22, www.mediafamily.org/research/Gentile_Lynch_Linder_Walsh_20041.pdf.

4 Ellen Wartella, 'Media and Problem Behaviours in Young People', *Psychosocial Disorders in Young People: Time Trends and Their Causes,* edited by Michael Rutter and David J. Smith, Academia Europa, John Wiley and Sons, Chichester, 1995, pp 296–319.

5 Santina Perrone and Rob White, 'Young People and Gangs', *Australian Institute of Criminology, Trends and Issues,* no. 167, Canberra, September 2000, www.aic.gov.au/publications/tandi/tandi167.html.

6 James C. Howell, 'Youth Gangs: An Overview', *Juvenile Justice Bulletin*, August 1998, www.ojjdp.ncjrs.org/jjbulletin/9808/contents.html.

7 James C. Howell, 'Youth Gangs: An Overview', *Juvenile Justice Bulletin*, August 1998, www.ojjdp.ncjrs.org/jjbulletin/9808/contents.html.

8 Jim Garbarino et al, transcript, 'Boys to Men: Questions of Violence', *Harvard Education Letter,* Research Online, Forum Feature, July/August 1999, www.edletter.org/past/issues/1999-ja/forum.shtml.

9 Santina Perrone and Rob White, 'Young People and Gangs', *Australian Institute of Criminology, Trends and Issues*, no. 167, Canberra, September 2000, www.aic.gov.au/publications/tandi/tandi167.html.

10 Deborah Tannen, *You Just Don't Understand: Women and Men in Conversation*, William Morrow, New York, 1990.

11 Dan Korem, *Suburban Gangs: The Affluent Rebels*, International Focus Press, Richardson, Texas, 1996.

12 Dan Korem, live update and addendum to *Suburban Gangs: The Affluent Rebels*, 7 February 2002, www.ifpinc.com/gangupdate.htm.

13 Interview with Father Dave Smith, 28 July 2005.

14 Interview with Father Dave Smith, 28 July 2005.

WHEN BOYS SUICIDE

1 William Pollack, *Real Boys: Rescuing Our Sons From the Myths of Boyhood*, Random House, New York, 1998.

2 Edwin Shneidman, *Suicide as Psychache: A Clinical Approach to Self-Destructive Behaviour*, Jason Aronson, Northvale, New Jersey, 1993.

3 National Health and Medical Research Council, *National Youth Suicide Prevention Strategy: Setting the Evidence-Based Research Agenda for Australia: A Literature Review*, March 1999.

4 World Health Organization statistics, www.who.int/mental_health/prevention/suicide/country_reports/en/.

5 World Health Organization statistics, www.who.int/mental_health/prevention/suicide/country_reports/en/.

6 Barry Maley, 'Youth Suicide and Youth Unemployment', paper presented at *From Industrial Relations To Personal Relations: The Coercion of Society*, Proceedings XVI Conference, H.R.Nicholls Society, Melbourne, December 1994, www.hrnicholls.com.au/nicholls/nichvo16/vol167yo.htm.

7 National Health and Medical Research Council, *National Youth Suicide Prevention Strategy: Setting the Evidence-Based Research Agenda for Australia: A Literature Review*, March 1999.

8 Bill O'Hehir, *Men's Health: Uncovering the Mystery – A Working Manual*, Open Book Publishers, Adelaide, 1996, p 140.

9 Bill O'Hehir, *Men's Health: Uncovering the Mystery – A Working Manual*, Open Book Publishers, Adelaide, 1996, p 142.

10 'Depression in Young and Teenage Boys', *Medicinenet.com*, 16 May 2003, www.medicinenet.com/script/main/art.asp?articlekey=23376.

11 National Health and Medical Research Council, *National Youth Suicide Prevention Strategy: Setting the Evidence-Based Research Agenda for Australia: A Literature Review*, March 1999.

12 Ellen Wartella, 'Media and Problem Behaviours in Young People', *Psychosocial Disorders in Young People: Time Trends and Their Causes*, edited by Michael Rutter and

David J. Smith, Academia Europa, John Wiley and Sons, Chichester, 1995, pp 296–319.
13 Gail Mason, *Youth Suicide in Australia: Prevention Strategies*, Department of Employment, Education, and Training, Youth Bureau, Canberra, 1990.
14 Interview with Father Dave Smith, 28 July 2005.
15 Jennifer Buckingham, 'Boy Troubles: Understanding Rising Suicide, Rising Crime and Educational Failure', *Centre For Independent Studies Policy Monographs 46*, St Leonards, 2000.

SONS AND THEIR MOTHERS
1 Jo Bailey, 'Making Good Men Out of Boys', *New Zealand Herald,* 1 March 2005.
2 Dan Kindlon, PhD. and Michael Thompson, PhD., with Teresa Barker, *Raising Cane: Protecting the Emotional Life of Boys*, Ballantine Books, New York, 1999.
3 Mark D'Arbanville, *The Naked Husband,* Bantam, Sydney, 2004, p 143.
4 Michael Gurian, *Mothers, Sons and Lovers: How A Man's Relationship With His Mother Affects The Rest Of His Life*, Shambhala, Boston, 1995, p 74.
5 Joe Tanenbaum, *Male and Female Realities: Understanding the Opposite Sex*, Candle Publishing Company, Sugar Land, Texas, 1989.
6 Barbara H. Fiese et al, 'The Stories That Families Tell: Narrative Coherence, Narrative Interaction and Relationship Beliefs', *Monographs of the Society for Research in Child Development*, serial no. 275, vol. 64, no 2., 1999, pp 105–123.

IN SEARCH OF THE PERFECT BODY
1 Peter West, 'From Tarzan to Terminator: Boys, Men and Body Image', a paper presented at the 7th Australian Institute of Family Studies Conference – *Family Futures: Issues in Research and Policy*, Sydney, July 2000, www.aifs.gov.au/institute/afrc7/west.html.
2 Harrison G. Pope Jnr., Katharine A. Phillips, and Roberto Olivardia, *The Adonis Complex: How To Identify, Treat And Prevent Body Obsession In Men And Boys*, Simon & Schuster, New York, 2002.
3 Jessica Bartlett, 'Bigger Isn't Always Better: Muscle Dysmorphia in Men', *American Fitness*, Aerobics and Fitness Association of America, January 2001, www.findarticles.com/p/articles/mi_m0675/is_1_19/ai_69651755.
4 Kendall Clarke and Michele Nardelli, 'The New Extreme – Buying Beauty', *UniSANews*, November 2004, www.unisa.edu.au/unisanews/2004/November/beauty.asp
5 Jacqueline Lunn and Denise Flaim, 'Gay Way Pays', *Sydney Morning Herald*, 25 October 2003.
6 Claire Briney, 'Men's Grooming Products Overview – Metrosexuals? Or Just Average Guys?', presentation *In-Cosmetics Show*, Berlin, 12 April 2005, www.in-cosmetics.com/files/in-cosmetics05_Euromonitor_%20Mens_Grooming_Market.pdf.

7   Renee A. Botta, 'For Your Health? The Relationship Between Magazine Reading And Adolescents' Body Image And Eating Disturbances', *Sex Roles: A Journal of Research*, May 2003, www.findarticles.com/p/articles/mi_m2294/ is_2003_May/ai_104635132.

8   Interview with Dr Murray Drummond, 29 July 2005.

9   B. Kassar, 'The Shape of Things: Men's Body Image and Eating Disorders', *Balance Journal*, Summer 2004, pp 16–21.

10   B. Kassar, 'The Shape of Things: Men's Body Image and Eating Disorders', *Balance Journal*, Summer 2004, pp 16–21.

11   Interview with Dr Murray Drummond, 29 July 2005.

12   Amanda Smith, 'Body Builders and Body Image', *The Sports Factor*, ABC Radio National, 13 December 2002, www.abc.net.au/rn/talks/8.30/sportsf/stories/ s746537.htm.

13   Amanda Smith, 'Body Builders and Body Image', *The Sports Factor*, ABC Radio National, 13 December 2002, www.abc.net.au/rn/talks/8.30/sportsf/stories/ s746537.htm.

14   Amanda Smith, 'Body Builders and Body Image', *The Sports Factor*, ABC Radio National, 13 December 2002, www.abc.net.au/rn/talks/8.30/sportsf/stories/ s746537.htm.

15   P.Y.L. Choi et al, 'Muscle Dysmorphia: A New Syndrome In Weightlifters', *British Journal of Sports Medicine*, vol. 36, 2002, pp 375–376, www.bjsm.bmjjournals. com/cgi/content/full/36/5/375.

16   Interview with Dr Murray Drummond, 29 July 2005.

17   Harrison G. Pope et al, 'Body Image Perception Among Men in Three Countries', *American Journal of Psychiatry*, vol. 157, August 2000, pp 1297–1301.

18   Interview with Dr Murray Drummond, 29 July 2005.

19   Kay Hawes, 'Is Bigger Better?', *National Collegiate Athletic Association News*, 24 September 2001, www.ncaa.org/news/2001/20010924/active/3820n27.html.

20   Murray J. N. Drummond, 'Men, Body Image, and Eating Disorders', *International Journal of Men's Health*, vol. 1, no. 1, January 2002, pp 79–93.

21   'Males and Eating Disorders: Some Basic Facts and Findings', *International Eating Disorder Referral Organisation,* www.edreferral.com/males_eating_disorders.htm.

22   Brendan J. Reed, 'Manorexia: Striving For Six Packs Men Are Losing Control', *FM Weekend Magazine*, Harvard Crimson, 7 December 2000, www.thecrimson. com/fmarchives/fm_12_07_2000/article11M.html.

23   Murray J. N. Drummond, 'Men, Body Image, and Eating Disorders', *International Journal of Men's Health*, vol. 1, no. 1, January 2002, pp 79–93.

24   Kay Hawes, 'Is Bigger Better?', *National Collegiate Athletic Association News*, 24 September 2001, www.ncaa.org/news/2001/20010924/active/3820n27.html.

25   Amanda Smith, 'Abused Bodies', a broadcast with Steven Ungerleider, *The Sports Factor*, ABC Radio National , 7 September 2001, www.abc.net.au/rn/ talks/8.30/sportsf/stories/s360029.htm.

26 P.A.F. McNulty, 'Prevalence and Contributing Factors of Eating Disorder Behaviours in Active Duty Navy Men', cited in 1LT Jennifer Rogers, 'Nutrition Therapy for Soldiers with Eating Disorders', *U.S. Army Medical Department Journal*, July–September 2004, pp 28–33.

27 1LT Jennifer Rogers, 'Nutrition Therapy for Soldiers with Eating Disorders', *U.S. Army Medical Department Journal*, July–September 2004, pp 28–33.

28 Interview with Dr Murray Drummond, 29 July 2005.

29 Department of Health, Housing and Community Services 1993, National Household Service Report, cited in Bruce Maycock and Andrea Beel, 'Anabolic Steroid Abuse and Violence', Contemporary Issues in Crime and Justice, *Crime and Justice Bulletin*, no. 35, July 1997, p 2.

30 A. McGufficke et al, 'Drug Use by Adolescent Athletes', *Youth Studies*, vol. 9, cited in Bruce Maycock and Andrea Beel, 'Anabolic Steroid Abuse and Violence', Contemporary Issues in Crime and Justice, *Crime and Justice Bulletin*, no. 35, July 1997, p 3.

31 Bruce Maycock and Andrea Beel, 'Anabolic Steroid Abuse and Violence', Contemporary Issues in Crime and Justice, *Crime and Justice Bulletin*, no. 35, July 1997, p 2.

32 Interview with Dr Murray Drummond, 29 July 2005.

33 Dr Doug Williamson, 'The Psychological Effects of Anabolic Steroids', *International Journal of Drug Policy*, vol. 5, no. 1, 1994, www.drugtext.org/library/articles/945104.htm.

34 Harrison G. Pope Jnr., Katharine A. Phillips and Roberto Olivardia, *The Adonis Complex: How To Identify, Treat And Prevent Body Obsession In Men And Boys*, Simon & Schuster, New York, 2002.

35 Harrison G. Pope Jnr., Katharine A. Phillips and Roberto Olivardia, *The Adonis Complex: How To Identify, Treat And Prevent Body Obsession In Men And Boys*, Simon & Schuster, New York, 2002.

36 Michele Nardelli, news release, 'UniSA Looks At The Pressure To Be Body Beautiful', University of South Australia, 12 September 2000, www.unisa.edu.au/news/media2000/120900.htm.

37 'Body Image Issues For Men', *Better Health Channel*, 19 April 2005, www.betterhealth.vic.gov.au/bhcv2/bhcarticles.nsf/AToZ?Openview&RestrictToCategory=B&Count=500.

38 Steven Gregor, 'The Man Behind the Mask: Male Body Image Dissatisfaction,' *In Psych 26(3)*, June 2004, pp 27–39, www.psychology.org.au/publications/inpsych/12.2_65.asp.

39 Hope Program, Memorial Hospital, South Bend, www.nd.edu/~wrc/eating.html.

40 Christine Sams, 'Anorexia almost killed me: Daniel Johns', *Sydney Morning Herald*, 6 June 2004.

41 Amanda Smith, 'Abused Bodies', a broadcast with Steven Ungleider, *The Sports Factor*, ABC Radio National, 7 September 2001, www.abc.net.au/rn/talks/8.30/sportsf/stories/s360029.htm.

42 Kendall Clarke and Michele Nardelli, 'The New Extreme – Buying Beauty', *UniSANews*, November 2004, www.unisa.edu.au/unisanews/2004/November/beauty.asp.

43 Interview with Alf Lewis, 28 July 2005.

44 Peter West, 'From Tarzan to Terminator: Boys, Men and Body Image', paper presented at the 7th Australian Institute of Family Studies Conference, *Family Futures: Issues in Research and Policy*, Sydney July 2000, www.aifs.gov.au/institute/afrc7/west.html.

45 Interview with Dr Murray Drummond, 29 July 2005.

46 Susan Faloudi, *Stiffed: The Betrayal of Modern Men*, Chatto & Windus, London, 1999, p 35.

WHEN MEN ARE VULNERABLE

1 Helen Garner, *Joe Cinque's Consolation*, Picador, Sydney, 2004.

2 Stan Dale, 'Why Are Men So "Crazy"?', *The Men's Journal*, Winter 1984/1985, reprinted in *From The Hearts of Men*, edited by Yevrah Ornstein, Ballantine, New York, 1991, p 70.

3 'Australian Crime: Facts and Figures 2003', *Australian Institute of Criminology 2005.*

4 Interview with Ray Lenton, 30 July 2005.

5 Dora Tsavdaridis, 'Killing On Camera', *The Daily Telegraph*, 4 November 2005.

6 'Victims of Sexual Assault, Australia, During the 12 Months Prior to April 2002', *National Crime and Safety Survey 2002*, Australian Bureau of Statistics.

7 Deborah Condon, '10% of Women and 3% of Men Have Been Raped', *Irish Health.com*, 19 April 2002, www.irishhealth.com/?level=4&id=3763.

8 Personal correspondence with Mairi M. Eadie, 7 May 2005.

9 Mairi M. Eadie, 'The Legal and Social Attitudes Towards Male Rape in Scotland and England', thesis, University of Paisley 2004, pp 17–19. Personal correspondence with Mairi M. Eadie, 7 May 2005.

10 Personal correspondence with Mairi M. Eadie, 7 May 2005.

11 Helen Nugent, 'Battered Husbands Trapped By Shame', *Times On Line*, 4 January 2005, www.timesonline.co.uk/article/0,,2-1353322,00.html.

12 David Mortimer, 'Domestic Violence Highlighted at Belfast Conference', *Northern Ireland News*, 26 November 2004, www.4ni.co.uk/forum2/forum/forum_posts.asp?TID=199&PN=1&get=last.

13 Email correspondence with Sotirios Sarantakos, 11 June 2005.

14 Email correspondence with Sotirios Sarantakos, 11 June 2005.

15 David Mortimer, 'Domestic Violence Highlighted at Belfast Conference', *Northern Ireland News*, 26 November 2004, www.4ni.co.uk/forum2/forum/forum_posts.asp?TID=199&PN=1&get=last.

16 Helen Nugent, 'Battered Husbands Trapped By Shame', *Times On Line*, 4 January 2005, www.timesonline.co.uk/article/0,,2-1353322,00.html.

17 Helen Nugent, 'Battered Husbands Trapped By Shame', *Times On Line*, 4 January 2005, www.timesonline.co.uk/article/0,,2-1353322,00.html.

18 Leslie Tutty, 'Husband Abuse: An Overview of Research and Perspectives', Family Violence Prevention Unit, *Health Canada*, 1999, www.phac-aspc. gc.ca/ncfv-cnivf/familyviolence/maleabus_e.html.

19 Matthew Fynes-Clinton, 'For All Mankind', *Brisbane Courier Mail*, 1 July 2000.

20 Marilyn I. Kwong et al, 'Gender Differences in Patterns of Relationship Violence in Alberta', *Canadian Journal of Behavioural Science*, vol. 31, no. 3, 1999, pp 150–160, www.fact.on.ca/Info/dom/kwong99.htm.

21 Marilyn I. Kwong et al, 'Gender Differences in Patterns of Relationship Violence in Alberta', *Canadian Journal of Behavioural Science*, vol. 31, no. 3, 1999, pp 150–160, www.fact.on.ca/Info/dom/kwong99.htm.

22 Email correspondence with Sotirios Sarantakos, 11 June 2005.

23 C. J. Simonelli and K. M. Ingram, 'Psychological Distress Among Men Experiencing Physical and Emotional Abuse in Heterosexual Dating Relationships', *Journal of Interpersonal Violence*, vol. 13, 1998, pp 667–681.

24 Matt Condon, *The Pillow Fight*, Vintage, Sydney, 2004, p 251.

25 Email correspondence with Sotirios Sarantakos, 11 June 2005.

26 Email correspondence with Sotirios Sarantakos, 11 June 2005.

27 Ann Lewis and Dr Sotirios Sarantakos, 'Domestic Violence and the Male Victim', *Nuance,* no. 3, December 2001, pp 1–15, www.nuancejournal.com. au/documents/three/saran.pdf.

28 Christopher H. Cantor et al, 'Australian Suicide Trends 1964–1997: Youth and Beyond?', *Medical Journal of Australia*, vol. 171, 1999, pp 137–141, www.mja.com. au/public/issues/171_3_020899/cantor/cantor.html.

29 Simon Castles, 'The Suicide Generation', the *Age*, 23 November 2004.

30 'Suicide – 41,000 in 20 years', media release, *Australian Institute of Health and Welfare*, 17 April 2001, www.aihw.gov.au/mediacentre/2001/ mr20010419.cfm.

31 Richard Jinman, 'Blokes v the Darkness', Health and Science Supplement, *Sydney Morning Herald*, 30 September 2004.

32 Sharon Hoogland and Randall Pieterse, *Suicide in Australia, A Dying Shame*, Wesley Mission, Sydney, 2000.

THE TRUTH ABOUT RELATIONSHIPS

1 Bill O'Hehir, *Men's Health: Uncovering the Mystery – A Working Manual*, Open Book Publishers, Adelaide, 1996, p 22.

2 Roger Horrocks, *Masculinity In Crisis: Myths, Fantasies and Realities*, St Martin's Press, New York, 1994, p 75.

3 Warren Farrell, Ph.D., *The Myth Of Male Power: Why Men Are the Disposable Sex*, second edition, Finch Publishing, Sydney, 2001.

4 Helen Garner, *The First Stone*, Pan Macmillan, Sydney, 1995.

5 Polly Shulman, 'Great Expectations', *Psychology Today,* doc. 3300, March/April 2004, www.cms.psychologytoday.com/articles/pto-20040301-000002.html.

6 Polly Shulman, 'Great Expectations', *Psychology Today,* doc. 3300, March/April 2004, www.cms.psychologytoday.com/articles/pto-20040301-000002.html.

7 Don Edgar, *Men, Mateship, Marriage: Exploring Macho Myths and the Way Forward,* HarperCollins, Sydney, 1997, p 77.

8 Don Edgar, *Men, Mateship, Marriage: Exploring Macho Myths and the Way Forward,* HarperCollins, Sydney, 1997, p 181.

WHAT HAPPENED TO THE CHEMISTRY?

1 Alon Gratch, *If Men Could Talk: Here's What They'd Say,* Little Brown and Company, New York, 2001.

2 Mark D'Arbanville, *The Naked Husband,* Bantam, Sydney, 2004, p 117.

3 Toby Green with Ray Welling, *The Men's Room: A Thinking Man's Guide For Surviving Women Of The Next Millennium,* Random House Australia, Sydney, 1999, p 90.

4 Deborah Tannen, *You Just Don't Understand: Women and Men in Conversation,* William Morrow, New York, 1990.

5 Bill O'Hehir, *Men's Health: Uncovering the Mystery – A Working Manual,* Open Book Publishers, Adelaide, 1996, p 31.

6 Toby Green with Ray Welling, *The Men's Room: A Thinking Man's Guide For Surviving Women Of The Next Millennium,* Random House Australia, Sydney, 1999, p xix.

7 Irma Kurtz, *Malespeak,* Jonathon Cape, London, 1986, p 14.

8 Michael Gurian, *Mothers, Sons and Lovers: How A Man's Relationship With His Mother Affects The Rest Of His Life,* Shambhala, Boston, 1995, p 95.

9 Alon Gratch, *If Men Could Talk: Here's What They'd Say,* Little Brown and Company, New York, 2001.

10 Steve Biddulph, *Manhood: An Action Plan For Changing Men's Lives,* Finch Publishing, Sydney, 1994, p 1.

11 Irma Kurtz, *Malespeak,* Jonathon Cape, London, 1986, p 3.

12 Alon Gratch, *If Men Could Talk: Here's What They'd Say,* Little Brown and Company, New York, 2001.

13 Toby Green with Ray Welling, *The Men's Room: A Thinking Man's Guide For Surviving Women Of The Next Millennium,* Random House Australia, Sydney, 1999.

14 Roger Horrocks, *Masculinity In Crisis: Myths, Fantasies and Realities,* St Martin's Press, New York, 1994, p 105.

15 Pat Conroy, *The Prince of Tides,* Houghton Mifflin, Boston, 1986, p 86.

16 Alon Gratch, *If Men Could Talk: Here's What They'd Say,* Little Brown and Company, New York, 2001.

17 Roger Horrocks, *Masculinity In Crisis: Myths, Fantasies and Realities,* St Martin's Press, New York, 1994, pp 123–124.

MEN AND SEX

1 Warren Farrell, Ph.D., *The Myth Of Male Power: Why Men Are the Disposable Sex*, second edition, Finch Publishing, Sydney, 2001.
2 Susan Faludi, *Stiffed: The Betrayal of Modern Men*, Chatto & Windus, London, 1999, p 35.
3 Bill O'Hehir, *Men's Health: Uncovering the Mystery — A Working Manual*, Open Book Publishers, Adelaide, 1996, p 21.
4 Susan Faludi, *Stiffed: The Betrayal of Modern Men*, Chatto & Windus, London, 1999, p 35.
5 'Your Best Sex Ever', *Men's Health*, Pacific Publications, Sydney, vol. 8, no.3, January 2005, pp 88–94.
6 Roger Horrocks, *Masculinity In Crisis: Myths, Fantasies and Realities*, St Martin's Press, New York, 1994, p 121.
7 Mark D'Arbanville, *The Naked Husband*, Bantam, Sydney, 2004, p 204.
8 Toby Green with Ray Welling, *The Men's Room: A Thinking Man's Guide For Surviving Women Of The Next Millennium*, Random House Australia, Sydney, 1999, p 70.
9 Helen Chryssides, 'Marriage in 2001: How Honest Are Couples Really?', *Reader's Digest*, December 2001, pp 24–35.
10 Stan Dale, 'Why Are Men So "Crazy"?', *The Men's Journal*, Winter 1984/1985, reprinted in *From The Hearts of Men*, edited by Yevrah Ornstein, Ballantine, New York, 1991, p 71.
11 Kent Hoffman, 'Hints and Guesses', *The Men's Journal*, Fall 1985, reprinted in *From The Hearts of Men*, edited by Yevrah Ornstein, Ballantine, New York, 1991, p 287.
12 Helen Garner, *The First Stone*, Pan Macmillan, Sydney, 1995, p 161.

WHEN THINGS FALL APART

1 Mark D'Arbanville, *The Naked Husband*, Bantam, Sydney, 2004, p 34.
2 Roger Horrocks, *Masculinity In Crisis: Myths, Fantasies and Realities*, St Martin's Press, New York, 1994, p 163.
3 Steve Biddulph, *Manhood: An Action Plan For Changing Men's Lives*, Finch Publishing, Sydney, 1994, p 13.
4 Don Edgar, *Men, Mateship, Marriage: Exploring Macho Myths And The Way Forward*, HarperCollins, Sydney, 1997, p 304.
5 P. Jordan, 'The Effects Of Marital Separation On Men — Men Hurt', *Family Court of Australia Principal Registry Research Report*, no. 5, 1985.
6 Toby Green with Ray Welling, *The Men's Room: A Thinking Man's Guide For Surviving Women Of The Next Millennium*, Random House Australia, Sydney, 1999, p 53.
7 P. Jordan, 'The Effects Of Marital Separation On Men — Men Hurt', *Family Court of Australia Principal Registry Research Report*, no. 5, 1985.
8 E. Mavis Hetherington and Margaret M. Stanley-Hagan, 'The Effects of Divorce on Fathers and Their Children', *The Role of Fathers in Child Development*, edited by Michael Lamb, Third Edition, John Wiley and Sons, New York, 1997, pp 212–226.

9 E. Mavis Hetherington and Margaret M. Stanley-Hagan, 'The Effects of Divorce on Fathers and Their Children', *The Role of Fathers in Child Development,* edited by Michael Lamb, Third Edition, John Wiley and Sons, New York, 1997, pp 212–226.

10 P. Jordan, 'The Effects Of Marital Separation On Men – Men Hurt', *Family Court of Australia Principal Registry Research Report,* no. 5, 1985.

11 Warren Farrell, Ph.D., *The Myth Of Male Power: Why Men Are the Disposable Sex,* second edition, Finch Publishing, Sydney, 2001.

12 Dan Jarvis, 'When Good Marriages Go Bad (and Good Again)', Michigan Family Forum. www.michiganfamily.org/main-resources/articles/ marriage_good%20bad%20good.htm.

13 P. Jordan, 'The Effects Of Marital Separation On Men – Men Hurt', *Family Court of Australia Principal Registry Research Report,* no. 5, 1985.

14 Toby Green with Ray Welling, *The Men's Room: A Thinking Man's Guide For Surviving Women Of The Next Millennium,* Random House Australia, Sydney, 1999, p 49.

15 BradleyH4 in Pat Gaudette, 'Divorce From His Viewpoint', www.divorcesupport. about.com/cs/forhusbands/a/aa121901.htm.

16 Dr David Crawford and Professor John Macdonald, 'Fathers and the Experience of Family Separation', First National Conference of Mental Health of Persons Affected By Family Separation, Liverpool Hospital, October 2002, www. menshealth.uws.edu.au/documents/Fathers%20sep%20ment%20hlth.htm.

17 P. Jordan, 'The Effects of Marital Separation on Men – Ten Years On', *Family Court of Australia Principal Registry Research Report,* no. 14, 1996.

18 Alan Close, talk on men at Byron Bay Writers Festival, 2004.

19 Darren Gray, 'Divorced Men Head Suicide List', the *Age,* 19 April 2001.

MEN AND THEIR HEALTH

1 Dr Ronald F. Levant with Gini Kopecky, *Masculinity Reconstructed: Changing the Rules of Manhood at Work, in Relationships, and in Family Life,* Penguin, New York, 1995.

2 Betsy Mason, 'Men Die Young – Even If Old', *NewScientist.com,* 25 July 2002, www.newscientist.com/article.ns?id=dn2586.

3 Bill O'Hehir, *Men's Health: Uncovering the Mystery – A Working Manual,* Open Book Publishers, Adelaide, 1996.

4 Dr Ronald F. Levant with Gini Kopecky, *Masculinity Reconstructed: Changing the Rules of Manhood at Work, in Relationships, and in Family Life,* Penguin, New York, 1995.

5 Micheal Woods et al, 'Men's Use of General Practitioner Services', *NSW Public Health Bulletin,* vol. 12, no. 12, 2001, pp 23–29, www.health.nsw.gov.au/ public-health/phb/dec01html/gpractdec01.html.

6 Felicity Goodyear-Smith, 'Gendered Approaches to Health Policy', *New Zealand Family Physician,* February 2003, pp 23–29, www.mzcgp.org.nz/news/nz/p/ Feb2003/Goodyear_Smith_Feb03.pdf.

7   Steve Dow, 'Body Report', *Sunday Life, Sun Herald*, 11 July 2004, pp 20–21.

8   Steve Dow, 'Body Report', *Sunday Life, Sun Herald*, 11 July 2004, pp 20–21.

9   *Facts About Testicular Cancer*, Andrology Australia, 2001, www.andrologyaustralia. org/testicular/default.htm.

10 'Osteoporosis and Men', Osteoporosis Australia, www.osteoporosis.org.au/ html/preventionmain.php.

11 Felicity Goodyear-Smith, 'Gendered Approaches to Health Policy', *New Zealand Family Physician*, February 2003, pp 23–29, www.mzcgp.org.nz/news/nz/p/ Feb2003/Goodyear_Smith_Feb03.pdf.

12 J. Jones, 'Understandings of Health: the Background to a Study of Rural Men's Perceptions of Health', proceedings of 3rd Biennial Australian Rural and Remote Health Scientific Conference, Toowoomba, Queensland, 8–9 August 1996.

13 Felicity Goodyear-Smith, 'Gendered Approaches to Health Policy', *New Zealand Family Physician*, February 2003, pp 23–29, www.mzcgp.org.nz/news/nz/p/ Feb2003/Goodyear_Smith_Feb03.pdf.

14 A. Wright, 'Men's Health: What Puts Men Off Visiting Their GP?', in proceedings of 3rd National Men's Health Conference, Alice Springs, 5–8 October 1999.

15 Micheal Woods et al, 'General Practitioners and Men's Health – Perceptions and Practicalities', NSW Men's Health Information and Resource Centre, University of Western Sydney, 2003, www.menshealth.uws.edu.au/documents/ GP%20ConfPaper.html.

16 See www.cancerresearchuk.org/menscancermonth.

17 NSW Health Department, *Moving Forward in Men's Health*, Sydney, 1999.

18 Micheal Woods et al, 'General Practitioners and Men's Health – Perceptions and Practicalities', NSW Men's Health Information and Resource Centre, University of Western Sydney, 2003, www.menshealth.uws.edu.au/documents/ GP%20ConfPaper.html.

19 'Unlocking Men's Secret Thoughts', press release, 30 May 2002, Cancer Research Council, www.info.cancerresearchuk.org/pressoffice/ pressreleases/2002/may/40529.

20 Bill O'Hehir, *Men's Health: Uncovering the Mystery – A Working Manual*, Open Book Publishers, Adelaide, 1996.

MEN'S TAKE ON WORK

1   Gore Vidal on work, cited in Adrienne Burgess, *Fatherhood Reclaimed: The Making Of The Modern Father*, Vermilion, London, 1997, p 15.

2   James Novak, 'Men and Dangerous Work', www.my.execpc.com/~buyright/ articles/men&danger.html.

3   Alon Gratch, *If Men Could Talk: Here's What They'd Say*, Little Brown and Company, New York, 2001.

4   John Markoff, 'Marketer's Dream, Engineer's Nightmare', *New York Times*, 12 December 1993.

RISKY BUSINESS

1 James Novak, 'Men and Dangerous Work', www.my.execpc.com/~buyright/articles/men&danger.html.
2 'Work-related Injuries, Australia', Australian Bureau of Statistics, cat.no.6324.0, September 2000.
3 'Work-related Injuries, Australia', Australian Bureau of Statistics cat.no. 6324.0, September 2000.
4 NSW Health Department, *Moving Forward in Men's Health*, Sydney, 1999, p 11.
5 David Barstow and Lowell Bergman, 'A Dangerous Business', *PBS Frontline*, written by Lowell Bergman, David Rummel and Linden MacIntyre, www.pbs.org/wgbh/pages/frontline/shows/workplace/mcwane/victims.html.
6 James Novak, 'Men and Dangerous Work', www.my.execpc.com/~buyright/articles/men&danger.html.
7 Warren Farrell, Ph.D., *The Myth Of Male Power: Why Men Are the Disposable Sex*, second edition, Finch Publishing, Sydney, 2001.
8 ABC Goldfields-Esperance and Peter Lavelle, 'Macho Miners', a feature based on a series of interviews broadcast on the ABC, June 2002, www.abc.net.au/health/regions/features/machominers/default.htm.
9 www.menatrisk.org/dangerousjobs.html, 12 August 2004.
10 Michelle McPhee, 'Sickly Saviors', *New York Daily News*, 26 May 2004, www.nydailynews.com/news/local/story/197084p-170233c.html.
11 Michelle McPhee, '1,700 Sue Over 9/11 Sickness', *New York Daily News*, 24 May 2004, www.nofirecuts.com/html/health_issues.html.
12 Michelle McPhee, '1,700 Sue Over 9/11 Sickness', *New York Daily News*, 24 May 2004, www.nofirecuts.com/html/health_issues.html.
13 Alan Mascarenhas, 'No Need to Cop it on the Chin', Health and Science Supplement, *Sydney Morning Herald*, 24 March 2005.
14 'The Images and Memories of War', interview with Don McCullin, originally aired on BBC Radio 4 programme *Open Country*, The Dart Center website, April 2005, www.dartcenter.org.
15 See www.dartcenter.org.

BECOMING A DAD

1 Don Edgar, *Men, Mateship, Marriage: Exploring Macho Myths And The Way Forward*, HarperCollins, Sydney, 1997, p 240.
2 Email correspondence with Colin George, director, The Fatherhood Project, 14 August 2005.
3 Professor Don Edgar, 'Emotional Competence is a Man's Business', keynote address, Fatherhood Conference, Perth, 14 February 2001, www.ngala.com.au/keynote_1_html.
4 Duncan Fisher, '21st Century Dad', speech at the National Conference of Working Fathers, London, 5 April 2004, www.fathersdirect.com/index.php?nID=43.

5 Jane Hutchinson, 'The Father Load', *Sunday Magazine, Sunday Telegraph*, 5 September 2004.
6 Ross D. Parke and Armin A. Brott, *Throwaway Dads: The Myths And Barriers That Keep Men From Being The Fathers They Want To Be*, Houghton Mifflin, Boston, 1999.
7 Email correspondence with Jared Fiel, 30 December 2004.
8 Michael Lamb, 'The Role of Fathers in Child Development', interview with Julie McCrossin, ABC *Life Matters*, ABC Radio National, 4 May 2004, www.abc.net.au/rn/talks/lm/stories/s1099987.htm.
9 Michael Lamb et al, 'Fathers' Influences on Children', *The Role of Fathers in Child Development,* edited by Michael Lamb, Fourth Edition, John Wiley and Sons, New York, 2004.
10 Irma Kurtz, *Malespeak*, Jonathon Cape, London, 1986.

THE MOMENT OF FATHERHOOD

1 Jay Turley, 'Fatherhood – The Journey', www.fatherville.com/Articles/New_Dads/Fatherhood_-_The_Journey/.
2 'Good Times, Bad Times', *Sunday Life, Sun-Herald*, 7 November 2004.
3 Email correspondence with Jared Fiel, 30 December 2004.
4 Gary Dornau, 'Children, Father and Families', workshop paper presented at the Australian Institute of Family Studies Conference, January 2003.
5 'Dads' Involvement with Their Babies and Pre-School Children', *Father Facts*, vol. 1, issue 1, www.fathersdirect.com, p 4.
6 Ross D. Parke and Armin A. Brott, *Throwaway Dads: The Myths And Barriers That Keep Men From Being The Fathers They Want To Be*, Houghton Mifflin, Boston, 1999.
7 Joane Hutchinson, 'The Father Load', *Sunday Magazine, Sunday Telegraph*, 5 September 2004.
8 Martin Greenberg M.D., *Birth of a Father*, Avon, New York, 1985.
9 Jay Turley, 'Fatherhood – The Journey', www.fatherville.com/Articles/New_Dads/Fatherhood_-_The_Journey/.
10 Duncan Fisher, '21st Century Dad', speech at the National Conference of Working Fathers, London, 5 April 2004, www.fathersdirect.com/index.php?nID=43.
11 Email correspondence with Julie Coates, 28 January 2005.
12 Email correspondence with Jared Fiel, 30 December 2004.
13 Shannon Quinn, 'Study: For Men, Family Comes First', *Harvard Gazette Archives*, 4 May 2000, www.news.harvard.edu/gazette/2000/05.04/radcliffe.html.
14 Don Edgar, *Men, Mateship, Marriage: Exploring Macho Myths And The Way Forward*, HarperCollins, Sydney, 1997, p 73.
15 Deirdre Macken, 'And Another Thing', *Sunday Life*, 6 March 2005.
16 Daniel Petre, *Father Time: Making Time For Your Children*, Jane Curry Publishing, Sydney, 2005, p xix.
17 Hogan Hilling, *A Father's Place is in the Home*, www.fatherville.com/Articles/Stay_At_Home_Dads/A_Father%27s_Place_Is_In_The_Home/.

[18] Hogan Hilling, *A Father's Place is in the Home*, www.fatherville.com/Articles/ Stay_At_Home_Dads/A_Father%27s_Place_Is_In_The_Home/.

[19] Hogan Hilling, *A Father's Place is in the Home*, www.fatherville.com/Articles/ Stay_At_Home_Dads/A_Father%27s_Place_Is_In_The_Home/.

WHAT DADS HAVE TO OFFER

[1] Adrienne Burgess, *Fatherhood Reclaimed: The Making Of The Modern Father*, Vermilion, London, 1997.

[2] Email correspondence with Colin George, director, The Fatherhood Project, 14 August 2005.

[3] Dr Ronald F. Levant, with Gini Kopeeky, *Masculinity Reconstructed: Changing the Rules of Manhood at Work, in Relationships, and in Family Life*, Penguin, New York, 1995.

[4] Michael Lamb, 'The Role of Fathers in Child Development', interview with Julie McCrossin, *Life Matters*, ABC Radio National, 4 May 2004, www.abc.net.au/rn/ talks/lm/stories/s1099987.htm.

[5] Kyle Pruett, M.D. 'Hands-On Dads Are Important', *Mensight Magazine*, 2003, www.mensightmagazine.com/Articles/Pruett.

[6] Kyle Pruett, M.D. 'Hands-On Dads Are Important', *Mensight Magazine*, 2003, www.mensightmagazine.com/Articles/Pruett.

[7] Daniel Petre, *Father Time: Making Time For Your Children*, Jane Curry Publishing, Sydney, 2005, p 102.

[8] Michael Gurian, *Mothers, Sons and Lovers: How A Man's Relationship With His Mother Affects The Rest Of His Life*, Shambhala, Boston, 1995, p 67.

[9] Jack O'Sullivan, 'Children Want To Do Ordinary Activities With Dad', press release, Father's Direct, 16 June 2004, www.fathersdirect.com/index. php?12&cID=78.

[10] Jack O'Sullivan, 'Children Want To Do Ordinary Activities With Dad', press release, Father's Direct, 16 June 2004, www.fathersdirect.com/index. php?12&cID=78.

[11] Email correspondence with Colin George, director, The Fatherhood Project, 14 August 2005.

BOYS AND THEIR DADS

[1] Steve Biddulph, *Manhood: An Action Plan For Changing Men's Lives*, Finch Publishing, Sydney, 1994, p 39.

[2] Interview with Father Dave Smith, 28 July 2005.

[3] Michael, E. Lamb, 'Fathers and Child Development: An Introductory Overview and Guide', *The Role of Fathers in Child Development*, edited by Michael Lamb, Third Edition, John Wiley and Sons, New York, 1997, pp 1–18.

[4] Frank C. Cardelle, *Journey to Brotherhood: Awakening and Healing Men's Hearts*, Gardner Press, New York, 1990.

5 Kyle Pruett, M.D. 'Hands-On Dads Are Important', *Mensight Magazine*, 2003. www.mensightmagazine.com/Articles/Pruett.

6 Madeleine Reiss, 'A Father's Last Letters', *Sydney Morning Herald*, 10 May 2005.

7 Michael Jacobson, *Windmill Hill*, Hodder Headline, Sydney, 2000.

8 Steve Biddulph, *Manhood: An Action Plan For Changing Men's Lives*, Finch Publishing, Sydney, 1994.

9 Email correspondence with Colin George, director, The Fatherhood Project, 14 August 2005.

10 Steve Biddulph, *Manhood: An Action Plan For Changing Men's Lives*, Finch Publishing, Sydney, 1994, p 42.

11 Don Edgar, *Men, Mateship, Marriage: Exploring Macho Myths And The Way Forward*, HarperCollins, Sydney, 1997, p 258.

12 Don Edgar, *Men, Mateship, Marriage: Exploring Macho Myths And The Way Forward*, HarperCollins, Sydney, 1997, p 259.

13 Yevrah Ornstein, ed., *From The Hearts of Men*, Ballantine, New York, 1991, p 127.

14 Pat Conroy, *The Prince of Tides*, Houghton Mifflin, Boston, 1986, p 155.

15 Yevrah Ornstein, ed., 'In Response to Robert Bly's Poem, "At My Father's Wedding"', *From The Hearts of Men*, edited by Yevrah Ornstein, Ballantine, New York, 1991, p 133.

16 Bill O'Hehir, *Men's Health: Uncovering the Mystery – A Working Manual*, Open Book Publishers, Adelaide, 1996, p 15.

17 Toby Green with Ray Welling, *The Men's Room: A Thinking Man's Guide For Surviving Women Of The Next Millennium*, Random House Australia, Sydney, 1999, p 59.

18 Yevrah Ornstein, ed., 'Once I heard My Real Dad', *From The Hearts of Men*, Ballantine, New York, 1991, pp 21–22.

FATHERS AND DAUGHTERS

1 Irma Kurtz, *Malespeak*, Jonathon Cape, London, 1986, p 65.

2 Irma Kurtz, *Malespeak*, Jonathon Cape, London, 1986, p 64.

3 Office of Alumni Affairs, 'Absent Fathers Faulted', *Duke Magazine*, vol. 85, no. 9, July–August 2003, www.dukemagazine.duke.edu/dukemag/issues/070803/depgaz6.html.

4 Jay Turley, 'Fatherhood – The Journey', www.fatherville.com/Articles/New_Dads/Fatherhood_-_The_Journey/.

OUT ON A LIMB

1 Jed Diamond, *The Myth of the Dangerous Dad*, San Rafael, 1998, reprinted in *From The Hearts of Men*, edited by Yevrah Ornstein, Ballantine, New York, 1991, p 105.

2 Tom Morton, *Altered Mates: The Man Question*, Allen & Unwin, Sydney, 1997, p 180.

3 Danae Clark, 'Father Figure', *Boys: Masculinities In Contemporary Culture*, edited by Paul Smith, Westview Press, Boulder, Colorado, 1996, pp 23–37.

4   Felicity Goodyear-Smith, 'Fathers – Myths and Realities about Child Maltreatment', *Perspectives on Fathering Issues*, no. 4, edited by Stuart Birks and Paul Callister, Centre for Public Policy Evaluation, Massey University, April 1999, www.econ.massey.ac.nz/cppe/papers/cppeip04/cppeip04.pdf.

5   Douglas Besharov, *Statement of Douglas Besharov Before the Select Committee on Children, Youth and Families*, 3 March 1987, www.liftingtheveil.org/beshar.htm.

6   Felicity Goodyear-Smith, 'Fathers – Myths and Realities about Child Maltreatment', *Perspectives on Fathering Issues*, no. 4, edited by Stuart Birks and Paul Callister, Centre for Public Policy Evaluation, Massey University, April 1999, www.econ.massey.ac.nz/cppe/papers/cppeip04/cppeip04.pdf.

7   D. Finkelhor, 'Early and Long-term Effects of Child Sexual Abuse: An update', *Professional Psychology: Research and Practice*, vol. 21, pp 325–330, cited in Felicity Goodyear-Smith, 'Fathers – Myths and Realities about Child Maltreatment', *Perspectives on Fathering Issues*, no. 4, edited by Stuart Birks and Paul Callister, Centre for Public Policy Evaluation, Massey University, April 1999, www.econ.massey.ac.nz/cppe/papers/cppeip04/cppeip04.pdf.

8   Michael Gordon, 'The Family Environment of Sexual Abuse: A Comparison of Natal and Stepfather Abuse', *Child Abuse and Neglect*, vol. 13, 1989, pp 121–130, cited in *Father Facts: Fatherless Families and Domestic Violence*, Palmetto Family Council, www.palmettofamily.org/Reports/Fatherhood/HTMLRpt/father02.htm.

DADS AND DIVORCE

1   Belinda Pascoe, Unifam Counselling and Mediation Service, *Shared Parenting: Working With Separated Fathers Workshop*, Burnside, March 2005.

2   Sanford Braver with Diane O'Connell, *Divorced Dads: Shattering the Myths*, Jeremy Tarcher/Putnam, 1998, pp 13–14.

3   Bruce Smyth, 'Postseparation Fathering: What Does Australian Research Tell Us?', paper presented at the Fatherhood Research in Australia Seminar, University of Newcastle, 4 December 2003, www.aifs.gov.au/institute/pubs/papers/smyth03.html.

4   Michael E. Lamb, 'Fathers and Child Development: An Introductory Overview and Guide', *The Role of Fathers in Child Development*, edited by Michael Lamb, Third Edition, John Wiley and Sons, New York, 1997, pp 1–18.

5   Bill O'Hehir, *Men's Health: Uncovering the Mystery – A Working Manual*, Open Book Publishers, Adelaide, 1996.

6   Interview with Ray Lenton, 30 July 2005.

7   Felicity Goodyear-Smith, 'Fathers – Myths and Realities about Child Maltreatment', *Perspectives on Fathering Issues*, no. 4, edited by Stuart Birks and Paul Callister, Centre for Public Policy Evaluation, Massey University, April 1999, www.econ.massey.ac.nz/cppe/papers/cppeip04/cppeip04.pdf.

8   Bruce Smyth, 'Postseparation Fathering: What Does Australian Research Tell Us?', paper presented at the Fatherhood Research in Australia Seminar,

University of Newcastle, 4 December 2003, www.aifs.gov.au/institute/pubs/
papers/smyth03.html.

9 Interview with Ray Lenton, 30 July 2005.

10 Sanford Braver with Diane O'Connell, *Divorced Dads: Shattering the Myths*,
Jeremy Tarcher/Putnam, 1998.

11 Michael Green, *Fathers After Divorce*, Finch Publishing, Sydney, 1998.

12 Bruce Smyth, 'Postseparation Fathering: What Does Australian Research
Tell Us?', paper presented at the Fatherhood Research in Australia Seminar,
University of Newcastle, 4 December 2003, www.aifs.gov.au/institute/pubs/
papers/smyth03.html.

13 Interview with Ray Lenton, 30 July 2005.

14 Bruce Hawthorne, 'Australian Men's Experience of Nonresident Fathering',
Australian Institute of Family Studies Conference, Melbourne, February 2005,
www.aifs.gov.au/institute/afrc9/hawthorne.html.

15 Terry Colling, *Beyond Mateship: Understanding Australian Men,* Simon & Schuster,
Sydney, 1992, p 105.

16 Bruce Smyth, 'Postseparation Fathering: What Does Australian Research Tell
Us?', paper presented at the Fatherhood Research in Australia Seminar, University
of Newcastle, 4 December 2003, www.aifs.gov.au/institute/pubs/papers/
smyth03.html.

17 Pat Gaudette, 'Divorce From His Viewpoint', www.divorcesupport.about.com/
cs/forhusbands/a/aa121901.htm.

18 Interview with Ray Lenton, 30 July 2005.

19 E. Mavis Hetherington and Margaret M. Stanley-Hagan, 'The Effects of Divorce
on Fathers and Their Children', *The Role of Fathers in Child Development,* edited by
Michael Lamb, Third Edition, John Wiley and Sons, New York, 1997,
pp 212–226.

20 Dr Wade F. Horn, 'Abusive Parents and Unhappy Marriages', keynote address,
Fatherhood Institute, Fifth Annual Smart Marriages Conference, Orlando,
June 2000, www.archives.his.com/smartmarriages/2000-December/
msg00013.html.

21 E. Mavis Hetherington and Margaret M. Stanley-Hagan, 'The Effects of Divorce
on Fathers and Their Children', *The Role of Fathers in Child Development,* edited by
Michael Lamb, Third Edition, John Wiley and Sons, New York, 1997, pp 212–226.

22 Bruce Smyth, 'Time to Rethink Time? The Experience of Time With Children
After Divorce', *Family Matters*, no. 71, Winter 2005.

23 Mark E.Cummings and Anne Watson O'Reilly, 'Fathers in Family Context:
Effects of Marital Quality on Child Adjustment', *The Role of Fathers in Child
Development,* edited by Michael Lamb, Third Edition, John Wiley and Sons,
New York, 1997, pp 49–65.

24 See www.campconnect.org.

25 Interview with Brad Mander, 25 June 2005.

26 E. Mavis Hetherington and Margaret M. Stanley-Hagan, 'The Effects of Divorce on Fathers and Their Children', *The Role of Fathers in Child Development,* edited by Michael Lamb, Third Edition, John Wiley and Sons, New York, 1997, pp 212–226.

27 Michael Flood, 'Mapping Loneliness in Australia', Discussion Paper 76, The Australian Institute, February 2005.

28 Farah Farouque, 'The Solitary Confinement of the Aussie Bloke', the *Age,* 26 February 2005.

LIFE AFTER DIVORCE

1 Bruce Hawthorne, 'Australian Men's Experience of Nonresident Fathering', Australian Institute of Family Studies Conference, Melbourne, February 2005, www.aifs.gov.au/institute/afrc9/hawthorne.html.

2 Dads in Distress website, www.dadsindistress.asn.au/stories.html.

3 Sanford Braver with Diane O'Connell, *Divorced Dads: Shattering the Myths,* Jeremy Tarcher/Putnam, 1998, p 37.

4 E. Mavis Hetherington and Margaret M. Stanley-Hagan, 'The Effects of Divorce on Fathers and Their Children', *The Role of Fathers in Child Development,* edited by Michael Lamb, Third Edition, John Wiley and Sons, New York, 1997, pp 212–226.

5 See www.geocities.com/stepfathers/issuesbestbond.html.

6 Awashen in Pat Gaudette, 'Divorce From His Viewpoint', www.divorcesupport. about.com/cs/forhusbands/a/aa121901.htm.

7 P. Jordan, 'The Effects Of Marital Separation On Men – Men Hurt', *Family Court of Australia Principal Registry Research Report,* no. 5, 1985.

8 Darren Gray, 'Divorced Men Head the Suicide List in Australia', the *Age,* 19 April 2001.

9 Dr David Crawford and Professor John Macdonald, 'Fathers and the Experience of Family Separation', First National Conference of Mental Health of Persons Affected By Family Separation, Liverpool Hospital, October 2002, www.google. com.au/search?hl=en&ie=ISO-8859-1&q=david+crawford+john+macdonald +fathers+separation&btnG=Search&meta=.

10 Bruce Hawthorne, 'Australian Men's Experience of Nonresident Fathering', Australian Institute of Family Studies Conference, Melbourne, February 2005, www.aifs.gov.au/institute/afrc9/hawthorne.html.

11 Sharon Hoogland and Randall Pieterse, *Suicide in Australia, A Dying Shame,* Wesley Mission, Sydney, 2000.

12 Sharon Hoogland and Randall Pieterse, *Suicide in Australia, A Dying Shame,* Wesley Mission, Sydney, 2000.

13 Andrew Renouf, www.fact.on.ca/renouf/r_letter.htm.

14 Interview with Ray Lenton, 30 July 2005.

15 Bruce Hawthorne, 'Australian Men's Experience of Nonresident Fathering', Australian Institute of Family Studies Conference, Melbourne, February 2005, www.aifs.gov.au/institute/afrc9/hawthorne.html.

PICKING UP THE PIECES

1 Julie Scelfo, 'Happy Divorce', *Newsweek*, 6 December 2004, www.fatherhood.about.com/b/a/132988.htm.
2 www.fatherville.com, www.divorcesupport.about.com.
3 Ron Miller, 'Take The High Road', 30 September 2002, www.fatherville.com/Articles/Divorced_Fathers/Take_The_High_Road/.
4 Ron Miller, 'The Impact of Divorce on Kids', 30 September 2002, www.fatherville.com/Articles/Divorced_Fathers/Take_The_High_Road/.
5 Chuck Houghton, 'My Story II, Divorced Dads – When Making A Difference Counts', www.geocities.com/Heartland/Meadows/1259/story2.htm.
6 Bill Klatte, 'A Letter to Live-Away Dads', *Connect For Kids*, www.connectforkids.org/node/237; William C. Klatte, *Live-Away Dads: Staying Part of Your Children's Lives When They Aren't Part of Your Home*, Penguin, New York, 1999.
7 Ray Lenton, Presentation, *Intensive Practice Workshop: Working With Separated Fathers*, Burnside, March 2005.
8 Chuck Houghton, 'My Story II, Divorced Dads – When Making A Difference Counts', www.geocities.com/Heartland/Meadows/1259/story2.htm.

WHEN MEN RETIRE

1 John Larkin, 'The Gnawing 40s', *Sunday Life*, Sun-Herald, 11 July 2004.
2 Jack Zinn, *Old Men's Business: Valuing Relationships, Living With Change*, Finch Publishing, Sydney, 2002, p vii.
3 Interview with Bob Nelson, 5 November, 2004.
4 Terry Colling, *Beyond Mateship: Understanding Australian Men*, Simon & Schuster, Sydney, 1992, pp 123–124.
5 NSW Health Department, *Moving Forward in Men's Health*, Sydney, 1999, p 16.
6 Tim Adams, 'Marriage Made in Heaven', *The Observer*, 18 March 2001, www.books.guardian.co.uk/departments/biography/story/0,6000,458429,00.html.
7 Robert James Waller, *The Bridges of Madison County*, Warner Books, New York, 1992, pp 100–101.

ON THEIR OWN

1 Steve Biddulph, *Manhood: An Action Plan For Changing Men's Lives*, Finch Publishing, Sydney, 1994
2 Interview with Bob Nelson, 5 November, 2004.
3 Sara Arbor, Kate Davidson et al, 'Older Men's Business: Their Social Worlds and Healthy Lifestyles', *GO Research Findings 12*, January 2003, pp 1–4, Economic and Social Research Council, www.esrcsocietytoday.ac.uk/ESRCInfoCentre/Plain_English_summaries//LLH/index154.aspx.
4 Irma Kurtz, *Malespeak*, Jonathon Cape, London, 1986, p 161.

ENDING IT

1 T. Salvatore, 'Elder Suicide: A Gatekeeper Strategy for Home Care',
Home Healthcare Nurse, vol. 18, no. 3, March 2000, pp 180–186.
2 WHO statistics, www.who.int/mental_health/prevention/suicide/
country_reports/en/.
3 WHO statistics, www.who.int/mental_health/prevention/suicide/
country_reports/en/.
4 Email correspondence with Professor Yeates Conwell, 12 November 2004.
5 John McIntosh, Ph.D., 'The Suicide of Elderly Men and Women: How You Can
Prevent the Tragedy', www.suicidereferencelibrary.com/test4~id~661.php.
6 Dr Eric Caine, press release, Ninth Congress of the International Psychogeriatric
Association, Vancouver, August 1999, www.suicidereferencelibrary.com/
test4~id~1320.php.
7 Dr Eric Caine, press release, Ninth Congress of the International Psychogeriatric
Association, Vancouver, August 1999, www.suicidereferencelibrary.com/
test4~id~1320.php.
8 'Suicide Among Older Persons – United States 1980–1992', *Morbidity and Mortality
Weekly Report,* vol. 45, no. 1, 12 January 1996, pp 3–6, Center for Disease Control
and Prevention, www.cdc.gov/mmwr/preview/mmwrhtml/00039937.htm.

OPENING UP

1 www.petsfortheelderly.org.
2 Odean Cusack, *Pets and Our Mental Health*, Hayworth Press, New York, 1988.
3 Karen Bullock, 'Grandfathers and The Impact of Raising Grandchildren',
Journal of Sociology and Social Welfare, vol. 32, no. 1, 43, 17 March 2005.
4 Interview with Jan Backhouse, 5 January 2005.

IN THE COMPANY OF MEN

1 Toby Green with Ray Welling, *The Men's Room: A Thinking Man's Guide For Surviving
Women Of The Next Millennium,* Random House Australia, Sydney, 1999, p 41.
2 Yevrah Ornstein, ed., *From The Hearts of Men*, Ballantine, New York, 1991.

THE WAY AHEAD

1 Suicide Fact Sheet, www.salvos.org.au/SALVOS/NEW/me.get?SITE.
sectionshow&FFFF358#australia.

Bibliography

Allen, Tim, *Don't Stand Too Close to a Naked Man*, Transworld Publishers, Sydney, 1995

Biddulph, Steve, *Manhood: An Action Plan For Changing Men's Lives*, Finch Publishing, Sydney, 1994

Biddulph, Steve, *Raising Boys: Why Boys Are Different and How To Help Them Become Happy and Well-Balanced Men*, Finch Publishing, Sydney, 1997

Blankenhorn, David, *Fatherless America: Confronting Our Most Urgent Social Problem*, Basic Books, New York, 1995

Braver, Sanford, with Diane O'Connell, *Divorced Dads: Shattering the Myths*, Jeremy Tarcher/Putnam, 1998

Brazelton, T. Berry et al, editors, *Affective Development in Infancy*, Ablex Publishing, Norwood, New Jersey, 1986

Buckingham, Jennifer, 'Boy Troubles: Understanding Rising Suicide, Rising Crime and Educational Failure', *Centre For Independent Studies Policy Monographs 46*, St Leonards, 2000

Burgess, Adrienne, *Fatherhood Reclaimed: The Making of The Modern Father*, Vermilion, London, 1997

Cardelle, Frank C., *Journey to Brotherhood: Awakening and Healing Men's Hearts*, Gardner Press, New York, 1990

Colling, Terry, *Beyond Mateship: Understanding Australian Men*, Simon & Schuster, Sydney, 1992

Condon, Matt, *The Pillow Fight*, Vintage, Sydney, 1998

Conroy, Pat, *The Prince of Tides*, Houghton Mifflin, Boston, 1986

Cusack, Odean, *Pets and Our Mental Health*, Haworth Press, New York, 1988

D'Arbanville, Mark, *The Naked Husband*, Bantam, Sydney, 2004

Edgar, Don, *Men Mateship, Marriage: Exploring Macho Myths And The Way Forward*, HarperCollins, Sydney, 1997

Edwards, Susan, *When Men Believe in Love: A Book for Men who Love Women and the Women they Love,* Element, Shaftsbury, Dorset, 1995

Emilo, Wayne, and Maria Palotto-Chiarolli, *Boys' Stuff: Boys Talking About What Matters,* Allen & Unwin, Sydney, 2001

Faludi, Susan, *Backlash: The Undeclared War Against American Women,* Anchor, New York, 1991

Faludi, Susan, *Stiffed: The Betrayal of Modern Men,* Chatto & Windus, London, 1999

Farrell, Warren, Ph.D., *The Myth Of Male Power: Why Men Are the Disposable Sex,* second edition, Finch Publishing, Sydney, 2001

Fiel, Jared, *Fumbling Through Fatherhood,* Atja Books, Greeley, Colorado, 2004

Flocker, Michael, *The Metrosexual Guide to Style: A Handbook For The Modern Man,* Perseus Books, Cambridge, Massachusetts, 2003

Friedman, Brook, *Boys Talk: A Program for Young Men about Masculinity, Non-Violence and Relationships,* Kookaburra Press, Adelaide, 1996

Garner, Helen, *The First Stone,* Pan Macmillan, Sydney, 1995

Garner, Helen, *Joe Cinque's Consolation,* Picador, Sydney, 2004

Gratch, Alon, *If Men Could Talk: Here's What They'd Say,* Little Brown and Company, New York, 2001

Gray, John, *Men Are From Mars, Women Are From Venus: A Practical Guide to Improving Communication and Getting What You Want in Your Relationships,* Thorsons, New York, 1993

Green, Michael, *Fathers After Divorce: Building A New Life and Becoming A Successful Separated Parent,* Finch Publishing, Sydney, 1998

Green, Toby, with Ray Welling, *The Men's Room: A Thinking Man's Guide For Surviving Women Of The Next Millennium,* Random House Australia, Sydney, 1999

Greenberg, Martin, M.D., *Birth of a Father,* Avon, New York, 1985

Gurian, Michael, *Mothers, Sons and Lovers: How A Man's Relationship With His Mother Affects The Rest Of His Life,* Shambhala, Boston, 1995

Henderson, Leila, *Step-Parent Survival Guide,* Gore and Osment Publications, Sydney, 1996

Horrocks, Roger, *Masculinity In Crisis: Myths, Fantasies and Realities,* St Emil's Press, New York, 1994

Jacobson, Michael, *Windmill Hill,* Hodder Headline, Sydney, 2002

Johnson, Robert A., *He: Understanding Masculine Psychology,* Harper & Row, New York, 1977

Kindlon, Dan, PhD. and Michael Thompson PhD., with Teresa Barker, *Raising Cane: Protecting the Emotional Life of Boys,* Ballantine Books, New York, 1999

Kurtz, Irma, *Malespeak,* Jonathon Cape, London, 1986

Lamb, Michael E., ed., *The Role of Fathers In Child Development,* Third Edition, John Wiley and Sons, New York, 1997

Levant, Ronald F. Dr with Gini Kopecky, *Masculinity Reconstructed: Changing the Rules of Manhood at Work, in Relationships, and in Family Life,* Penguin, New York, 1995

Marsden, John, *Secret Men's Business: Manhood: The Big Gig*, Pan Macmillan, Sydney, 1998

Mason, Gail, *Youth Suicide in Australia: Prevention Strategies*, Department of Employment, Education and Training, Youth Bureau, Canberra, 1990

Mate, Gabor, *When The Body Says No*, Scribe, Melbourne, 2003

Miedzian, Myriam, *Boys Will Be Boys: Breaking the Link Between Masculinity and Violence*, Anchor, Bantam, Doubleday, New York, 1991

Morton, Tom, *Altered Mates: The Man Question*, Allen & Unwin, Sydney, 1997

National Health and Medical Research Council, *National Youth Suicide Prevention Strategy: Setting the Evidence-Based Research Agenda for Australia: A Literature Review*, March 1999

Nelson, Bob, *Mateship and Meaningful Community Contribution: Promoting the Sound Mental Health of Retired Men*, paper presented at the NSW Elderly Suicide Prevention Network Conference, Sydney, November 2003

NSW Health Department, *Moving Forward in Men's Health*, Sydney, 1999

O'Hehir, Bill, *Men's Health: Uncovering the Mystery – A Working Manual,* Open Book Publishers, Adelaide, 1996

Ornstein, Yevrah, *From The Hearts of Men*, Ballantine, New York, 1991

Parke, Ross.D. & Brott, Armin A., *Throwaway Dads: The Myths and Barriers that Keep Men from Being the Fathers They Want to Be*, Houghton Mifflin, Boston, 1999

Parsons, Tony, *Man and Boy*, HarperCollins, London, 2002

Peck, Michael L. et al, eds., *Youth Suicide*, Springer Publishing Company, New York, 1985

Petre, Daniel, *Father Time: Making Time for Your Children*, Jane Curry Publishing, Sydney, 2005

Phillips, Katharine A., *The Broken Mirror: Understanding and Treating BDD*, Oxford University Press, New York, 1996

Pollack, William, *Real Boys: Rescuing Our Sons From the Myths of Boyhood*, Random House, New York, 1998

Pope, Harrison G. Jnr., Katharine A. Phillips, and Roberto Olivardia, *The Adonis Complex: How To Identify, Treat And Prevent Body Obsession In Men And Boys*, Simon & Schuster, New York, 2002

Rutter, Michael and David J. Smith, eds., *Psychosocial Disorders in Young People: Time Trends and Their Causes*, Academia Europa, John Wiley and Sons, Chichester, 1995

Shneidman, Edwin, *Suicide as Psychache: A Clinical Approach to Self-Destructive Behaviour*, Jason Aronson, Northvale, New Jersey, 1993

Silverstein Olga, and Beth Rashbaum, *The Courage To Raise Good Men*, Viking, New York, 1994

Smith, David B., Rev., *Sex, The Ring and The Eucharist: Reflections on Life, Ministry and Fighting in the Inner City*, Hippo Books, Sydney, Australia, 2003

Smith, Paul, ed., *Boys: Masculinities in Contemporary Culture*, Westview Press, Boulder Colorado, 1996

Stoltenberg, Jon, *Refusing to Be A Man*, Fontana, London, 1990

Tanenbaum, Joe, *Male and Female Realities: Understanding the Opposite Sex*, Candle Publishing Company, Sugar Land, Texas, 1989

Tannen, Deborah, *You Just Don't Understand: Women and Men in Conversation*, William Morrow, New York, 1990

Waller, Robert James, *The Bridges of Madison County*, Warner Books, New York, 1992

West, Peter, *What IS the Matter With Boys? Showing Boys The Way Towards Manhood*, Choice Books, Sydney, 2002

Zinn, Jack, *Older Men's Business: Valuing Relationships, Living With Change*, Finch Publishing, Sydney, 2002

Resources

Battered men: www.batteredmen.com, www.mensrights.com.au
Boys: www.boysforward.com, www.pathwaysfoundation.com.au
Counselling: www.dadsindistress.asn.as, www.mensworkshop.com.au,
    www.lifeworks.com.au
Fathers: www.fatherhood.com.au, www.fathersdirect.com, www.fathermag.com,
    www.fathers.com, www.fatherhood.org, www.fathersonline.org
Fathers' weekends away with their kids: www.campconnect.org
Male rape: www.vix.com/men/abuse/abuse.html, www.actabuse.com/malerape.
    html, www.XRIS.com
Manhood: www.mensworkproject.com, www.manhood.com.au, www.
    mtmaustralia.org.au
ManKind: www.mankind.org.uk
Men's cancer: www.cancerresearchuk.org/menscancermonth
Men's e-magazines: EMALE – free subscription – gmillan@bigpond.net.au,
    www.mensightmagazine.com
Men's groups: www.mensgroups.com.au
Men's Internet radio show: www.glennsacks.com
Men's issues: www.menatrisk.org, www.menweb.org, www.menalive.com.au
Pets for the elderly: www.petsfortheelderly.org
Relationships: www.rels-about.com
Separated dads: www.sos-family.org.au, www.weekendparent.com.au
Shared parenting: www.spig.clara.net
Solo dads: www.lonefathers.com.au, www.oneparent.freeservers.com/index/html
Stay-at-home dads: www.slowlane.com, www.daddyshome.com
Stepfathers: www.stepdads.com, www.positive-way.com, www.geocities.
    com/stepfathers
Suicide: www.suicidereferencelibrary.com
Testicular Cancer: www.andrologyaustralia.org

Permissions

The author and publisher would like to thank the following copyright holders for permission to reproduce text.

Extracts reprinted with the permission of The Free Press, a Division of Simon & Schuster Adult Publishing Group, from *The Adonis Complex: The Secret Crisis of Male Body Obsession* by Harrison G. Pope, Jnr., M.D., Katherine A. Phillips, M.D., Roberto Olivardia, Ph.D. Copyright © 2000 by Harrison G. Pope, Jnr., M.D., Katherine A. Phillips, M.D., Roberto Olivardia, Ph.D.

Boys to Men: Questions of Violence, by Michael Thompson et all, Harvard Education Letter, reproduced by kind permission of Harvard Education Publishing Group.

Boys Will Be Boys: Breaking the Link Between Masculinity and Violence, by Myriam Miedzian, Anchor, Bantam, Doubleday, New York, 1991, reproduced by kind permission of Lantern Books, revised edition 2002.

The Bridges of Madison County, Robert James Waller, Warner Books, New York, 1992, reproduced by kind permission of Warner Books.

From *The Courage to Raise Good Men* by Olga Silverstein and Beth Rashbaum, copyright © 1994 by Olga Silverstein and Beth Rashbaum. Used by permission of Viking Penguin, a division of Penguin Group (USA) Inc.

Divorced Dads: Shattering the Myths, by Sanford Braver, with Diane O'Connell, Jeremy Tarcher/Putnam, 1998, reproduced with kind permission of Penguin Group (USA) Inc.

From *Stiffed: The Betrayal of Modern Men*, by Susan Faludi, published by Chatto & Windus. Reprinted by kind permission of the Random House Group Ltd.

'Suburban Violence', by Dan Korem, *Suburban Gangs: The Affluent Rebels*, International Focus Press, Richardson, Texas, 1996, reproduced with kind permission of Dan Korem.

'Teenage Boys' Perceptions of the Influence of Teachers and School Experiences On Their Understanding of Masculinity', by Dr John R Lee, Association for Research in Education Conference, reproduced with kind permission of Dr John Lee.

Every effort has been made to locate the copyright holders of printed material. The publisher welcomes hearing from anyone in this regard.

Coming Home: Rediscovering our sacred selves

Maggie Hamilton

Where, beyond the stress and fatigue, is the space to be who we most long to be?

Most of us yearn for more depth and meaning, only to feel empty much of the time. Life's fulfilment is only a heartbeat away.

Discover effortless and effective ways to:

- Connect with your inner wisdom
- Transform your relationships at home and at work
- Respond positively to those who are hard to love
- Re-align your aspirations
- Celebrate your innate creativity
- Use your emotions as they were intended
- Navigate your way through the dark chapters of life

When we dare to move beyond the things that limit us, we are able to discover who we are and all we are capable of – and now is the perfect time to do just that.

Love Your Work, Reclaim Your Life
Maggie Hamilton

Most of us not only have to work, we want to work. But we sometimes feel so stressed and exhausted that we're afraid we can't continue living at this pace. If you're feeling down about your job right now, you are standing on the threshold of a whole new way of experiencing your work. Discover how even subtle changes to your day can make a huge difference, and explore the many resources you already possess that can help you create a rich and fulfilling life within and beyond work.

Learn new, easy-to-implement techniques for:

- overcoming manic work patterns
- handling constant changes and cutbacks
- coping with retrenchments and takeovers
- thriving in a challenging work culture
- tackling your boss
- being a good boss
- dealing with customer and workmate conflicts
- managing a career change, and
- breathing new life into your home, your passions and your friendships

Once you've read *Love Your Work, Reclaim Your Life*, you'll never see work the same way again.

Magic of the Moment
Maggie Hamilton

It's time now to let go of the past and embrace all that awaits you!

Every moment is a miracle. Your life is a miracle. Learn to recognise all the signposts around you and move beyond your current limitations, so you can begin to experience the magic of each moment and live the life you dream of.

Motherguilt

Ita Buttrose and Dr Penny Adams

Today's mothers are suffering from an epidemic of guilt that is so powerful and so uniquely related to motherhood that it has its own name – Motherguilt! But what causes them to feel this way and why are fathers seemingly immune from the condition? Wanting only the very best for their families, mothers run themselves ragged, taking care of everyone and everything else before considering their own needs. When things go wrong, as they inevitably do, they blame themselves and Motherguilt takes over.

So is it possible for women to deprogram themselves from this oppressive guilt? Yes, say Ita Buttrose and Dr Penny Adams, who have combined their respective talents to examine this phenomenon and offer positive solutions for a permanent cure.